Growing Industrial Clusters in Asia

Growing Industrial Clusters in Asia

Serendipity and Science

Edited by
Shahid Yusuf, Kaoru Nabeshima, and Shoichi Yamashita

THE WORLD BANK
Washington, D.C.

This volume is a product of the staff of the International Bank for Reconstruction and Development / The World Bank. The findings, interpretations, and conclusions expressed in this volume do not necessarily reflect the views of the Executive Directors of The World Bank or the governments they represent.

The World Bank does not guarantee the accuracy of the data included in this work. The boundaries, colors, denominations, and other information shown on any map in this work do not imply any judgement on the part of The World Bank concerning the legal status of any territory or the endorsement or acceptance of such boundaries.

ISBN: 978-0-8213-7213-5
eISBN: 978-0-8213-7214-2
DOI: 10.1596/978-0-8213-7213-5

Cover photo: Gary L. Friedman (www.FriedmanArchives.com)

Library of Congress Cataloging-in-Publication Data has been requested.

Contents

Boxes

Figures

Tables

Preface

As competition increases within an ever more globalized world, the appeal of industrial clusters not only remains strong but has become even more urgent. Policy makers in both developed and developing countries are searching for better ways to create new clusters, sustain existing ones, and revive those that are losing their vigor. But even after almost three decades of research, the formation and maintenance of dynamic industrial clusters remain something of a mystery. This book is part of the ongoing effort by researchers to unravel that mystery.

The question underlying the entirety of the book is, "Can viable clusters be called into existence by dint of policy?" The authors go about answering this question by examining the experience of clusters—including policies employed to induce their formation—in Asia and the United States. Their analysis results in a wealth of insights into the dynamics of clusters and helps to identify many of the conditions necessary for their formation. These findings, along with the detailed evidence from which they are derived, will be particularly valuable to policy makers and development specialists.

While we believe that this book moves us closer to the science of cluster building, it is nonetheless obvious that there is much work yet for others to do. However, we hope that this volume will make their task a little easier.

The chapters in this volume were initially prepared for the conference "ICT Industrial Clusters in Asia and the Problems in Japan," held in the City of Kitakyushu, Japan, on December 14–16, 2005. The papers were subsequently revised and updated by the authors based on the comments received from conference participants and other suggestions. Our thanks to all those who have helped us improve the contents. The conference was organized by the City of Kitakyushu and the International Centre for the Study of East Asian Development (ICSEAD), Kitakyushu, supported by the Council of Local Authorities for International Relations, the World Bank, and the Asian Development Bank. We are grateful to those who helped us in organizing the event and provided logistical assistance, including city officials and many ICSEAD staff.

We would also like to express our appreciation to the former adviser to ICSEAD, Professor Shin-ichi Ichimura, and the former vice president of the World Bank, Mr. Yukio Yoshimura, for helping us initiate this project and for supporting it with sound advice through to the end.

Last but not least, we are greatly indebted to the team who assisted us in preparing the volume for publication: our assistants, Marinella Yadao and Rebecca Sugui, and the World Bank Office of the Publisher.

Contributors

Rakesh Basant is Professor of Economics at the Indian Institute of Management, Ahmedabad.

Tain-Jy Chen is President, Chun-Hua Institution for Economic Research.

Maryann P. Feldman is Miller Distinguished Professor, Institute of Higher Education, University of Georgia.

Martin Kenney is a Professor at the University of California (UC), Davis, and a Senior Project Director at the Berkeley Roundtable on the International Economy. He is a fellow at the Center for Entrepreneurship at UC Davis.

Kaoru Nabeshima is a Consultant for the Development Research Group, World Bank.

Sam Ock Park is Professor of Economic Geography, Department of Geography, Seoul National University.

Poh-Kam Wong holds a joint appointment as Associate Professor at the National University of Singapore (NUS) Business School and the Lee Kuan Yew School of Public Policy. He concurrently serves as Director, Entrepreneurship Centre, NUS.

Shoichi Yamashita is Director, International Centre for the Study of East Asian Development, Kitakyushu (ICSEAD); Professor Emeritus, Hiroshima University; and Advisory Professor, Fudan University, China.

Shahid Yusuf is Economic Adviser, Development Research Group, World Bank.

Abbreviations

AMD	Advanced Micro Devices
ASE	Advanced Semiconductor Engineering
ASEAN	Association of Southeast Asian Nations
ASIC	application-specific integrated circuit
ASSP	application-specific standard product
B2B	business-to-business
B2C	business-to-consumer
BIOS	basic input/output system
CAD	computer-aided design
CDMA	code division multiple access
CERN	European Organization for Nuclear Research
CIGS	copper, indium, gallium, and selenium
CMOS	complementary metal-oxide semiconductor
CPU	central processing unit
CRT	cathode ray tube
DoE	Department of Electronics (India)
DRAM	dynamic random access memory
DSL	digital subscriber line

The treatment of all country names within this book complies with World Bank policy.

DSP	digital signal processing
DVD	digital video disc
EDB	Economic Development Board (Singapore)
EPROM	erasable programmable read-only memory
EPZ	export processing zone
ERSO	Electronics Research and Service Organization
ESN	entrepreneurial support network
FAIS	Foundation for the Advancement of Industry, Science, and Technology (Kitakyushu, Japan)
GDP	gross domestic product
GE	General Electric
GLC	government-linked corporation
GSM	Global System for Mobile
HP	Hewlett-Packard
HSP	Hsinchu Science Park
iN2015	Intelligent Nation by 2015 (Singapore)
IC	integrated circuit
ICE	information, computer, and electronics (technologies)
ICT	information and communication technology
IDA	Infocomm Development Authority (Singapore)
IP	intellectual property
IPDC	India Product Development Center
ISI	Information Society Index
ISO	India Software Operations
IT	information technology
ITRI	Industrial Technology Research Institute
KSRP	Kitakyushu Science and Research Park
LAN	local area network
LCD	liquid crystal display
LSI	large-scale integration
MDA	Media Development Authority (Singapore)
METI	Ministry of Economy, Trade, and Industry (Japan)
MEXT	Ministry of Education, Culture, Sports, Science, and Technology (Japan)
MICO	Motor Industries Company
MNC	multinational corporation
MS-DOS	Microsoft disk operating system
NCB	National Computer Board (Singapore)
NFN	national fiber network
NRF	National Research Foundation (Singapore)

NRI	Networked Readiness Index
OECD	Organisation for Economic Co-operation and Development
PARC	Palo Alto Research Center
PC	personal computer
PTT	postal, telegraph, and telephone
PV	photovoltaic
R&D	research and development
RFID	radio frequency identification
ROM	read-only memory
SBA	Singapore Broadcasting Authority
SDA	Solomon Design Automation
SDIC	Seoul Digital Industrial Complex
SIC	Standard Industrial Classification
SiS	Silicon Integrated Systems
SoC	system-on-a-chip
SMIC	Semiconductor Manufacturing International Corporation
SPIL	Silicon Precision Industries Limited
STP	software technology park
TAS	Telecommunications Authority of Singapore
TCS	Tata Consultancy Services
TI	Texas Instruments
TSMC	Taiwan Semiconductor Manufacturing Corporation
UMC	United Microelectronics Corporation
VC	venture capital
VLSI	Very-Large-Scale IC (project)
VSAT	very-small-aperture terminal
VSNL	Videsh Sanchar Nigam Limited
WBN	wireless broadband network

CHAPTER 1

Can Clusters Be Made to Order?

Shahid Yusuf

Industrial hollowing and the emergence of rust belts have signaled the end of a cycle of urban development for many mature industrial centers, triggering the search for business models and policies that can attract new industries and rejuvenate local economies.[1] Many urban centers confronting this predicament, such as those in Japan, are enthused by the industrial cluster model for several reasons.[2] Policy makers are influenced by the experience of iconic clusters in Silicon Valley in California; Boston,

My thanks to Kaoru Nabeshima for his valuable suggestions and to Ella Yadao for producing the manuscript.

1 The term *rust belt* was first associated with the decline of manufacturing industries in the states of Illinois, Indiana, Michigan, Ohio, and Pennsylvania in the 1970s and 1980s. The term was coined and popularized by Walter Mondale. Hollowing out of industries through their migration to countries with lower wages has been a concern of the more advanced countries for decades. In Japan, this concern has been repeatedly underscored since the 1980s (see, for example, Horaguchi 2004). Since the 1990s, it has also become a concern for the Republic of Korea and Taiwan (China) as industries have migrated first to Southeast Asia and increasingly to China, beginning with textiles, footwear, and consumer electronics and now extending to semiconductors, integrated circuits, and automotive parts (see Kang 2007; Kim 2007; Kobayashi 2007). The process of hollowing out in China's neighbors and its implications for their capacity to upgrade are analyzed through a model presented by Kim (2007).

2 An *industrial cluster* is a geographically contiguous concentration of related and supporting industries that are rendered more competitive because of synergies arising from participation in a value-adding supply chain. This definition is based on the several definitions presented in Martin and Sunley (2003).

Massachusetts;[3] Cambridge, United Kingdom; Medicon Valley in the Greater Copenhagen area;[4] the Emilia-Romagna region in Italy;[5] the Bavarian region in Germany, centered in Munich; the Sophia Antipolis technology park in France;[6] and Hsinchu Science Park near Taipei. These clusters are responsible for sustaining the momentum of the urban economies in which they have emerged. As Cortright (2006: 1) observes, "Clusters represent a fundamental organizing framework for understanding regional economies and for developing economic strategies." In particular, their appeal derives from three attributes that can be grouped under the concepts of agglomeration economies and externalities (Johansson 2005).

The Allure of Clusters

First, the co-location of numerous firms can generate substantial direct and indirect employment; give rise to numerous links, including fiscal links; and crowd in many other services. The most successful clusters embrace hundreds of firms and achieve substantial localization economies.[7]

Second, where clustered firms achieve a high degree of networking and interconnectedness within a fundamentally competitive milieu, they generate spillovers, which stimulate productivity, and they acquire a self-sustaining dynamic arising from a resilient comparative advantage in a specific range of products or services.[8]

Third, innovative clusters are able to diversify and to acquire the capacity to make the transition to a fresh line of products if the demand for the existing product mix enters a downward spiral. The ability to rebound by

---

3 According to a BankBoston report in 1997, the income from businesses started by former and current Massachusetts Institute of Technology staff members and students, if combined, would equal the world's 24th largest economy (Kelly 2001).

4 The Medicon Valley life science cluster extends from Copenhagen into the Malmo and Lund regions of Sweden, an area with 3 million people. The area derives its research capabilities from the universities of Copenhagen and Lund, and its commercial orientation is assisted by the presence of the firm Novo Nordisk (Lembke and Osthol 2005).

5 This site was described in a classic work by Piore and Sabel (1984), which extolled the advantages of small, flexible specialized manufacturers.

6 Sophia Antipolis, located 9 kilometers from Cannes, has been a cluster in the making since the early 1970s, drawing talent from the Institute Eurécom, Sciences et Technologies de l'Information et de la Communication, and CERAM Business School (see Saperstein and Rouach 2002).

7 Localization economies accrue when the concentration of firms belonging to one industrial subsector promotes specialization and incremental innovation.

8 See Chang and Harrington (2005) for issues associated with networking—both the gains from shared knowledge and the risk of homogenization.

diversifying is a distinctive attribute of clusters in Silicon Valley and in the Boston area, and it has been invaluable for the health of local economies.[9]

For these reasons, the nurturing of clusters has become a focus of regional and urban policies in both industrial and industrializing economies. A cluster with adequate industrial mass and associated support services can be a local engine of growth, and an innovative cluster, by evolving and diversifying, can also dampen the swings in growth over time.[10] Urban centers, which already host clusters, are seeking to enhance their size and innovativeness. Those with nascent clusters are attempting to grow them through a variety of public and private initiatives. And cities casting about for a leading industrial sector are eagerly experimenting with policies that will germinate a cluster, either a freestanding group or a cluster that is pegged to an existing area of competence and production base.[11]

Inevitably, it is easier to devise policies for a functioning cluster and devilishly hard to call a cluster into existence, especially when the essential industrial nuclei are difficult to identify (see Cooke 2002).[12] Unless it achieves flexibility and innovativeness, even a successful cluster can suffer from lock-in, and like a large and specialized firm with a mature product line, businesses in the cluster often cannot perceive or are reluctant to acknowledge when an industry is past its prime and there is a need to change tracks.[13] Recognizing the warning signs of an impending slowdown and helping a cluster to reorient or evolve its economic activities also requires a great deal of policy foresight, careful application of policy instruments to support a desirable change in product mix by some of the more dynamic firms, and a healthy dose of luck.

---

9 Glaeser (2003) shows that Boston was able to recover from the downturn of the 1970s because of the presence of a skilled and entrepreneurial labor force. See also Glaeser and Berry (2006) and Glaeser and Saiz (2003) on the growth advantages of *smart cities*—those with a higher percentage of highly educated workers. Human capital is also instrumental in enabling firms to bring ideas to commercial fruition (Leiponen 2005).

10 A model devised by Martin and Ottaviano (2001) indicates that growth and agglomeration can result in a self-reinforcing virtuous spiral, assisted by innovation, as economic activity becomes more concentrated.

11 The multimedia cluster in New York, known as Silicon Alley, drew its ideas and entrepreneurship from the local culture system and the publishing and information technology industry. Its capital came from New York's unrivaled financial market (Currid 2007; Indergaard 2004).

12 A study of technology-intensive firms in Germany found little evidence of tendencies toward the clustering of high-tech firms and discounted the case for localization economies arising from knowledge spillovers and labor market pooling (Alecke and others 2005).

13 This problem is discussed by Christensen (2003). For cluster lock-in, see Cooke (2002).

The purpose of this introductory chapter is to examine the formation and evolution of clusters and to relate this progression to the experience of nascent and mature clusters in Silicon Valley, California; Singapore; Seoul, Republic of Korea; Bangalore, India; and Hsinchu Science Park, Taiwan (China)—all of which are explored by the contributors to this volume.

Moreover, the chapter attempts to determine whether the current wealth of knowledge about clusters provides us with a recipe that could induce formation of a cluster in the city of Kitakyushu, the subject of the final chapter and also, in many ways, a city typical of postindustrial areas seeking a new growth engine. Because clusters do not exist in isolation, the chapter will bring out the significance of the regional context and of regional development efforts. Although industrial clusters flourish in rural areas, as in the case of manufacturers of wood and cane furniture in Indonesia and the Philippines,[14] and in small towns, as has happened in Japan,[15] the focus here is on clusters in large urban centers. Such clusters are more likely to emerge or grow in the future, they will have potentially greater economic significance and contribute more to the overall economic performance of their locale, and current urban clusters in the major cities engage the attention of policy makers to a far greater degree than do their cousins in the rural areas.[16]

The Chemistry of Clusters

Clusters[17] come in several different forms, and various authors have attempted typologies, but all clusters share a family resemblance: they are composed of a multitude of firms of different sizes belonging to one branch of industry, they are broadly defined, and membership is open and elastic.[18] Markusen (1994), for instance, has classified clusters into four categories: Marshallian, hub and spoke, satellite platform, and state anchored (see table 1.1). Others have described them as competitive, strategic, emerging,

---

14 See Geenhuizen and Indarti (2006) on the Jeppara cluster in Indonesia and Beerepoot (2005) on the furniture cluster in Cebu, Philippines.

15 See Yamawaki (2002) for a review of clusters in Japan covering a wide range of industries.

16 Larger cities, at least in the United States, are quicker to accumulate skills and have proven to be more fertile sources of innovation (see Bettencourt, Lobo, and Strumsky 2007; Glaeser and Mare 2001). Moreover, the density of employment is correlated with the number of patents generated (Carlino, Chatterjee, and Hunt 2007).

17 Many researchers complain about the vagueness of the term *clusters* (see Cortright 2006).

18 It is appropriate at the outset to heed the warning note struck by Feldman and Francis (2005: 128), who note, "The attributes observed in a mature and fully functioning cluster are artifacts of the formation process and reflect attributes and relationships formed as the cluster developed rather than pre-conditions for cluster development."

Table 1.1. Markusen's Typology of Industry Clusters

Cluster type growth	Characteristics of member firms	Intracluster interdependencies	Prospects for employment
Marshallian	Small and medium-size locally owned firms	Substantial interfirm trade and collaboration; strong institutional support	Dependent on synergies and economies provided by cluster
Hub and spoke	One or several large firms with numerous smaller supplier and service firms	Cooperation between large firms and smaller suppliers on terms of the large firms (hub firms)	Dependent on growth prospects of large firms
Satellite platform	Medium-size and large branch plants	Minimum interfirm trade and networking	Dependent on ability to recruit and retain branch plants
State anchored	Large public or nonprofit entity related supplier and service firms	Restricted to purchase-sale relationships between public entity and suppliers	Dependent on region's ability to expand political support for public facility

Source: Markusen 1996.

potential, and mature. Clustered firms are assumed to be grouped within a fairly compact geographic area; the firms enjoy not only the localization economies from spatial contiguity but also the benefits from varying degrees of interaction through myriad reciprocal relationships as competitors, collaborators, buyers, or suppliers. Furthermore, the cluster contributes to and feeds off the growth of dense and localized markets for products, labor, and technology. Competition among clustered firms serves to weed out the weaker firms but also encourages all participants to innovate and evolve as organizations in order to survive, as noted in the case of the hard disk drive industry.[19]

The most successful of existing clusters—and those with a potentially bright future—also have distinct locational advantages, and such attributes are likely to be even more important for new clusters.[20] A large urban area, well served by an efficient information and communication

19 For more on the hard disk drive industry, see McKendrick and Barnett (2001). McKendrick (as quoted by Durbin 2003) observes that "in the hard disk drive industry, organizations became both more viable and more competitive the more they had survived competition in the past. Isolation from competition can have current-time benefits, but it also has the less obvious downside in that it deprives the organization of the engine of development."

20 Silicon Valley benefits to no small extent from the local weather—for instance, San Francisco is known as the *air-conditioned city*, which is pleasant year-round. The importance of local weather conditions in determining individual choices has been growing and is likely to increase in importance (Rappaport 2007).

technology (ICT) infrastructure and transport facilities, ensures access to product and factor markets and offers a wide range of producer services. Attractive urban amenities are increasingly essential to retain locally trained workers and to attract knowledge workers from other areas.[21]

For a cluster to expand and to reap the economies of scale and scope, the urban area must have the space for firms to establish facilities and find nearby housing for workers at an affordable cost. The opportunities for growth and entrepreneurship[22] are also linked to the demographics of the urban region. An increasing population that is heterogeneous and has a greater percentage of younger people has higher levels of energy and initiative and is more likely to generate a buzz,[23] which is a wonderful marketing instrument and can quickly raise the profile of a cluster. Silicon Valley, for example, has derived tremendous leverage both from heterogeneity that stimulates innovation (see Cooke 2002) and from the buzz about its innovativeness, the money to be made there, and the quality of life. Hsinchu Science Park in Taiwan (China), Bangalore in India,[24] and Cambridge in the United Kingdom are all beneficiaries of a buzz that, with some support from professional marketing, accounts for the successful branding of those clusters.

There is another dimension to location as well. The most promising and durable clusters are not just in major urban centers, but also in cities situated in regions that have acquired strong economic momentum by combining economic legacies and resource endowment with good policies. In the words of Feldman (chapter 7; see also Feldman and Martin 2004), they have created a "jurisdictional advantage" that provides the enabling environment for a cluster. The regional hinterland is a vital factor in many respects.[25] First, the size of the potential market within a 200-mile radius matters; in other words, a day's drive can be an important

---

21 Florida (2002) is responsible for some of the recent pathbreaking work in this area. Webster (2006) provides a useful juxtaposition of geographic characteristics and cluster development in the Thai context.

22 The role of entrepreneurs in assembling the building blocks of clusters is stressed by Feldman, Francis, and Bercovitz (2005).

23 *Buzz*—the word-of-mouth communication led by (alpha) trendsetters with high group connectivity—can be immensely effective in the urban context in propagating ideas promoting clusters (see Leamer and Storper 2001).

24 However, Bangalore city is struggling to accommodate the influx of people, which has caused severe congestion and compromised its past attractions and the quality of life. Many of the new high-tech campuses are emerging outside the city.

25 For more on the regional dimension, see Cooke (2002). For a critical review of the city-region literature, see Harrison (2007).

determinant of prospects.[26] Although some clusters that have formed around foreign-invested enterprises have a strong export orientation and function as enclave economies (such as the electronics cluster in Subic Bay near Manila), many—possibly most—clusters derive much of their growth impetus, at least initially, from local or regional markets. Larger, affluent, and faster-growing markets are advantageous for clusters as they are for most kinds of industrial activity. For all these reasons, research on the Organisation for Economic Co-operation and Development member countries finds that high-tech spinoff firms are rare, except in the United States; that they arise from a few of the leading research institutions; and, most importantly, that they are prominent mainly in the large established clusters. In small boutique clusters, firms do not grow much (Degroof and Roberts 2004).

Second, in many large countries, fiscal and administrative decentralization has pushed the locus of decision making with respect to fiscal incentives, land-use policy, regulation, industrial licensing, and infrastructure development to the regional level or to municipal decision makers. The central authorities retain control of macro level policies and over the development of the trunk infrastructure, but these authorities have increasingly delegated regional and urban projects, their implementation, and some of their financing to subnational governments, as has occurred in China and Brazil. In the absence of a robust system for interprovincial transfers, this approach creates serious problems for the poorer, less industrialized subnational entities, as in the case in China (Ming and Quanhou 2007).

Third, most new industrial clusters[27] are emerging or have emerged not in core cities—because rental costs are high and space is a severe constraint—but in the peri-urban fringes of the cities. Hsinchu Science Park is almost 70 kilometers from Taipei, the Boston area cluster is along Route 128 outside the city, new software parks are springing up in the suburbs of Bangalore, and the electronics and biotech clusters in Shanghai are in the new areas developed in Pudong across the river from downtown Huang-pu. In some cases, clusters can straddle two or more municipalities. Thus, provincial- or state-level governments are very likely to be engaged in the development of clusters and in the coordination of intermunicipal policies supporting those clusters. Moreover, sustaining high-level research-intensive clusters, such as Silicon Valley, or aspiring clusters, such as the one

---

26 Shanghai-based clusters are boosted by the presence of 200 million people living within a day's drive in the Yangtze Valley area.

27 Older clusters, as in the "Third Italy," (which covers the area in the northeast and central part of Italy) are located in the core cities.

in Pudong—all of which are skill- and research-intensive and require expensive infrastructure—calls for resources and planning that generally exceed the capacities of a single municipality. A joint approach by central, subnational, and private bodies can be essential in these cases, with the national innovation system providing a framework for the orchestration of a number of policy initiatives, ranging from tertiary education to ICT infrastructure. Such an approach minimizes the coordination failures, highlighted by Rodrik (1996), that can hobble industrial change.

Necessary Conditions

There is enough empirical material to cobble together a checklist of necessary conditions to bring a new cluster into existence. However, these apparently straightforward conditions are inherently complex, and fulfilling each of them adequately can be a substantial policy exercise in itself. Even after the conditions have been met to a greater or lesser degree, a true functioning cluster might not arise—in fact, it seldom emerges. Perhaps the only way of apprehending the magnitude of the task is to examine the nine key conditions for a cluster and to understand what they entail, taking into account the limits of our knowledge of causal relationships and the consequences of policy actions:

- Identification of products
- Cluster geography
- Capability to lead, finance, and do business
- Incentives
- Urban labor market
- Innovation
- Angel investors and venture capitalists
- Urban setting and infrastructure
- Anchor firms

Identification of Products

The future of a cluster depends first and foremost on the category of products or services to be produced. Clusters are defined by such categories. The range of items produced can be broad or relatively narrow, but in any meaningful cluster, the items fall within a specific class, such as electronic components, software, or bioengineering.

The market prospects of a product are crucial, whether they are domestic or international, and increasingly these are not mutually exclusive. A high income elasticity of demand, which ensures a good longer-term increase in revenues, is a sine qua non, and in high-tech industries, domestic market penetration needs to be supplemented by sales overseas. The product itself must have, potentially at least, a protean quality that opens the door to extensive product differentiation and the spawning of numerous next-generation products that will create new niche markets, thereby expanding the sales of cluster-based firms and creating openings for new firms. Electronics and ICT-based activities have been unusually fertile sources of new products. Moreover, it is highly advantageous if the class of products accommodates continuous innovation and comprises many subcomponents that can be refined, elaborated on, and evolved in incremental or radical ways. The more dense and technologically fruitful are the backward links to suppliers of components, services, and manufacturing equipment—such as with a thin-film transistor–liquid crystal display—the more a cluster can grow and the greater the room for innovations.[28]

Identifying a product or a service that fulfills these characteristics is no easy task. It requires a careful reading of trends in the development of and the markets for candidate products and decomposition of the product itself, in its current and prospective forms, to tease out the potential links that could thicken the cluster. In addition, identification demands some enlightened forecasting grounded in a sophisticated knowledge of the product, the often several intersecting underlying technologies, and the educated guesses as to how these technologies might evolve and shape the future of the product. Any product or service can encounter trade, regulatory, or ethical obstacles, and the more novel the product the greater the likelihood of bumps in the road ahead, as with the approval of biotech drugs, ICT-enabled services, and genetically modified crops. The possibility of those obstacles must be factored into the process. If barriers to entry into a product category are relatively low—as with call centers, low-tech electronics products, furniture or watch making, or apparel or leather goods—they will have a bearing on future revenue and growth prospects and will influence the longer-term viability of the cluster. Italian firms that are leaders in furniture, luxury apparel, and leather goods are attempting to maintain their competitiveness through sophisticated

---

28 Companies such as Applied Materials, which established a presence in Hsinchu Park after the electronics cluster took off, are the key suppliers of production equipment. Others include ASML, Varian Semiconductor, Hitachi, Canon, Horiba Manufacturing, Shimadzu, and Novellus Systems. Applied Materials, founded in 1967, is the world's largest supplier of semiconductor manufacturing equipment. Its subsidiary, Applied Materials Taiwan, was established in 1989 and within a decade became the preeminent supplier to local firms (see Chen, Wu, and Lin 2006; Trompenaars and others 2002).

production methods and innovation in design.[29] Swiss watchmakers rely on extraordinary technical skills, design, exclusive brand names, marketing skills, the cachet acquired over centuries, and a stable market of well-heeled buyers who collect premium timepieces. For mature products and services, intangible assets are beginning to bolster competitiveness more and more. For instance, countries attempting to jump-start a medical biotech cluster, such as Singapore, must factor in all these considerations in addition to the start-up costs of a cluster, which are discussed later (see Yusuf and Nabeshima 2006).

Cluster Geography

When a product has been identified as the possible basis for a cluster, how can it be matched with a suitable urban venue? It almost goes without saying that clusters will not emerge in just any urban setting, no matter how large, and that for specific types of products the suitability of urban centers or regions is likely to vary significantly depending on a host of considerations. Most countries are targeting the higher-technology industries with the potential to innovate and the prospect of expanding domestic and global markets. Almost all of these industries are skill intensive, and some, such as engineering and manufacturing equipment, also require a fund of tacit knowledge and craft skills that are acquired through learning and experimentation over a lengthy span of time. A knowledge-intensive cluster can grow only in an urban region that has or can attract a pool of entrepreneurs and technical and professional people, many of whom now have sophisticated lifestyle preferences and plenty of options. This growth can be a slow process, which commenced in Silicon Valley in the early 20th century (Sturgeon 2000) and took 70 years to come to fruition even in the Research Triangle in North Carolina. Thus, an urban center pursuing a cluster-based development strategy must at the minimum be capable of supplying the housing and public services and the quality infrastructure expected by mobile knowledge workers and entrepreneurs. The physical location of the urban center is important but not critical as long as the transportation infrastructure permits easy access to travel within and between the countryside. Clusters have emerged in South Dakota and Utah; in parts of Finland; in Austin, Texas; and in the Research Triangle in North Carolina because facilities were created together with a rich suite of urban amenities.[30] In Austin,

---

29 They have also come to rely on low-wage immigrant workers, many from China. However, doing so is a two-edged sword, because these workers are transferring Italian production and design skills to China (Kynge 2006).

30 Cluster development in Finland has occurred in Oulu and Tampere. For more on the Research Triangle, see Lembke and Osthol (2005).

public officials, university administrators, and private developers worked together to build local research capability and to craft an urban environment that would attract knowledge workers with diverse skills and induce them to stay and invest their energies in building a mixed, high-tech cluster (Smilor and others 2005).[31]

Capability to Lead, Finance, and Do Business

Tailoring an environment for an industrial cluster is a costly and risky enterprise. The payback might never materialize,[32] and even if it does, years may pass before the urban region begins to derive substantial benefits from the new industrial activity. The process calls for a vision of development centered on an industrial engine with specific characteristics, on the planning and coordination of projects and people, on the mobilization of resources, on an efficient administrative and regulatory regime, on a large dose of entrepreneurship, and on determined leadership by local or regional champions. The success of the clusters in Silicon Valley; Cambridge, United Kingdom; and San Diego, California, is associated with the efforts of Fred Terman, Alec Broers, and Roger Revelle, respectively,[33] who provided the leadership and vision that helped to attract investors and leading researchers. When resources are marshaled, the role of the province or the state and of foreign investors becomes especially important. But even here, leaders with a vision and a strong commitment to a plausible development strategy must convince a host of others to cooperate and to finance the large, often long-term costs of local high-tech industrialization. In turn, leaders speak for and rely on a local community of businesses, developers, and aspiring entrepreneurs who constitute the social and political bedrock of the cluster. Their numbers, the backing they provide, and the social capital they engender strengthen a leader's hand and ultimately determine outcomes.

Any financing plan involving large-scale reshaping of an urban environment to accommodate a new industrial engine has many parts to it. Raising money from local taxes, fees, and charges is one factor. Obtaining long-term resource transfers from provincial or central authorities is a second factor, which can have problematic and time-consuming legislative implications.

---

31 Urban land ownership and land development are discussed by the contributors to Perry and Wiewel (2005).

32 The attempt by New Jersey to build a high-tech cluster failed (see Leslie and Kargon 1997).

33 Fred Terman was provost of Stanford University, Alec Broers was vice chancellor of Cambridge University, and Roger Revelle was director of the Scripps Institute and a founder of the University of California–San Diego campus.

Tapping the financial markets is a third factor, and here, too, municipalities must take steps to ensure that they meet market-determined standards of creditworthiness. Harnessing the resources of private financiers through promises and tax concessions is a fourth factor. Foreign direct investment is a fifth factor, and there are yet more. As Basant notes in chapter 5 and as has been widely cited by others, Bangalore confronts severe infrastructure bottlenecks because of difficulties raising financing and surmounting political as well as administrative hurdles.[34]

In short, the financial lead-up to an urban industrial cluster can be long and arduous. Before the ground is broken for a single new manufacturing firm, many of the critical details of financing need to be in place so that a nascent cluster is not strangled by a funding drought that results in infrastructure bottlenecks or by a shortage of serviced land at a critical juncture. The latter issue is a problem faced by land-deficient Singapore (Yusuf 2007).

Building alliances among the several stakeholders—including, of course, the business community whose entrepreneurship drives the cluster—depends, in the first place, on leadership and a compelling business model. However, a wealth of research now convincingly shows that business activity—and in particular the formation of new clusters—can be severely hobbled by local regulatory and administrative requirements, which can slow down decision making and introduce uncertainties about property rights, rent controls, contracts, tax laws, dispute resolution, labor regulations, and the stability of rules.[35] No urban center is perfect, although Singapore has struggled vigorously to minimize each of these problems, and businesses worldwide are inured to a degree of corruption, delays in approval, lack of transparency, and the normal bureaucratic frictions of doing business. However, the lower the threshold of discomfort, the easier it is for businesses to take root. More facilitation and less red tape can be great assets. Singapore and Hong Kong (China) have both managed to entice and retain clusters of service providers—and, in the case of Singapore, manufacturers of electronics and pharmaceuticals—because businesses find that the transaction costs of operating in those cities are unusually low and the amenities are exceptional. Transaction costs are higher in Shanghai, for example, but

---

34 See Heitzman (2004) for an additional account of Bangalore's emergence as a center for the information industry.

35 These uncertainties have been explored in depth by World Bank studies, which have assessed the costs of doing business in areas such as Chinese cities (see Dollar and others 2003). Some of these hurdles, such as rent control, land-use restrictions, and labor regulations are very apparent in Mumbai, for example.

other offsetting factors tip the scales in the city's favor, as discussed later. However, in cities such as Manila, Mumbai, and São Paulo, the environment is much less conducive to the growth of high-tech clusters.

Incentives

Both national and subnational governments put great store in incentive policies to promote industries. There is a lengthy list of incentives that governments deploy. Table 1.2 lists the main industrial promotion policies in the United States. They include tax credits, exemptions, and depreciation allowances on equipment; subsidies for various inputs, including land, water, and electricity; and rent ceilings and training grants. They embrace science parks and incubators, which provide space and services at competitive rates, and they include a variety of financing packages, ranging from outright grants to subsidized credit for specific activities or investments.[36] Accessing these incentives, where they are offered, depends on the quality of systems in place and the volume of red tape. Many firms, especially smaller ones, are unaware of the incentives or find it too time consuming and onerous to actually apply for them. Training grants in Malaysia are only partially used (World Bank 2005), and incentives for research and development (R&D) in Thailand are often left untouched by large and small firms alike (World Bank 2008).

Moreover, there is only limited country-specific research that rigorously analyzes the effects of the incentives provided for urban industrialization that are targeted toward specific types of technology-intensive firms. There is little or no knowledge of what works, what type of incentive has the greatest effect at the least cost to the authorities, and what type creates the smallest amount of distortion. The track record of assessing the efficacy of individual incentives or incentive policies grouped as a package is virtually nonexistent. As a consequence, there is no systematic body of empirical evidence on incentives and their outcomes that can guide policy makers on how to design policies for specific purposes under particular circumstances or, for that matter, how to evaluate and refine the policies so as to achieve the best results. In most cases, urban centers and regional and national governments[37] offer a raft of incentives because their competitors

---

36 The Multimedia Super Corridor in Malaysia offers eligible firms a generous package of incentives, and similar packages are provided by urban regions in China and Singapore.

37 Administrative and fiscal decentralization—along with, in the European Union, the importance of structured grants—has encouraged regional governments to play a more active role in pursuing science and technology policies (Sanz-Menendez and Cruz-Castro 2005).

Table 1.2. State-Level Industrial Promotion Policies in the United States

Entrepreneurial policy	Industrial recruitment incentive	Labor regulations
Public venture capital funds	Bond-based financing	Minimum-wage laws
Technical assistance center	Loans for building, construction, equipment, and machinery	Fair employment laws
Business incubators	Loan guarantees for building, construction, equipment, and machinery	Absence of right-to-work laws
Research parks	Aid for existing plant expansion	
Research and development tax incentives	Matching funds for city-county industrial financing	
	Funds for development-related public works	
	Incentives for establishing industrial plants	
	Tax exemption on land-capital improvements	
	Tax exemption on equipment and machinery	
	Inventory tax exemption for goods in transit and in manufacturing inventories	
	Tax exemption on new equipment and raw materials	
	Tax incentive for job creation and industrial investment	
	Accelerated depreciation for industrial equipment	
	State-supported training and retraining of industrial workers	
	State-financed speculative building	
	Free land for industry	
	State and city-owned industrial park sites	
	State funding of city-county master plans	
	Feasibility studies for recruitment of plants	
	Recruiting and screening of industrial employees	
	Training of the long-term unemployed population	
	Technical assistance with procurement bids	

Source: Jenkins, Leicht, and Wendt 2006: table 1, 1127.

are doing so, and they add to or subtract from the incentive regime on fiscal grounds, in response to idiosyncratic information or to actions taken by their neighbors, or in the face of demands from industrial pressure groups, which can include powerful firms playing off one urban center and government against another. Feldman and Francis (2005) doubt that industrial incentives influenced locational choices, especially for high-tech firms. In their view, high-tech clusters have "developed endogenously using their ability to leverage location specific assets to induce new investment and create new value; no incentive program can be identified a priori" (Feldman and Francis 2005: 128).

In other words, the menu of incentive mechanisms is rich and is widely applied. Unfortunately, no one knows what works, how it works, or what might make policies more effective. Policy makers rarely have a good sense of the counterfactual: what might happen if a different approach were adopted that eschewed the traditional fiscal and financial incentives and focused mainly or exclusively on other instruments for inducing clusters. This is not to deny that, in certain instances, government industrial policies can be effective. As Chen points out in chapter 3, the R&D investment by the government of Taiwan (China) in Hsinchu Science Park and in the establishment of the wafer fabs, which brought fabless chip designers to the park, motivated cluster formation. Similarly, as Wong notes in chapter 4, the Singapore authorities are the driving force behind the effort to create a biomedical cluster using a range of investments and incentives.

Urban Labor Market

A knowledge-intensive cluster needs ready access to a deep pool of skilled and technical workers and the sources of research and industrial extension.[38] (Basant, in chapter 5, describes how such clusters were brought into existence in Bangalore.) For these two vital reasons, high-tech clusters, where they exist, are invariably to be found in urban regions thickly populated with universities that contribute to the formation and growth of the cluster and to its innovation capability.[39] Not only have universities supplied the skills and the professional talent, but they are also the principal source of scientific findings that firms, sometimes

---

38 Large urban centers confer the advantages of agglomeration economies, which include thick labor markets that facilitate a matching of jobs with skills (Andersson, Burgess, and Lane 2007).

39 Together with universities, vocational and other training institutions have a large role in nurturing skills. For example, the Penang Skills Development Centre in Malaysia and comparable institutions in Singapore have played a vital role in developing and upgrading the hard disk drive industry in both locations (McKendrick, Doner, and Haggard 2000).

with the assistance of university-based researchers, have been able to commercialize.[40] In recent years, university-industry links have multiplied as firms in leading clusters have found it advantageous to collaborate with universities in conducting basic research and in designing courses offered by the university so as to better meet their own requirements.[41] Stanford University, for example, offers courses prompted by the expressed needs of firms in Silicon Valley (see chapter 2 by Kenney). The firms, in turn, contribute to the university endowment and infrastructure, and business personnel enroll in courses and give lectures and presentations. Even the largest firms are finding that research is becoming too costly, and a sharing of the research effort with other firms and with universities is emerging as a necessity (*Economist* 2007). Because the proximity of researchers is especially important for work done on the cutting edge of science, where much of the knowledge is not codified, the clustering of firms and the proximity of a cluster to centers of teaching and research is doubly advantageous (Adams 2001). Firms collaborate among themselves to conduct R&D and to engage in the incremental innovations that are essential for competitiveness, and they can forge alliances with universities and tap the highly specialized pool of multidisciplinary skills in universities through a variety of contractual arrangements. Moreover, the circulation of workers among firms is an important aspect of networking and technology transfer (Casper 2007).

It is a known fact that universities and major research centers such as the Palo Alto Research Center (in Silicon Valley), the Salk Institute (in San Diego), and the Industrial Technology Research Institute's Electronics Research and Service Organization (ITRI/ERSO) (in Hsinchu Science Park) lie at the heart of clusters. But what role universities can play in triggering cluster formation remains uncertain. There are leading universities in Brazil, Japan, Korea, and the United States and in Europe that have not generated significant spillovers or been responsible for a host of start-ups.[42]

---

40 For more on the role of universities, see Yusuf and Nabeshima (2007) and the symposium papers in *World Development* (2007).

41 Proximity to a university is an asset because knowledge spillovers are highly localized, as shown by Adams (2001), Fu (2007), and Keller (2002). On the evolution of technology exchanges between universities and the business sector, see Colyvas (2007) on Stanford University and Etzkowitz (2002) on the Massachusetts Institute of Technology.

42 A major survey of firms in the United States and the United Kingdom showed that in both countries, but more so in the United Kingdom, universities rank very low as sources of knowledge for firms. Industrial sources such as suppliers and customers dominate. Nevertheless, there is a perception that universities are likely to become more prominent in this respect because the knowledge intensity of productive activities is on the rise (Centre for Business Research 2004).

There are also notable examples of universities that have promoted the formation of clusters. These include the University of Texas at Austin, the University of California–San Diego, Peking University, and Technion in Haifa,[43] and several universities in Denmark and Finland. The truth is that the university as a driver of cluster development has only a few instruments that it can bring to bear.

Undoubtedly, the scale, disciplinary breadth, quality, and research intensity of the university system in an urban center powerfully affect the local labor market, especially if a sizable percentage of graduates remain in the area. Universities can set up incubators for start-up activities; set aside small amounts of seed money for new ventures; and provide incentives to their researchers to conduct research, develop their findings, and attempt to commercialize promising innovations. For example, Massachusetts Institute of Technology, the American land grant universities, and Peking University and Qinghua University in China have provided such encouragement (Chen and Kenney 2007; Wu 2007). Universities with resources, strong local support, and access to conveniently located real estate can also carve out a science park that can host a cluster, as Stanford was able to do. There are cases of these initiatives, in conjunction with others, having delivered good results. However, one does not frequently hear about the many more instances of failure because they are not advertised. But there are plenty of costly failures, and perhaps the majority of attempts at creating industrial clusters in science parks founder. A few firms are attracted by promises and juicy subsidies, but a cluster never materializes.

The supply of skills from local sources or elsewhere is certainly a plus for cluster formation, but whether one or several universities and research institutes can serve as the nucleus of a cluster is far from obvious. Often the most entrepreneurial and ambitious graduates move on to other more appealing cities, as they do from midwestern U.S. universities and now also from cities such as Harbin, Qiqihar, Daqing, and Shenyang in Northeastern China. The research done in universities generally has no immediate commercial relevance (it usually does not extend beyond early-stage technology development), and creating multidisciplinary teams in universities to do applied research so as to evolve technologies with practical applications can be an uphill task. Universities such as Johns Hopkins (in Baltimore) and the University of Pennsylvania (in Philadelphia) were unable to acquire land contiguous to their campuses

---

43 Founded in 1924, Technion claims that its graduates account for 70 percent of all the founders and managers of high-tech firms in Israel.

where a cluster could have materialized.[44] And with the exception of biotechnology, pharmaceuticals, and some branches of electronics, close links with a university or a major research establishment are of minor significance for industrial clusters. In today's world, with the ICT that is now so widely accessible, scientific knowledge and expertise can be harvested from around the world with only a little effort. It need not be on the doorsteps of the cluster. Nevertheless, policy makers, if not industrialists, are increasingly convinced that the university can play an axial role in high-tech clusters and that links between firms and universities will be critical to the growth and clustering of science-based industries. The current status of such links in Singapore, Hsinchu Science Park, and Bangalore—and of the efforts to enhance their efficacy—is discussed by Chen (in chapter 3), Wong (in chapter 4), and Basant (in chapter 5), respectively (see also Yusuf and Nabeshima 2007). Kenney (in chapter 2) and Park (in chapter 6) also highlight the role of universities in Silicon Valley and Seoul, respectively.

Innovation

In this volume, Chen and Kenney argue persuasively that clusters that survive and grow are conspicuous for their fertile innovativeness. A finely honed innovation capability enables clusters to expand, diversify the markets for their products, and make the transition to a fresh range of products or services as an existing product range matures and becomes commodified and quasi rents are competed away. The center of gravity of the Silicon Valley cluster has shifted through time from semiconductors, to integrated circuits, to software and Web-based services, to biotechnology, bioinformatics, and the rich new technological development at the intersection of electronics, biotechnology, nanotechnology, and ICT. The clusters in the Boston area have similarly diversified away from electronics and computers toward the life sciences and electro- and bioengineering products, plus a wide spectrum of ICT-based services. As Chen notes, the Hsinchu Science Park cluster took off only when the silicon foundry model was in place, thanks to the efforts of ITRI and the experienced leadership of Morris Chang and others who supported Taiwan Semiconductor Manufacturing Corporation and provided the financing. Now that the silicon foundry and fabless designer model is being embraced by urban centers in China, Hsinchu Science Park is scrambling to diversify into the life sciences and nanotechnology.

---

44 Both universities have now managed to acquire land nearby and are working with developers, such as Forest City, to create functioning clusters.

It is difficult enough to bring a cluster into existence by dint of policy; it is doubly difficult to make it innovative. Italian furniture, silk, footwear,[45] and tile clusters are struggling to survive under competitive pressure from China and are finding it hard to transform themselves through radical innovations that substantially broaden their product lines. However, their experience and the lessons from Silicon Valley and Boston provide a few clues as to how a cluster can position itself so as to maximize the likelihood of serial innovation.

First, clusters adjacent to world-class research-oriented universities with an emphasis on science and engineering, which attract the most talented students and faculty members, have an edge when it comes to innovation. This edge is likely to be further sharpened if the culture of the area—and of the cluster—powerfully supports entrepreneurship, offers many role models, generously rewards success, and is tolerant of failure but not of incompetence.[46]

Second, diversified clusters that host several interlinked industrial subsectors, such as engineering, electronics, and automotive parts, multiply the opportunities for innovation. It is now almost a cliché that more and more innovations are the outcome of multidisciplinary efforts by teams of researchers. But cliché or not, narrowly specialized clusters are at greater risk of atrophy than broader-based clusters—especially now (Adams and others 2004). For example, take the ICT sector. Many manufactured items now contain some semiconductor products. More and more goods are integrating features offered by ICT. Nanotechnology will also have a broad effect on many materials we use. Adding new industrial facets to a cluster is no ordinary challenge, but again it is more likely to happen in the mega urban area, which benefits from the economies of agglomeration and urbanization.

---

45 There are a few examples of remarkable success based on product innovations, supplemented by innovations in the supply chain and marketing to a broad range of customers. Geox shoes, with headquarters in Treviso, Italy, is a manufacturer of shoes made of waterproof but breathable fabric and is one such example (Camuffo, Furlan, Romano, and Vinelli 2005). Because most small Italian firms have concentrated on manufacturing, they have often been unsuccessful in introducing complementary innovations in design, engineering, and marketing (Camuffo, Furlan, and Grandinetti 2005).

46 Safford (2004) examines two instances of urban industrial hollowing out that have been partially reversed with the help of local universities. In one example, Akron, Ohio, the former tire capital of the United States accumulated expertise and new technological learning that has helped create firms producing polymers, fibers, and engineered plastics. In Rochester, New York, a center for optoelectronics, the vacancies left by the departure of traditional industries have been filled by firms producing lasers and photonic equipment.

An urban center can further facilitate innovation through its openness to ideas and heterogeneity and through urban spatial topography, amenities, and a culture that encourages face-to-face interaction—a mechanism conducive to the sparking of and spread of ideas (see Yusuf 2007). In other words, an urban area that functions as an open innovation system[47] is likely to have spillovers for the clusters in its midst, assisting their efforts to innovate and helping to nudge them in new directions through the infusion of fresh thinking and the opportunity to test market new products and ideas. Tokyo is a good example of a mega urban region that is home to many clusters—for consumer electronics, animation, robotics, apparel, and the life sciences—and that is full of adventurous consumers ready to experiment with novel offerings that could lead to niche markets (Yusuf and Nabeshima 2006). Again, these are broad observations grounded in casual empiricism that are not readily translated into policies for clusters. Strictly speaking, they would argue against attempting to pursue cluster-led development in smaller cities that lack an advanced infrastructure of research and tertiary education and a rich, open cultural environment—conditions that cannot be cultivated overnight through investments in an opera house and an enclave waterfront development, as in Baltimore.

Angel Investors and Venture Capitalists

Cluster diversification and innovation, whether by new business models or technologies, is the outcome of entrepreneurial endeavors that come to fruition only if financing is forthcoming. In chapter 2, Kenney emphasizes the central role of venture capital (VC) in the birth of Silicon Valley and the rejuvenation of Silicon Valley–based clusters when earlier lines of business lost steam. The contribution of VC has been underscored by others as well in connection with the entry of new firms, and it is widely believed that the ready availability of risk capital is one of the keys to cluster development—especially so of technology-intensive firms. However, a closer look at the data on financing of start-ups in the United States show that those firms that receive seed capital from investors rely mainly, if not exclusively, on angel investors[48]—and this was true of the early start-ups

---

47 New York, with its many creative industries, flourishes for this reason (see Currid 2007).
48 A few years ago, it was estimated that of the 200,000 technology-based ventures in the United States, one-tenth had received funding from angel investors in amounts ranging from US$100,000 to US$1 million. Only 500 companies received seed-stage financing from venture capitalists (Auerswald and Branscomb 2003; Branscomb 2004).

in Silicon Valley. Venture capitalists, by and large, provide later-stage mezzanine financing, once firms have established a performance record and the chances of their product succeeding and the viability of their business model are clearer. When a cluster has matured and become much larger, as in Silicon Valley,[49] Hsinchu Science Park, and Boston, venture capitalists can become more active in supporting start-ups.

A second characteristic of venture capitalists—particularly those operating in industrializing economies—is that they are likely to put only a small fraction of their resources in the new, technology-intensive sectors and to seek out the safer bets, those with a more assured near-term cash flow. Public sector venture capitalists or venture funds run by banks or institutional investors are even more inclined to play it safe, in part because their investment philosophy is conservative and in part because their knowledge of the industry is frequently shallow.

A third aspect of risk capital is that angel or VC financing adds value only when the financier has the experience to assist the start-up with specific advice regarding the industry. That assistance occurs when the financier mentors, coaches, and guides the embryonic firm on the basis of his or her hands-on experience; provides valuable management inputs and contacts; and paves the way to additional financing. In other words, the financier does a significant amount of handholding so as to help the new firm surmount the early and more difficult thresholds. Usually, only the angel investors and venture capitalists who have had or have direct personal involvement with a particular line of business—who have been successful and have acquired a certain standing in the business community—are in a position to groom new entrants. Most venture capitalists do not render such services.

The lesson is not that risk capital is of secondary importance for a high-tech cluster. Instead, the lesson is that angel investors emerge and local venture capitalists become most useful after the industry has gained some traction. And there is an accumulating fund of managerial experience and technological capacity (Heirman and Clarysse 2007) through which a few firms have bloomed into success stories and the learning process has progressed a few years. Foreign angel investors and venture capitalists with such experience, if they are prepared to invest in acquiring local knowledge, can serve as partial substitutes, but because of insufficient local

---

49 The multiple channels through which venture capitalists assist firms and work with management is discussed and analyzed by Bottazzi, Da Rin, and Hellman (2004) and Hellman and Puri (2002).

knowledge and contacts, they are rarely in a position to play the leading role that homegrown venture capitalists and angel investors can assume.[50]

East Asian economies have attempted to jumpstart the VC industry by setting up public sector funds and by encouraging initial public offerings so as to provide exit options (Kenney, Han, and Tanaka 2002). Singapore has taken a lead in this respect (see chapter 4 by Wong), joined by Korea, Taiwan (China), and Malaysia, all of which are scrambling to diversify into knowledge-based activities. The results thus far are not particularly encouraging, although risk capital is flowing to emerging sectors.[51] What is lacking is a solid core of angel investors, drawn from the seasoned veterans of high-tech businesses, who have accumulated wealth, acquired a reputation of expertise, and know the nuts and bolts of the business so intimately that they can coach new companies.

Another feature that is emerging slowly in industrializing economies is the well-tested exit option for angel investors and venture capitalists. Exit options depend on the existence of financial market institutions and a level of market activity that is fueled by large numbers of institutional investors and that permits the floating of initial public offerings for high-tech firms. They also depend on market mechanisms and a business culture that embraces mergers and acquisitions of rising new firms as a normal path for the growth of corporations.

Urban Setting and Infrastructure

Urban amenities are important attractions, as noted earlier. The cluster of creative industries being assembled in central Seoul, described in chapter 6 by Park, would be almost inconceivable in any other Korean city. In fact, virtually all the concentrations of creative industries, such as publishing, multimedia, video games, movie making, animation, design, and advertising, are gathered in a very few megacities, lured there by the promise of skilled labor and affordable housing,[52] recreational facilities, a clean and crime-free environment, and efficient services. However,

---

50 Historically, the financing for small firms and new start-ups has come from local inter-mediaries who mobilize resources also from local sources and are well acquainted with their borrowers' businesses prospects and risk profiles (Cull and others 2005).

51 In fact, there may be too much capital of this kind that is not being efficiently allocated with a keen sense for technological potential. There may not be a funding gap (Cressy 2002). Heirman and Clarysse (2007) find, for instance, that the volume of initial financing received is unrelated to the innovativeness of a firm.

52 The lack of affordable housing has become a major concern in the Boston area and in Silicon Valley, and it is inhibiting the influx of workers (Muro and others 2007). Inexpensive housing is one of the attractions of Austin and the Research Triangle area.

industrial clusters require more than just amenities for their employees; the quality of the physical infrastructure is an equally critical factor. With online communication, information gathering, and transactions becoming the rule in any high-tech industry, the sophistication of the ICT infrastructure and user costs are an important element in industry calculations. One of Seoul's attractions for the video game, movie-making, and Web-content industry relative to other East Asian cities is the quality and reach of the ICT infrastructure and the highly affordable user costs.

Clusters associated with electronics, the life sciences, and materials technologies demand reliable supplies of power and clean water (Mazurek 2003). Producing their own power and filtering their own water is always an option for clusters, but it is expensive and is usually viewed as a supplement to (reliable) municipal supplies. Producers of high-value items depend on ultramodern and convenient transportation facilities, particularly an airport with numerous connections such as Singapore's Changi, which allows them to ship their products quickly and to bring in inputs, spare parts, and skilled labor as needed. Cumbersome visa and customs formalities and sparse airline services are a grave handicap.

At one level, furnishing an urban area with infrastructure of the requisite quality is simpler than building a skilled workforce, but experience suggests that infrastructure remains the Achilles' heel of many cities. The cost of ensuring round-the-clock supplies of high-quality power and potable water is enormous, as is the cost of upgrading the transportation system. India's leading cities, including Bangalore, are falling far short of meeting even quite modest targets. Neither Bangalore nor Mumbai have yet been able to build modern airport facilities comparable to those in other major East Asian urban centers. Putting together the financing package for long-lived projects with extended payback periods is one hurdle, and even in times of abundant global liquidity, urban centers with weak credit ratings struggle to find the necessary capital from private and budgetary sources. A second hurdle is the replacement of old and worn-out facilities and the extension of these facilities to serve new customers. Infrastructure renewal can face intense opposition in major cities that are subject to many land-use restrictions, difficulties in acquiring land, and strongly entrenched interest groups. Projects can drag on for years and are complicated to implement, and cost overruns are frequent. When the projects have been completed, managing and maintaining the infrastructure so that it performs at or near its designed capabilities is taxing for municipal authorities and private providers. Regulating and pricing services and enforcing rules governing pollution and emissions pose yet more challenges. Cities in China that have constructed new water and sanitation infrastructure find that the skills and institutional framework to manage it can take years to mobilize. Perhaps the least problematic is the ICT infrastructure, but cities such as Bangkok and Kuala Lumpur are still unable to provide sufficient international bandwidth at competitive prices.

Municipal authorities in China have generally assigned priority to basic physical infrastructure and have moved aggressively to supply it in the high-tech zones in Beijing, Shanghai, Tianjin, and other leading cities. This emphasis on infrastructure has apparently facilitated the emergence of industry and underscores the supporting role that good infrastructure can play. But infrastructure projects are expensive and demanding, and infrastructure does not lead inevitably to cluster formation, as Malaysia has discovered, or to industrialization, as the Mezzogiorno in Italy has come to realize. It is just one stepping stone.

Anchor Firms

As stated at the beginning of this chapter, clusters come in many forms. They can be composed mainly of small firms, as in the Ota engineering cluster in the Tokyo metro area, and they can include a hierarchy of firms. An interesting feature of some of the most dynamic clusters is that one or several parent firms have had a large role in populating the cluster, as described by Kenney in chapter 2. This pattern was repeated in the Boston area, in North Carolina when IBM exited from that area, in San Diego with Hybritech,[53] in Bangalore when IBM shuttered its operations in that country and released its staff (see chapter 5 by Basant), and in Hsinchu Park with Taiwan Semiconductor Manufacturing Corporation. In Cambridge, United Kingdom, many of the clustered firms can be traced back to Cambridge Consultants, Acorn Computers, and Top Express (Myint, Vyakarnam, and New 2005).[54]

The growth of the Silicon Valley cluster is entwined with the histories of four firms: Shockley Semiconductor Laboratory, Fairchild, Hewlett-Packard (HP), and Lockheed. At different times, these companies were a dominant force in the valley, and HP remains a major presence. Former employees of these firms were responsible for starting scores of companies, and the demands generated by these corporate entities spawned networks

---

53 For more on Hybritech, see Smilor and others (2005). For details on the Hybritech spinoff tree, see Maeda (2005).

54 However, the Cambridge cluster has failed to create large global firms such as those that have proliferated in Silicon Valley (Athreye 2001).

of suppliers that fitted out the cluster. As Tim Sturgeon (2000) has shown, chance brought these firms to the Santa Clara, California, area. No municipal entity—and not Stanford University—had conceived in the 1940s and 1950s of electronics clusters. As Lécuyer (2006), O'Mara (2005), Sturgeon (2000) have described, the San Francisco Bay area cluster arose out of an unscripted sequence of events, as a result of many decisions and policies that also included those of U.S. federal agencies. No single architect anticipated and planned the valley cluster. Nevertheless, for cities aspiring to grow clusters, the role that large high-tech corporations and research institutes can play deserves close attention. In the case of Silicon Valley, the companies responsible for many start-ups had a strong bias toward research and innovation, recruited employees of high caliber, cultivated an informal and entrepreneurial culture, conducted research on a broad front opening up many new lines of development, and—with respect to Fairchild and HP at least—were tolerant and even supportive of employees who left to start their own firms.

So far, few if any such parent firms have appeared in East Asia. Until very recently, there were no examples of major Japanese corporations playing the role of Fairchild. As Maeda (2007) has pointed out, employees of Japanese firms rarely leave to launch companies of their own, partly because they are too comfortable in their lifetime jobs and partly because the risk of failure carries a lasting stigma. Start-ups that could populate a high-tech cluster are few in Japan.[55] Korean *chaebol* also have not spawned start-ups that could provide the makings of a cluster, and large firms in Southeast Asia have been equally barren. The cluster in Seoul, which Park describes in chapter 6, is not directly linked to Korea's leading chaebol.

Multinational corporations (MNCs), which have a significant and expanding presence in all of the industrializing Southeast Asia economies and China, have not induced start-ups either. Subsidiaries of MNCs have generated vertical spillovers affecting suppliers of inputs; however, horizontal intra-industry spillovers are far fewer.[56] Research institutes set up by MNCs, as in Penang, Malaysia, have also failed to initiate a start-up culture. Although there are exceptions, MNCs in East Asia have not served as hubs for high-tech clusters comprising networked suppliers. Most often,

---

55 Maeda (2005) observes that a crop of new firms has begun to appear.
56 For more on spillovers, see Kugler (2006). Liu and Buck (2007) observe that technology uptake by local firms depends on their preparedness and proactive seeking of new technology. Yeung, Liu, and Dicken (2006) find that MNCs and their foreign suppliers (for example, the telecommunication industry in China) can have spillover effects on firms and customers outside the cluster with which they trade.

MNCs persuade their key suppliers from their home countries to locate branch plants adjacent to their overseas facilities—as Japanese automobile assemblers have done in China, Indonesia, and Thailand—and farm out lesser-value, lower-tech components to local suppliers (see Takayasu and Mori 2004). Similarly, foreign first-tier suppliers also minimize their reliance on local producers for important components. The reasons usually are a lack of confidence in design and manufacturing capabilities and an unwillingness to share technology. Even in industrial centers such as Penang and Singapore, where MNCs have a long-standing presence, innovative and self-sustaining clusters made up of local firms have not emerged. When MNCs leave, as they do with some regularity, the local supplier base generally collapses. It lacks large innovative firms that can help it survive and chart a new and independent course. Were the multinational manufacturers, pharmaceutical majors, and producers of electronics to pull out of Indonesia, Malaysia, Singapore, or Thailand, the supplier base catering to their needs would be quickly depleted.

If MNCs have failed to spark cluster formation, so also have major research institutes, with the exception of ITRI/ERSO in Taiwan (China). Only the Korea Advanced Institute of Science and Technology and Korea Institute of Technology are possible contenders. In time, institutes in China might be able to achieve results equivalent to those of ITRI.[57] However, it is too early to tell. This start-up gap in much of East Asia for higher-tech activities may have several causes, of which three could be uppermost. First, neither the MNCs nor the research institutes are instilling much of an entrepreneurial spirit in their most talented engineers and technical personnel. As in Japan, the best people are reluctant to strike out on their own and take risks. There is the lack of a particular kind of entrepreneurship, not of entrepreneurship overall. This situation is changing in China and to an extent in Korea, albeit slowly.

Second, and with respect to the earlier reference to the importance of angel investors, there are extremely few role models—people who have successfully built up a high-tech and innovative company. East Asia has plenty of millionaires, but it has yet to find its Steve Jobs, Paul Allen, and Vinod Khosla. Masayoshi Son in Japan is a possible contender.[58] Success,

---

57 In the United States, the National Institutes of Health in Washington, D.C., has been responsible for the biotech cluster development in the Rockville-Bethesda area of Maryland. Other federal agencies, most notably the Pentagon, have underpinned the expanding cluster along the Dulles Airport access road and Reston in Virginia.

58 See Studwell (2007) on the characteristics of wealthy East Asian businessmen, the richest of whom have accumulated their wealth often through association with governments.

thus far, has rested on harnessing codified technologies; raising money through connections with officialdom, the extended family, or the clan; using protection afforded by local tariff regulations; and selling the products using mainly buyer-driven production chains, especially U.S. retailers and firms such as Nike.

Third, innovation capability is still weak. Potential entrepreneurs with ideas cannot connect with a critical mass of others with a variety of skills and penchant for experimentation and tinkering. East Asia is steadily learning and deepening its technical skills, but as has been noted repeatedly, the skills permit rapid and effective imitation, not innovation. The frequently voiced call by leaders in China, Korea, Singapore, and now Japan points to a persistent perceived shortfall. These rapidly growing economies that have demonstrated the capacity to invent—as numerous patents awarded to East Asian applicants testify (see table 1.3)—have not learned to innovate. If innovation is the dynamic that causes a cluster to

Table 1.3. Patents Granted by the U.S. Patent and Trademark Office to Selected Economies, 1963–2006

		2006	1963–2006
Total patents granted by USPTO		173,771	4,065,671
Patents of U.S. origin		89,823	2,381,249
Patents of foreign origin		83,948	1,684,422
Rank	*Economy*	*2006*	*1963–2006*
1	Japan	36,807	658,827
2	Germany	10,005	295,110
3	United Kingdom	3,585	123,371
4	France	3,431	110,839
6	Taiwan (China)	6,360	58,162
7	Switzerland	1,201	52,201
8	Korea, Republic of	5,908	44,125
10	Sweden	1,243	38,456
14	Israel	1,218	14,534
16	Finland	950	12,596
22	Singapore	412	3,305
23	China	661	3,178
24	Hong Kong (China)	308	3,156
25	India	481	2,899
38	Malaysia	113	637
43	Philippines	35	319
45	Thailand	31	270
56	Indonesia	3	168

Source: USPTO 2006.

enter a virtuous spiral, then routinizing innovation will be as essential as building infrastructure or enhancing the supply of risk capital.

Clues for Kitakyushu

In summary, what are the messages that the chapters in this volume and the literature on clusters can offer a mature industrial city such as Kitakyushu, the topic of the final chapter by Nabeshima and Yamashita and a focus of chapter 7 by Feldman? First, the questions to be posed are whether cluster development is even feasible and, moreover, whether one or two clusters can grow to a size and create enough highly paid jobs[59] to drive the economy. This question can be answered with some qualifications by looking at the acquired jurisdictional comparative advantages of technological capabilities, the level and distribution of local investment, the emergence of new firms, and the strategies being adopted by existing major firms, and then studying what is happening in comparable economies. If it does not appear that clusters offer a convincing long-term strategy, alternative approaches should be scrutinized and juxtaposed with urban resource endowments (including the university system) and industrial capabilities to arrive at a better match. Potential nuclei for cluster formation, or development more broadly, should be identified in the urban areas. These nuclei are the appropriate starting points, depending on corporate strategic objectives and product life cycles for specific products. In the case of Kitakyushu, they could include solar cells; green technologies, including those for recycling; mechatronics, which are an intersection of automotive parts and electronics technologies; and robotics—all of which draw on the existing industrial base described by Nabeshima and Yamashita.[60]

Second, a city may not be an appropriate unit of analysis. High-tech industrial clusters must be viewed in a regional or broader context. In most instances, a single city is too small in terms of market size and

---

59 The highly paid jobs typically have the largest multiple general equilibrium effects (Beaudry, Green, and Sand 2007).

60 The case of Hamamatsu, a city with approximately half the population of Kitakyushu, offers a useful point of comparison. The city's textile, musical instrument, and automobile industries have either departed or are fast disappearing. However, technological inputs from Shizuoka University enabled a world-class optoelectronics firm, Hamamatsu Photonics, to establish itself, assisted also by municipal investment in infrastructure. But only a few new firms have followed, in part because Shizuoka University "ceased to foster new spinouts or to forge deep ties with other companies, as it became more academically oriented" (Hatakenaka 2004: 2).

resource base. Silicon Valley embraces an urban region of Santa Clara Valley and the San Jose area that had a population of about 7 million in 2006.[61] Even if it were anchored in Kitakyushu, an industrial cluster would also draw its energy and resources from nearby Fukuoka and the rest of the island. Fukuoka's logistics infrastructure would provide valuable additional support. Thus, the planning for such a cluster would require coordination among the principal jurisdictions. In chapter 4, Wong underlines the roles of the state and the government-linked corporations in building ICT activities in Singapore, and in chapter 5, Basant points to the contribution of a succession of government actions that cumulatively created the ICT cluster–friendly environment in Bangalore.

Third, even in a mature region, retaining and augmenting human and social capital is vital to nurturing existing technological capabilities and preparing the ground for diversification. There are three parts to this lesson. One is that increased expenditure on local education and training can raise volume and quality. Wong and Basant both draw attention to the significance of human capital and of links between universities and businesses. A second part to the lesson is that widening the attractive employment opportunities in industry and research can help to retain the talented workers.[62] Creating opportunities is the most difficult part of all, and it is tied with local entrepreneurship and access to VC (which is the principal theme of chapter 2 by Kenney), access to risk capital, formation of new startups, and expansion of existing businesses and public sector–supported employment in research, teaching, and other service occupations. Pouring money into the ICT and research infrastructure and into new business ventures—as Seoul and the Beijing and Shanghai municipalities are doing and as Singapore is doing in the biomedical industry—are gambles that might work if they actually succeed in igniting entrepreneurship and innovation while steadily augmenting technological capability (see Yusuf and Nabeshima 2006). A third part is the formation of local, regional, and international networks that can serve as the social conduits for the transfer of technology and tacit knowledge. In chapter 6, Park discusses the role of such networks in the context of creative industries in Seoul.

---

61 This figure represents the estimated population of the Bay Area (Lelchuk 2007). Compare it with the population of Cambridgeshire in the United Kingdom, which is less than 600,000 (Athreye 2001).

62 China's northeastern provinces are now having to cope with a brain drain as the country's labor market becomes more flexible and integrated.

All of this is terrain that is largely uncharted. There are no tested hypotheses, only conjectures, and all are entwined with vague concepts such as culture, openness, and social capital. Can societies where freedoms are circumscribed behave as though they are open? Can technological innovation be cultivated independently of innovation in other areas? Can risk taking be taught and practiced in a society where the majority of professionals shun risk? There are no answers to these questions yet, and none may arrive soon.

Fourth, and finally, are the infrastructure, urban amenities, and services required by clusters. In both Singapore and Seoul, the quality of the ICT infrastructure has promoted cluster development. Even mature industrial cities such as Kitakyushu must ensure that infrastructure and services match the levels attained by leading competitors. Kitakyushu must also reverse a perception that it is a declining city with an aging population and a history of severe industrial pollution. Now that Kitakyushu has ushered out most of the polluting industries and rebuilt the downtown areas, it needs to project a fresh image and to create a buzz.

References

Adams, James D. 2001. "Comparative Localization of Academic and Industrial Spillovers." NBER Working Paper 8292, National Bureau of Economic Research, Cambridge, MA.

Adams, James D., Grant C. Black, Roger J. Clemmons, and Paula E. Stephan. 2004. "Scientific Teams and Institution Collaborations: Evidence from U.S. Universities, 1981–1999." NBER Working Paper 10640, National Bureau of Economic Research, Cambridge, MA.

Alecke, Björn, Christoph Alsleben, Frank Scharr, and Gerhard Untiedt. 2005. "New Evidence on the Geographic Concentration of German Industries." In *Industrial Clusters and Inter-Firm Networks*, ed. Charlie Karlsson, Börje Johansson, and Roger Stough, 321–57. Northampton, MA: Edward Elgar.

Andersson, Fredrik, Simon Burgess, and Julia I. Lane. 2007. "Cities, Matching, and the Productivity Gains of Agglomeration." *Journal of Urban Economics* 61: 112–28.

Athreye, Suma S. 2001. "Agglomeration and Growth: A Study of the Cambridge Hi-Tech Cluster." SIEPR Discussion Paper 00-42, Stanford Institute for Economic Policy Research, Stanford, CA.

Auerswald, Philip, and Lewis Branscomb. 2003. "Spin-Offs and Start-Ups: The Role of the Entrepreneur in Technology-Based Innovation." In *The Emergence of Entrepreneurship Policy: Governance, Start-Ups, and Growth in the Knowledge Economy*, ed. David M. Hart, 61–91. Cambridge, U.K.: Cambridge University Press.

Beaudry, Paul, David A. Green, and Benjamin Sand. 2007. "Spill-Overs from Good Jobs." NBER Working Paper 13006, National Bureau of Economic Research, Cambridge, MA.

Beerepoot, Niels. 2005. "Collective Learning by Artisanal Subcontractors in a Philippine Furniture Cluster." *Tijdschrift voor Economische en Sociale Geografie* 96 (5): 573–84.

Bettencourt, Luis M. A., José Lobo, and Deborah Strumsky. 2007. "Invention in the City: Increasing Returns to Patenting as a Scaling Function of Metropolitan Size." *Research Policy* 36 (1): 107–20.

Bottazzi, Laura, Marco Da Rin, and Thomas F. Hellman. 2004. "Active Financial Intermediation: Evidence on the Role of Organizational Specialization and Human Capital." CEPR Discussion Paper 4794, Centre for Economic Policy Research, London.

Branscomb, Lewis M. 2004. "Where Do High Tech Commercial Innovations Come From?" *Duke Law and Technology Review* (5).

Camuffo, Arnaldo, Andrea Furlan, and Roberto Grandinetti. 2005. "Knowledge and Capabilities in Subcontractor's Evolution: The Italian Case." MIT-IPC Working Paper 05-004, Massachusetts Institute of Technology–Industrial Performance Center, Cambridge, MA.

Camuffo, Arnaldo, Andrea Furlan, Pietro Romano, and Andrea Vinelli. 2005. "Breathing Shoes and Complementarities: How Geox Has Rejuvenated the Footwear Industry." MIT-IPC Working Paper 05-005, Massachusetts Institute of Technology–Industrial Performance Center, Cambridge, MA.

Carlino, Gerald A., Satyajit Chatterjee, and Robert M. Hunt. 2007. "Urban Density and the Rate of Invention." *Journal of Urban Economics* 61 (3): 389–419.

Casper, Steven. 2007. "How Do Technology Clusters Emerge and Become Sustainable? Social Network Formation and Inter-Firm Mobility within the San Diego Biotechnology Cluster." *Research Policy* 36 (4): 438–55.

Centre for Business Research. 2004. "UK Plc: Just How Innovative Are We?" University of Cambridge, Cambridge, U.K.

Chang, Myong-Hun, and Joseph E. Harrington. 2005. "Discovery and Diffusion of Knowledge in an Endogenous Social Network." *American Journal of Sociology* 110 (4): 937–76.

Chen, Chung-Jen, Hsueh-Liang Wu, and Bou-Wen Lin. 2006. "Evaluating the Development of High-Tech Industries: Taiwan's Science Park." *Technological Forecasting and Social Change* 73 (4): 452–65.

Chen, Kun, and Martin Kenney. 2007. "Universities/Research Institutes and Regional Innovation Systems: The Cases of Beijing and Shenzhen." *World Development* 35 (6): 1056–74.

Christensen, Clayton M. 2003. *The Innovator's Dilemma: The Revolutionary Book That Will Change the Way You Do Business.* New York: HarperCollins.

Colyvas, Jeannette A. 2007. "From Divergent Meanings to Common Practices: The Early Institutionalization of Technology Transfer in the Life Sciences at Stanford University." *Research Policy* 36 (4): 456–76.

Cooke, Philip. 2002. *Knowledge Economies: Clusters, Learning, and Cooperative Advantage.* London: Routledge.

Cortright, Joseph. 2006. *Making Sense of Clusters: Regional Competitiveness and Economic Development.* Washington, DC: Brookings Institute.

Cressy, Robert. 2002. "Funding Gaps: A Symposium." *Economic Journal* 112 (477): F1–F16.

Cull, Robert, Lance E. Davis, Naomi R. Lamoreaux, and Jean-Laurent Rosenthal. 2005. "Historical Financing of Small- and Medium-Sized Enterprises." NBER Working Paper 11695, National Bureau of Economic Research, Cambridge, MA.

Currid, Elizabeth. 2007. *The Warhol Economy: How Fashion, Art, and Music Drive New York City.* Princeton, NJ: Princeton University Press.

Degroof, Jean-Jacques, and Edward B. Roberts. 2004. "Overcoming Weak Entrepreneurial Infrastructures for Academic Spin-Off Ventures." MIT-IPC Working Paper 04-005, Massachusetts Institute of Technology–Industrial Performance Center, Cambridge, MA.

Dollar, David, Anqing Shi, Shuilin Wang, and Lixin Colin Xu. 2003. *Improving City Competitiveness through the Investment Climate: Ranking 23 Chinese Cities.* Washington, DC: World Bank.

Durbin, Ron. 2003. "The Competition Getting You Down? Feed Your Head." *ISIC Quarterly* 1 (1). http://isic.ucsd.edu/newsletter/comp.shtml.

Economist. 2007. "The Rise and Fall of Corporate R&D: Out of the Dusty Labs," *Economist* 382 (8518): 74–76.

Etzkowitz, Henry. 2002. *MIT and the Rise of Entrepreneurial Science.* London: Routledge.

Feldman, Maryann P., and Johanna Francis. 2005. "Homegrown Solutions: Fostering Cluster Formation." *Economic Development Quarterly* 18 (2): 127–37.

Feldman, Maryann P., Johanna Francis, and Janet E. L. Bercovitz. 2005. "Creating a Cluster While Building a Firm: Entrepreneurs and the Formation of Industrial Clusters." *Regional Studies* 39 (1): 129–41.

Feldman, Maryann P., and Roger Martin. 2004. "Jurisdictional Advantage." NBER Working Paper 10802, National Bureau of Economic Research, Cambridge, MA.

Florida, Richard. 2002. *The Rise of the Creative Class and How It's Transforming Work, Leisure, and Everyday Life.* New York: Basic Books.

Fu, Shihe. 2007. "Smart Café Cities: Testing Human Capital Externalities in the Boston Metropolitan Area." *Journal of Urban Economics* 61 (1): 86–111.

Geenhuizen, Marina van, and Nurul Indarti. 2006. "Knowledge and Innovation in the Indonesian Artisanal Furniture Industry." European Regional Science Association, Vienna. http://www.ersa.org/ersaconfs/ersa06/papers/847.pdf.

Glaeser, Edward L. 2003. "Reinventing Boston: 1640–2003." NBER Working Paper 10166, National Bureau of Economic Research, Cambridge, MA.

Glaeser, Edward L., and Christopher Berry. 2006. "Why Are Smarter Places Getting Smarter?" Policy Brief PB-2006-2, Harvard University, Cambridge, MA.

Glaeser, Edward L., and David C. Mare. 2001. "Cities and Skills." *Journal of Labor Economics* 19 (2): 316–42.

Glaeser, Edward L., and Albert Saiz. 2003. "The Rise of the Skilled City." NBER Working Paper 10191, National Bureau of Economic Research, Cambridge, MA.

Harrison, John. 2007. "From Competitive Regions to Competitive City-Regions: A New Orthodoxy, but Some Old Mistakes." *Journal of Economic Geography* 7 (3): 311–32.

Hatakenaka, Sachi. 2004. "Optoelectronics in Hamamatsu: In Search of a Photon Valley." MIT-IPC Working Paper 04-004, Massachusetts Institute of Technology–Industrial Performance Center, Cambridge, MA.

Heirman, Ans, and Bart Clarysse. 2007. "Which Tangible and Intangible Assets Matter for Innovation Speed in Start-Ups?" *Journal of Product Innovation Management* 24 (4): 303–15.

Heitzman, James 2004. *Network City: Planning the Information Society in Bangalore.* New York: Oxford University Press.

Hellman, Thomas, and Manju Puri. 2002. "Venture Capital and the Professionalization of Start-Up Firms: Empirical Evidence." *Journal of Finance* 57 (1): 169–97.

Horaguchi, Haruo. 2004. "Hollowing-Out of Japanese Industries and Creation of Knowledge-Intensive Clusters." Paper presented at Globalization and Revitalization of Industrial and Regional Employment: Comparison of Germany and Japan Symposium, Tokyo, March 26.

Indergaard, Mich. 2004. *Silicon Alley: The Rise and Fall of a New Media District.* London: Routledge.

Jenkins, J. Craig, Kevin T. Leicht, and Heather Wendt. 2006. "Class Forces, Political Institutions, and State Intervention: Subnational Economic Development Policy in the United States, 1971–1990." *American Journal of Sociology* 111 (4): 1122–80.

Johansson, Börje. 2005. "Parsing the Menagerie of Agglomeration and Network Externalities." In *Industrial Clusters and Inter-Firm Networks*, ed. Charlie Karlsson, Börje Johansson, and Roger Stough, 107–47. Northampton, MA: Edward Elgar.

Kang, Du Yong. 2007. "A Quantitative Estimation of Industrial Hollowing-Out." *Economic Papers* 8 (1): 32–49.

Keller, Wolfgang. 2002. "Geographic Localization of International Technology Diffusion." *American Economic Review* 92 (1): 120–42.

Kelly, Jim. 2001. "The Lively Chemistry of Transatlantic Enterprise." *Financial Times*, November 1, p. 14.

Kenney, Martin, Kyonghee Han, and Shoko Tanaka. 2002. "Scattering Geese: The Venture Capital Industries of East Asia: A Report to the World Bank." BRIE Working Paper 146, Berkeley Roundtable on the International Economy, University of California, Berkeley, CA.

Kim, Yong Jin. 2007. "A Model of Industrial Hollowing-Out of Neighboring Countries by the Economic Growth in China." *China Economic Review* 18 (2): 122–38.

Kobayashi, Hideo. 2007. "Responses of South Korea, Taiwan, and Japan to the Hollowing Out of Industry." Contemporary Asian Studies Center of Excellence, Waseda University, Tokyo.

Kugler, Maurice. 2006. "Spillovers from Foreign Direct Investment: Within or Between Industries." *Journal of Development Economics* 80 (2): 444–77.

Kynge, James 2006. *China Shakes the World: A Titan's Rise and Troubled Future— and the Challenge for America*. New York: Houghton Mifflin.

Leamer, Edward E., and Michael Storper. 2001. "The Economic Geography of the Internet Age." NBER Working Paper 8450, National Bureau of Economic Research, Cambridge, MA.

Lécuyer, Christophe. 2006. *Making Silicon Valley: Innovation and the Growth of High Tech, 1930–1970*. Cambridge, MA: MIT Press.

Leiponen, Aija. 2005. "Skills and Innovation." *International Journal of Industrial Organization* 23: 303–23.

Lelchuk, Ilene. 2007. "Bay Area: After Several Years of Decline, Population Starts to Grow Again." *San Francisco Chronicle*, B-3. http://www.sfgate.com/cgi-bin/article.cgi?f=/c/a/2007/04/05/BAGGVP2QD31.DTL.

Lembke, Johan, and Anders Osthol. 2005. "Regional Partnerships for the Biotech Sector: North Carolina and Sweden." In *Industrial Clusters and Inter-Firm Networks*, ed. Charlie Karlsson, Börje Johansson, and Roger Stough, 361–89. Northampton, MA: Edward Elgar.

Leslie, Stuart W., and Robert H. Kargon. 1997. "Selling Silicon Valley: Frederick Terman's Model for Regional Advantage." *Business History Review* 70 (4): 435–472.

Liu, Xiaohui, and Trevor Buck. 2007. "Innovation Performance and Channels for International Technology Spillovers: Evidence from Chinese High-Tech Industries." *Research Policy* 36 (3): 355–66.

Maeda, Noboru. 2005. "ICT Cluster Development: The Role of Start-Ups." Paper presented at the Second International Conference on ICT Clusters in East Asia, Kitakyushu, Japan, December 12.

———. 2007. "Japan Actually Has Start-Ups." In *Making It: The Rise of Asia in High Tech*, ed. Henry S. Rowen, Marguerite Gong Hancock, and William F. Miller, 74–86. Stanford, CA: Stanford University Press.

Markusen, Ann R. 1994. "Sticky Places in Slippery Space: The Political Economy of Postwar Fast-Growth Regions." Working Paper 79, Center for Urban Policy Research, New Brunswick, NJ.

———. 1996. "Sticky Places in Slippery Space: A Typology of Industrial Districts." *Economic Geography* 72 (3): 293–313.

Martin, Philippe, and Gianmarco I. P. Ottaviano. 2001. "Growth and Agglomeration." *International Economic Review* 42 (4): 947–68.

Martin, Ron, and Peter Sunley. 2003. "Deconstructing Clusters: Chaotic Concept or Policy Panacea?" *Journal of Economic Geography* 3 (1): 5–35.

Mazurek, Jan. 2003. *Making Microchips*. Cambridge, MA: MIT Press.

McKendrick, David G., and William P. Barnett. 2001. "The Organizational Evolution of Global Technological Competition." Report 2001-02, Information Storage Industry Center, La Jolla, CA.

McKendrick, David G., Richard F. Doner, and Stephan Haggard. 2000. *From Silicon Valley to Singapore: Location and Competitive Advantage in the Hard Disk Drive Industry*. Stanford, CA: Stanford University Press.

Ming, Su, and Zhao Quanhou. 2007. "China: Fiscal Framework and Urban Infrastructure Finance." In *Financing Cities*, ed. George E. Peterson and Patricia Clarke Annez, 74–107. Washington, DC: Sage.

Muro, Mark, John Schneider, David Warren, Eric McLean-Shinaman, Rebecca Sohmer, and Benjamin Forman. 2007. *Reconnecting Massachusetts Gateway Cities: Lessons Learned and an Agenda for Renewal*. Boston: MassInc.

Myint, Yin M., Shailendra Vyakarnam, and Mary J. New. 2005. "The Effect of Social Capital in New Venture Creation: The Cambridge High-Technology Cluster." *Strategic Change* 14 (3): 165–77.

O'Mara, Margaret Pugh. 2005. *Cities of Knowledge: Cold War Science and the Search for the Next Silicon Valley*. Princeton, NJ: Princeton University Press.

Perry, David, and Wim Wiewel, eds. 2005. *The University as Urban Developer*. New York: M. E. Sharpe.

Piore, Michael J., and Charles F. Sabel. 1984. *The Second Industrial Divide*. New York: Basic Books.

Rappaport, Jordan. 2007. "Moving to Nice Weather." *Regional Science and Urban Economics* 37 (3): 375–98.

Rodrik, Dani. 1996. "Coordination Failures and Government Policy: A Model with Applications to East Asia and Eastern Europe." *Journal of International Economics* 40 (1–2): 1–22.

Safford, Sean. 2004. "Searching for Silicon Valley in the RustBelt: The Evolution of Knowledge Networks in Akron and Rochester." MIT-IPC Working Paper 04-001, Massachusetts Institute of Technology–Industrial Performance Center, Cambridge, MA.

Sanz-Menendez, Luis, and Laura Cruz-Castro. 2005. "Critical Surveys." *Regional Studies* 39 (7): 939–54.

Saperstein, Jeff, and Daniel Rouach. 2002. *Creating Regional Wealth in the Innovation Economy*. Upper Saddle River, NJ: Financial Times Prentice Hall.

Smilor, Raymond, Niall O'Donnell, Gregory Stein, and Robert Welborn. 2005. "The Research University and the Development of High Technology Centers in the U.S." Paper presented at the Conference on University Industry Linkages in Metropolitan Areas in Asia, Washington, DC, November 17.

Studwell, Joe. 2007. *Asian Godfathers: Money and Power in Hong Kong and Southeast Asia*. Berkeley, CA: Atlantic Monthly Press.

Sturgeon, Timothy J. 2000. "How Silicon Valley Came to Be." In *Understanding Silicon Valley: Anatomy of an Entrepreneurial Region*, ed. Martin Kenney, 15–47. Stanford, CA: Stanford University Press.

Takayasu, Ken'ichi, and Minako Mori. 2004. "The Global Strategies of Japanese Vehicle Assemblers and the Implications for the Thai Automobile Industry." In *Global Production Networking and Technological Change in East Asia*, ed. Shahid Yusuf, Kaoru Nabeshima, and M. Anjum Altaf, 209–54. New York: Oxford University Press.

Trompenaars, Fons, Peter Prud'homme, Jae Ho Park, and Charles Hampden-Turner. 2002. "Pioneering the New Organization: Jim Morgan, Applied Materials." In *21 Leaders for the 21st Century: How Innovative Leaders Manage in the Digital Age*, ed. Fons Trompenaars and Charles Hampden-Turner, 215–38. New York: McGraw-Hill.

USPTO (United States Patent and Trademark Office). 2006. "Patents by Country, State, and Year: Utility Patents (December 2006)." USPTO, Washington, DC. http://www.uspto.gov/web/offices/ac/ido/oeip/taf/cst_utl.htm.

Webster, Douglas. 2006. "Supporting Sustainable Development in Thailand: A Geographic Clusters Approach." National Economic and Social Development Board of Thailand and World Bank, Bangkok.

World Bank. 2005. *Malaysia: Firm Competitiveness, Investment Climate, and Growth*. Report No. 26841-MA. Washington, DC: World Bank.

———. 2008. *Towards a Knowledge Economy in Thailand*. Washington, DC: World Bank.

World Development. 2007. "Special Issue: University-Industry Linkages in Metropolitan Areas in Asia." *World Development* 35 (6): 931–1097.

Wu, Weiping. 2007. "Building Research Universities for Knowledge Transfer: The Case of China." In *How Universities Promote Economic Growth*, ed. Shahid Yusuf and Kaoru Nabeshima, 185–98. Washington, DC: World Bank.

Yamawaki, Hideki. 2002. "The Evolution and Structure of Industrial Clusters in Japan." *Small Business Economics* 18 (1–3): 121–40.

Yeung, Henry Wai-Chung, Weidong Liu, and Peter Dicken. 2006. "Transnational Corporations and Network Effects of a Local Manufacturing Cluster in Mobile Telecommunications Equipment in China." *World Development* 34 (3): 520–40.

Yusuf, Shahid. 2007. "About Urban Mega Regions: Knowns and Unknowns." Policy Research Working Paper 4252, World Bank, Washington, DC.

Yusuf, Shahid, and Kaoru Nabeshima. 2006. *Postindustrial East Asian Cities*. Palo Alto, CA: Stanford University Press.

———, eds. 2007. *How Universities Promote Economic Growth*. Washington, DC: World Bank.

CHAPTER 2

Lessons from the Development of Silicon Valley and Its Entrepreneurial Support Network for Japan

Martin Kenney

In the 1990s, Silicon Valley achieved iconic status for economic development planners globally. But how did Silicon Valley come into being? And how can the development of the industrial clusters responsible for the success of Silicon Valley inform efforts in East Asia to create new clusters or to enable existing ones to retain their vigor through diversification? This chapter argues that the rise of Silicon Valley was a social process of bricolage in which not only did actors fashion solutions for various problems that they confronted (Garud and Karnøe 2003), but also new actors were called into being to support entrepreneurial activities. Frequently, the solutions were adapted from existing business practices and then applied to new purposes. Similarly, the new actors were mainly preexisting businesses, such as law firms, that acquired new specializations. For the most part, the solutions were responses to immediate problems or path-dependent drifts, rather than wisely considered, far-sighted answers by prescient economic actors maximizing their utility functions. Like the Panda's thumb, solutions that worked were diffused, repeated, and adjusted, gradually evolving into routines and institutions (Nelson and Winter 1982). These routines and institutions enabled and encouraged further experimentation even as a stable repertoire of actions came into being. If one borrows from Spender's (1989) notion of industrial recipes, Silicon Valley actors developed, through an unplanned iterated learning process, a "regional recipe" for creating and nurturing start-ups. Technology and institutions coevolved to create an entrepreneurial support network (ESN) within which entrepreneurs were able to encapsulate many new innovations in separate firms, as opposed to having all of the innovations being commercialized by existing firms. Similar support networks are likely to influence the diversification of clusters in regions such as Kyushu in Japan and places elsewhere in East Asia (Rowen, Hancock, and Miller 2007).

In discussions of regions that derive dynamism from new firms commercializing new technologies, the technologies and their trajectories should be examined (Dosi 1984). The technologies are the raw material that entrepreneurs use to create their firms, but these technologies are socially constructed and shaped. One argument for the importance of seeing this process as socially constructed is that the most successful Silicon Valley entrepreneurs, such as Larry Ellison, William Hewlett, Steven Jobs, William Joy, Robert Noyce, and David Packard, have been marketers as much as technologists.[1] Unfortunately, beyond a few popular press articles, the role of marketing in helping to create markets for new technology is little understood.

Information, computer, and electronics (ICE) technologies and, to a far lesser degree, biomedical technologies formed the technical base of the venture capital–financed start-up economy. For the past five decades, ICE technologies have experienced exponential rates of improvement in cost and functionality. Also, ICE technologies have frequently experienced (or, alternatively, entrepreneurs have created) moments when entry barriers have been decreased sufficiently to allow well-placed and nimble entrepreneurs to enter new market niches. Thus, understanding Silicon Valley is predicated, on one dimension, on tracing the evolution of technologies and the industries based on them and, on another dimension, on the evolution of the institutions, practices, and cultural understandings that orient action.

---

1 See Hargadon and Douglas (2001) for a discussion of Edison's marketing genius or Lampel's (2001) suggestive work on the use of technological spectacles.

Joseph Schumpeter recognized that technological change offers possibilities to entrepreneurs, but establishing a new firm is difficult and risky. During the past five decades, in regions like Silicon Valley, a support infrastructure of institutions that assist in new firm creation has evolved to mitigate the liabilities of newness (Stinchcombe 1965). In Silicon Valley, successful entrepreneurship preceded the creation of supporting institutions, such as venture capital firms (Feldman 2001; Kenney 2000), and after these support organizations came into existence, they incited further entrepreneurship by creating more demand for start-ups. Creating demand was not their only contribution. They also lowered entry barriers by simplifying the process for forming firms and by speeding the growth of start-ups by providing capital, services, and advice.[2] Gradually, the institutions providing such assistance became part of the environment, thereby altering the trajectory of further evolution. Institutions and agents within Silicon Valley have survived repeated downturns that have winnowed participants and business models.

This chapter examines the building of Silicon Valley's entrepreneurial support infrastructure and its coevolution with local high-tech industries. It highlights the way entrepreneurs developed new business models and often combined different technologies to create fresh business opportunities. It also considers the importance of culture as an explanatory variable, arguing that culture is as much a dependent variable as it is an independent variable. Culture coevolved with the regional business activity—and, in the case of Silicon Valley culture, it might better be seen as a learned set of guides to action, rather than as some ethereal force emanating from a "Gold Rush" mentality or set of personal attributes. The conclusion examines the implications of these findings for the encouragement of entrepreneurship in regions such as Kyushu in Japan, which to date has seen minimal entrepreneurial activity.

Formation of Silicon Valley

Entrepreneurship in Silicon Valley involves two separate sets of organizations formed over time in tandem with the industries that were developed in the region (Kenney and von Burg 1999). The first set of organizations produces entrepreneurs, and the second specializes in supporting the

---

2 There is considerable debate as to whether location in the cluster increases survival rates.

entrepreneurial process. The primary source of entrepreneurs for Silicon Valley start-ups has been other firms (Gompers, Lerner, and Scharfstein 2003; Zhang 2003). Though Gordon Moore, a founder of Intel, argues that university and corporate research institutions contributed little to the evolution of the semiconductor industry (Moore and Davis 2001), he may underestimate the role of universities and corporate research laboratories in providing the support and intellectual space for the seeds of new industries to develop (National Research Council 1999). A number of pacesetting firms in individual industries can be attributed to universities and corporate research laboratories. For example, 3Com, Cisco, Yahoo!, Seagate, Google, Sun Microsystems, and Cadence are directly linked to San Francisco Bay Area corporate research institutes and universities, a set of interdependent institutions specialized in supporting firms (Kenney and Goe 2004).

The decision by William Shockley in 1956 to establish Shockley Semiconductor Laboratory in Santa Clara, California, was a defining moment for the Silicon Valley cluster. Shockley had also considered the Boston area, where a number of transistor firms were already using germanium as their substrate, MIT was producing numerous technically capable personnel, and a group of early technology adopters (the mini-computer firms) were on the verge of being established. On reflection, there seems little doubt that a number of other regions, such as Los Angeles, Long Island, or northern New Jersey, would have had sufficient technical personnel, lead customers, and other institutional supports to allow an industry to take root. For example, the germanium-based transistor firms on the East Coast, particularly in Boston, might have switched to silicon, which ultimately became the substrate of choice for the most important technology of the late 20th century—the silicon semiconductor. Alternatively, Texas Instruments, in Dallas, might have begun to spin off firms. Texas Instruments was not as badly managed as Shockley Semiconductor, and unlike Shockley Semiconductor, it never experienced mass resignations like those leading to the creation of Fairchild Semiconductor. Later, Fairchild Semiconductor also began leaking people, who created the start-ups that eventually transformed the region into what the editor of *Electronic News* first described in 1971 as "Silicon Valley."[3]

If Shockley Semiconductor was the "bad seed" that soon failed, Fairchild was the most fecund seed of all, producing numerous start-ups.

---

3 See http://www.netvalley.com for a history of the term.

However, in some sense, fecundity is also a function of the environment, and the environment into which Fairchild was born was significant. The existing electronics industry could be traced back as far as Lee De Forest and the invention of the vacuum tube (Lécuyer 2006; Sturgeon 2000). Other entrepreneur-based, high-tech electronics firms—the most salient of which were Hewlett-Packard (HP) and Varian—were located in the region. Though these firms were not semiconductor firms, they were electronics firms, and HP was especially important because it produced basic equipment, such as oscilloscopes and potentiometers, that all electronic firms needed.

Shockley was not alone in deciding to locate a high-technology electronics firm in the Bay Area. In 1952, IBM decided to establish a branch of its Yorktown Heights research laboratory in San Jose to tap the skilled personnel in the area.[4] Approximately 18 years later, in July 1970, Xerox established its West Coast research facility in Palo Alto (called the Palo Alto Research Center, or PARC) to secure access to the now even more skilled labor pool. But even in the 1950s, there were compelling business reasons to establish a new high-technology electronics firm in the region.

William Shockley's relocation to Palo Alto was serendipitous and was at least partially motivated by his desire to live close to his mother. However, the history of Silicon Valley must also encompass key regional actors. Among them, Frederick Terman, initially dean of engineering and then provost at Stanford University, was a near-mythical figure in its development (Lécuyer 2006; Sturgeon 2000). A professor of electrical engineering, Terman admired the MIT model of university interaction with business. He was also a fervent believer in the economic potential of electronics, championing the establishment of electronics firms in the region and assiduously working to attract them and encourage entrepreneurship among students and faculty. He had early success in encouraging Stanford graduates William Hewlett and David Packard and the Varian brothers to establish firms. However, though HP would become the largest electronics firm in region, it was the decision by Shockley to establish his semiconductor firm in the Palo Alto area that was the key to the creation of Silicon Valley. Serendipity brought Shockley to the region, and Frederick Terman encouraged him in his

---

4 The San Jose laboratory would pioneer magnetic data storage media and became IBM's global center of excellence for magnetic media. Much later, many key Silicon Valley disk drive entrepreneurs spun out of IBM to create new disk drive firms (McKendrick, Doner, and Haggard 2000). Later, IBM's laboratory was an important source of the relational database technology that firms such as Oracle and Sybase commercialized in the mid-1980s.

decision. Terman was a centrally located actor actively trying to affect the trajectory of events. At its root, the success of the cluster in the region was the result of the strategies of key actors, happenstance, and institutional evolution.

Business Models and Regional Recipes

An ESN emerged in concert with the success of new firms. The creation of the venture capital industry has often been directly attributed to Fairchild Semiconductor, and Fairchild and its progeny did play an important part. Although there were already a number of informal investors in the region who were willing to invest in new electronics start-ups, the capital required to start Fairchild was secured by Arthur Rock, who, at the time, was a manager at the New York investment bank Hayden Stone and active in arranging the private placement of securities issued by small technology-based firms. The practice of angel investing had a long history: in 1909 Stanford professors and administrators invested in a start-up, Federal Telegraph (Sturgeon 2000). Though it is difficult to be certain, there is anecdotal evidence that the Bay Area was already in the 1950s one of the national centers for angel investing in electronics.[5]

Whether Fairchild should be considered irreplaceable in the formation of the Silicon Valley high-technology cluster is probably unanswerable. Leslie (2000) argues that a microwave technology cluster was established in the region at roughly the same time (the 1950s) on the basis of U.S. Defense Department research. From 1955 through the early 1960s, there was a high-technology electronics boom, and many firms were formed in the region with funding from informal investors. There is reason to believe that a high-technology cluster of some sort was evolving and would have continued to evolve. However, the region is named "Silicon Valley" with good reason. The semiconductor was the most important technology of the 20th century, and it was a critical input that made new industries such as workstations, personal computers, and computer networking possible. There can be little doubt that the semiconductor is at the heart of the technological dominance that Silicon Valley has shown in the sphere of ICE for the past three decades.

---

5 The historical record suggests that in Boston there were very few angels, and this lack of investors is, in fact, cited as one of the reasons for the formation of the first formal venture capital firm, American Research and Development (Hsu and Kenney 2005).

Entrepreneurs, Technologies, Firms, and Industries in Silicon Valley

The evolution of Silicon Valley is based on its entrepreneurs, the technologies they commercialize, and the firms they create. Figure 2.1 illustrates the most significant technologies that have fueled the region's growth. In some cases, a technology was developed in Silicon Valley but eventually shifted out of the region entirely. Technology also came in from outside Silicon Valley; for example, semiconductor technology was imported from Bell Laboratories in New Jersey.

Levels of employment are a good measure of which industries were most important. Figure 2.2 shows that software currently employs the greatest numbers in the region, having overtaken components (such as semiconductors) in 1996. Software continued to grow very rapidly in the late 1990s, fueled by the dot-com boom. Employment in the aerospace sector, represented by guided missiles, has been largely steady at 20,000 through the entire period, with the exception of the 1980s, when it doubled because of President Ronald Reagan's Star Wars plans. The growth of computer and peripherals employment is interesting because it peaked in the early 1980s and then decreased to approximately 25,000 in 2001. Benefiting from the dot-com boom, communication equipment employment grew from approximately 20,000 in the 1980s to more than 50,000 in the late 1990s. Scientific instruments also have been an important contributor to Bay Area employment since the 1970s. However, the most noteworthy growth has been in software, an industry that did not even merit a separate category until the early 1970s, a few years after IBM signed the consent decree unbundling software and hardware.

Employment provides one perspective on the structure of the Bay Area high-technology industries. Figure 2.3 indicates the number of establishments in each industry and thus provides a different perspective. The numbers differ so radically that a logarithmic scale was required to present the data. Notice that during the entire period, there were no more than six establishments in guided missiles. In the case of components, instruments, communication equipment, and computer and peripherals, the number of firms was in the hundreds, though obviously there was great turnover. In absolute terms, the number of computer establishments has declined since its high-water mark in the 1980s. This decline corresponds with the proliferation and later shakeout of microcomputer and workstation manufacturers. The one industry showing a continuing high rate of entry is software, which despite the collapse

Figure 2.1. Genealogy of Silicon Valley Technologies: Stanford University, Hewlett-Packard, University of California–Berkeley, Xerox PARC, IBM San Jose, and University of California–San Francisco

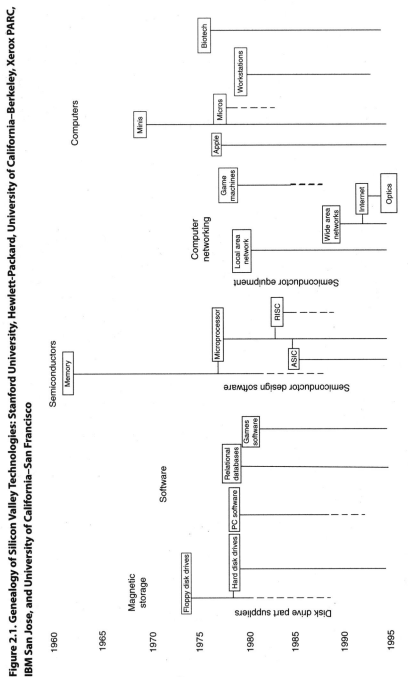

Source: Author's compilation.

Note: ASIC = application-specific integrated circuits; RISC = reduced instruction set computer.

Figure 2.2. Employment in Four Bay Area Counties, 1959–2001

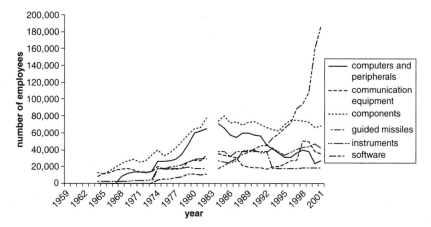

Source: Author's compilation.
Note: Data before 1998 were collected by Standard Industrial Classification (SIC) code. For 1998 to 2001, data were not available in SIC codes. Therefore, data were collected in North American Industrial Classification codes, which approximate SIC codes.

Figure 2.3. Establishments in Four Bay Area Counties, 1959–2001

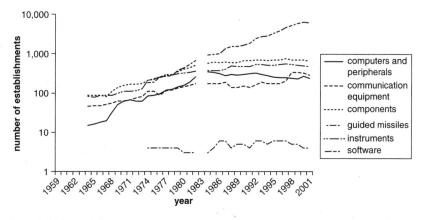

Source: Author's compilation.
Note: Data before 1998 were collected by SIC code. For 1998 to 2001, data were not available in SIC codes. Therefore, data were collected in North American Industrial Classification codes, which approximate SIC codes.

of the dot-com bubble in 2001 has continually grown in the number of establishments and employment since entering the Census of Manufacturing in 1974.

The quantitative indicators and Figure 2.1 provide an overview of the development of the region. In the following sections, the development of the most salient industries and firms will be examined, providing a richer description of the coevolution of the region, technologies, and industries responsible for the Silicon Valley cluster.

Semiconductors and Ancillary Industries

Over the past four decades, semiconductor technology has had a single overwhelming dynamic, namely Moore's Law, which correctly predicted that the areal density of transistors would double every 18 months. Because the cost of a semiconductor device is roughly comparable to the chip's dimensions, either performance increases for the same price or price drops accordingly. Thus, each new generation of semiconductor devices is able to process more data than the previous generation, providing the opportunity to increase the speed and capability of any artifact containing semiconductors. As a result, products containing integrated circuits (ICs) experience constant improvements in functionality, and functionality that formerly was too expensive or even impossible to achieve continually becomes less expensive and enters the realm of the possible.

Semiconductor technology was so fecund in opening new economic spaces that new business opportunities repeatedly emerged, and experts in the field had opportunities to create their own firms. This fecundity is illustrated by the fact that Fairchild and its successor firms experienced 134 spinoffs by 1986 (SEMI 1986), and there have been more since then. Even as the increase in areal density made ICs less expensive per transistor, the cost of a fabrication facility doubled every four years (Leachman and Leachman 2004). When Fairchild began producing chips, converted pizza ovens were used for the baking process. By 1975, a fabrication facility cost approximately US$50 million (ÓhUallacháin 1997: 220), and in keeping with the predictions of life-cycle theory, entry costs increased to the point at which there were far fewer entrants.[6] According to Semiconductor Equipment and Materials International's genealogy (SEMI 1986), during 1974 to 1980 there were 21 entrants in Silicon Valley (or an average of 3 per year). In the seven prior years, 1967 to 1973, there were 43 start-ups (an average of 6.1 per year). Yet in the following six years, 1981 to 1986, a total of 46 firms were established (an average of 7.7 firms per year).

The increased rate of entry after 1981 was the result of a collective action solution to the increasing cost of fabrication. Beginning in the

---

6 The classic citations on industry and product life-cycle theories are Abernathy (1978), Abernathy and Utterback (1978), and, most recently, Klepper (1996).

early 1980s, venture capitalists funded a number of start-ups to design and market new ICs. However, they contracted for manufacturing from the integrated producers that had spare capacity, thus circumventing the entry barrier created by the capital cost of fabrication. The IC producers benefited, because their expensive fabrication facilities could be fully used. The difficulty with this solution was that during semiconductor market booms, the integrated manufacturers reclaimed their capacity, and the fabless firms often lost their access to the fabrication capacity. A market-based solution was the silicon foundry, which specialized in contract manufacturing. These foundries, which were established in Taiwan (China), were pure contractors that did not compete with their customers. As specialists, they had to be willing to invest in providing excellent service and rapid turnaround (Leachman and Leachman 2004). Soon, a number of firms were established in Taiwan (China) to produce chips designed by other firms. A symbiotic relationship developed that eliminated the high cost of manufacturing as an entry barrier and unleashed a plethora of new Silicon Valley semiconductor start-ups that specialized in design and marketing.

The key to continuing Silicon Valley entrepreneurship in the semiconductor industry has been the ability to create new business models. The solution to the problem of high entry costs for fabrication reopened the industry to start-ups, and the pace of start-up formation, once again, accelerated. This solution was possible only because the actors in the support infrastructure were willing to back start-ups that were pioneering new business models.

Frequently, an industrial cluster will both attract and spawn supplier firms for the core industry (Porter 1998). The roots of the semiconductor equipment industry can also be traced to Fairchild Semiconductor. Fairchild initially built its equipment internally but soon decided to divest these activities and assist with the spinoff of firms like Electroglas, Kasper, and Micro Tech Manufacturing (Moore and Davis 2001; von Hippel 1988: 173). The most significant surviving Fairchild-linked equipment firms are Applied Materials (established in 1967), which is the largest semiconductor equipment maker in the world; KLA (established in 1976) and Tencor (established in 1976), which merged in 1997 to form KLA-Tencor; Lam Research (established in 1980); and Novellus (established in 1984)—all of which are located in Silicon Valley. Though very few ICs are made in Silicon Valley, it shares with Japan the distinction of being the global center for semiconductor production equipment design and manufacturing. In fact, the headquarters of Semiconductor Equipment and Materials International, an industrial association, is in San Jose.

In the past three decades, a merchant IC design automation software industry emerged. This software was a response to the fact that increasingly complex IC designs could no longer be done on paper without an unacceptable number of errors. Thus, in the late 1960s, integrated semiconductor firms began developing software tools for design automation. Fairchild was an early leader, as its engineers developed computer-aided design (CAD) software (Walker 1998). At the beginning of the 1980s, a number of IC design software start-ups were established. Many of the advances were made at the University of California–Berkeley and certain Berkeley professors participated in forming start-ups. For example, in 1982, James Solomon, who was assisted by a number of Berkeley professors, established Solomon Design Automation (SDA). SDA merged with ECAD, a start-up that was publicly traded, to form Cadence Design Systems (interview with James Solomon by Richard Florida and Martin Kenney, Santa Clara, CA, March 31, 1988). Today, Cadence is the world's largest supplier of electronic design technologies, methodology services, and design services. In 1986, Synopsys, a major competitor, was founded in North Carolina as a spinout from a General Electric acquisition, Calma. However, at the suggestion of its venture capital investors, Synopsys relocated to Silicon Valley (interview with Aart J. de Geus by Richard Florida and Martin Kenney, Cupertino, CA, March 30). As the software improved, an ever-greater number of the IC firms abandoned their in-house software and purchased software from the design software vendors. Design software standardization facilitated the rise of fabless semiconductor firms, because they could purchase their design tools, releasing them from the onerous task of creating their own software. The software also allowed the foundries to stipulate their manufacturing parameters in the software to be used by the designers. In other words, the design software became the interface between the designers and the manufacturers.

The development of a supplier industry enriched the semiconductor industry ecosystem. A number of these firms were very successful, benefiting the venture capitalists investing in them and contributing to the growth of the venture capital industry. Each new division of labor reinforced not only the semiconductor industry, but also the ESN.

The semiconductor industry was important for a number of reasons beyond its technological fecundity. First, the large number of spinoffs in the 1960s encouraged the already-existing entrepreneurial culture.

Second, the semiconductor industry provided significant investment opportunities for venture capital. Third, it attracted attention to the region and many of the region's entrepreneurs, including Gordon Moore, Robert Noyce, and Jerry Sanders, achieved fame as the region became known as "Silicon Valley."

Computers

Silicon Valley was the birthplace of computer firms that served a wide variety of product classes (IBM-compatible mainframes, minicomputers, workstations, personal computers, and so forth), though, interestingly enough, Silicon Valley became dominant only in workstations. Of particular importance was a class of small computers based on microprocessors, a new category of ICs that were pioneered by Silicon Valley semiconductor firms in the early 1970s. These small computers, dedicated to individuals, were central to the establishment of the networked, distributed computing paradigm that dominates contemporary computing. This period is also interesting because Silicon Valley firms produce many of the crucial components in personal computers (PCs) today, even though Silicon Valley is no longer the center of the PC industry.

Initially, of course, IBM and the various other mainframe producers dominated the computing industry. It was with the minicomputer, which was so important for the building of Route 128, that Silicon Valley firms began to experience success in computing. The greatest success was HP, but many other venture capital–financed start-ups entered the market. Some of them, such as Tandem Computer, established in 1975 to offer fail-safe computing, captured unique niches, while others were me-too firms. Another important firm was Amdahl, which was founded in 1970 by Eugene Amdahl, a key IBM computer designer, and which offered an IBM plug-compatible computer. A number of these computing firms were successful, but they did not spawn waves of new firm creation and entirely new industries; rather, they occupied niches and created large capital gains for investors.

For Silicon Valley, the great wave of new firm creation in computing would begin in the late 1970s when two technological trajectories combined to create personal computing. The first trajectory was the work at Xerox PARC, which developed an expensive workstation that was a personal computer (that is, not a time-shared computer). The Xerox effort, in fact, created a workstation designed by engineers for engineers. Xerox failed to capture the market, but many start-ups entered the market to try where Xerox was failing. Very quickly, a market for workstations developed, and an industry emerged, led by Sun (Stanford University Network) Microsystems, which was based in Silicon Valley, and Apollo Computer, which was based on Route 128. Sun became the dominant workstation provider, though in the late 1980s and early 1990s, it was challenged by another Stanford spinout, Silicon Graphics, which specialized in graphics computing. Eventually, the workstation firms would morph into the computer server providers.

The other personal computing trajectory was what was then called the *microcomputer*, and it led directly to the PC. Beginning in the mid-1970s, hobbyists and engineers, including Apple's Steve Jobs and Steve Wozniak, began building computers using the newly introduced microprocessors from Silicon Valley firms, such as Intel and Zilog, and the non–Silicon Valley firm Motorola. Silicon Valley soon became a hotbed of hobbyist computer start-ups with their locus in the now-famous Homebrew Computer Club that met at Stanford University (Freiberger and Swaine 1984; Langlois 1990).[7] Of all the start-ups, Apple Computer was the most strategic, because Steve Jobs actively tapped the Silicon Valley entrepreneurial support structure (Young 1988: 151). By using this infrastructure and conforming to its requirements, Jobs transformed Apple, as investors required the appointment of experienced management and made other changes necessary to establish a real business. This support helped tip the scales for Apple's survival and growth.

During the early 1980s, microcomputer start-ups proliferated. By all measures, the region was on its way to becoming the industry center. New firms were being established to provide software (for example, VisiCalc was developed by Bay Area entrepreneurs) and components. Then, in August 1981, IBM introduced its PC, which rapidly became the dominant design, and nearly all the non-IBM-compatible microcomputer firms in Silicon Valley and other places disappeared. Within three short years, most Silicon Valley microcomputer firms, with the notable exception of Apple, left the business (Angel and Engstrom 1995). After the mid-1980s, Silicon Valley would not host any new PC companies, with the exception of HP, which entered during that period.

The demise of the PC industry did not mean that Silicon Valley would not benefit from the diffusion of PCs. Numerous start-ups found opportunities to supply components, including microprocessors (Intel and Advanced Micro Devices); BIOS (basic input/output system) chips (American Megatrends Inc., Phoenix Technologies, and Chips and

---

7 Bill Gates was also far more closely related to this hobbyist stream than he was to PARC.

Technologies); graphics chips (S3 Graphics, NVIDIA, and Cirrus Logic); hard disk drives (Seagate, Quantum, and Conner Peripherals); and even computer mice (Logitech and Kensington). The loss of the PC industry to IBM and then the cloners created new markets for peripherals and components that Silicon Valley firms could supply.

When the IBM PC, with its simple architecture, was introduced and low-cost cloners began to enter the market, Silicon Valley's technological prowess no longer provided any particular advantage for PC assembly. Apple survived, in an ever-narrowing niche, on the basis of marketing and some desirable software features. Silicon Valley's position as a center for computing systems firms deteriorated as the PC turned computing hardware into a commodity and eroded the workstation market. In historical terms, with each new computing category, Silicon Valley firms were early leaders, and yet, in some cases, the industry evolved in ways that prevented them from remaining in that industry.

Computer Networking

The first computer networking firms in Silicon Valley were established in the early 1970s (von Burg 2001).[8] Time-sharing of minicomputer capacity was one of the earliest forms of computer networking, and a number of start-ups were established in Silicon Valley and other regions to exploit it. As a greater number of computers were installed on corporate campuses, an opportunity arose to provide technologies that would allow for faster data transfer rates through local area networks (LANs). The initial opportunity was in exchanging data between mainframes.

The proximate cause for dramatically increased interest in computer networking was an effort that began in the early 1970s to automate the office. This "office of the future" required a network to share files between computers and expensive peripherals such as printers and data storage devices. A pioneer in this quest was Xerox PARC, which in the mid-1970s created a system of small computers, laser printers, and data storage devices networked by what would be called *Ethernet*. PARC was not alone in this effort; minicomputer firms such as Wang Laboratories were also experimenting with the future office.

At the end of the 1980s, computers were proliferating, and entrepreneurs began forming firms to design and produce networking equipment, which, interestingly enough, depended on semiconductors capable of signal processing. At the time, the market was still small, and there

---

8 This section is largely drawn from von Burg (2001).

were no standards to ensure computer interoperability. The critical event that catalyzed the formation of an industry was the 1980 decision by Xerox to offer low-cost licenses for the Ethernet standard. In 1978, Robert Metcalfe left Xerox PARC and in 1979 started 3Com. In rapid succession, three groups of Zilog employees left to establish LAN firms. As Ethernet became the de facto standard, a positive feedback loop ensued as the increasing number of users created a growing market for yet other innovations (von Burg and Kenney 2003), and venture capitalists became more confident in funding firms (von Burg and Kenney 2000). The proliferation of LANs, many running different protocols, created an opportunity for an interconnection solution. A number of firms were created to solve this problem. The most successful would be Cisco Systems, a Stanford University spinoff that commercialized a multiprotocol router.

In the early 1990s, data communications traffic exploded as LANs proliferated and wide area networks were created. File sharing and e-mail became standard business applications, and corporations began interconnecting their global operations. The increasing standardization of the datastream meant that a simpler, cheaper, and faster solution, the switch, could be deployed. In typical fashion, entrepreneurs began leaving existing firms to establish switching firms with venture capital financing. To ensure that they did not miss this new technology, established networking firms such as Cisco, SynOptics, and 3Com acquired many of these switching start-ups for large premiums, thereby encouraging greater investment and yet more spinouts.

In the 1990s, the networking firms—especially Cisco—developed a strategy of scanning their "ecosystem" to identify firms developing important new technologies and markets. Start-ups that were experiencing the greatest success were then acquired. In effect, firms such as Cisco began using the venture capital financing system as an integral component of their research and development strategies (Mayer and Kenney 2004). This technique encouraged a further proliferation of networking start-ups, established by entrepreneurs who hoped that they too would be acquired. The opportunities in networking were not limited to simply increasing speed and bandwidth. Networks also became more complicated, thereby providing entrepreneurial opportunities for network management, security, and other software and hardware, such as specialized ICs. Many of these opportunities were exploited by start-ups.

By the mid-1990s, computer networking had become one of the core Silicon Valley industries. A business model emerged in which venture capitalists funded start-ups that were established with acquisition as an exit strategy. Cisco pioneered a new corporate strategy of using the Silicon Valley start-up ecosystem to identify new technologies that would augment its business. As firms were formed, competed, and grew, Silicon Valley increasingly became the knowledge center for computer networking. This deep knowledge meant that Silicon Valley firms, entrepreneurs, and venture capitalists would be uniquely positioned to see the "next big thing."

The World Wide Web

The World Wide Web protocols were not a product of Silicon Valley. They were developed in 1991 and 1992 at CERN (the European Organization for Nuclear Research) in Geneva (Abbate 1999; Kenney 2003). At the time, few start-ups aimed to exploit the Internet, which was still largely an academic operation funded and controlled by the U.S. federal government. In 1993, entrepreneurs did not yet comprehend the opportunities that the Internet represented. There was also a delay in convincing venture capitalists that the Internet presented an investment opportunity (Ferguson 1999). However, the lag in comprehension did not last long, especially in Silicon Valley, and by early 1994, venture capitalists were receiving business plans from entrepreneurs with ideas for the commercial exploitation of the Web. The first easy-to-use Web browser, Mosaic, was developed at the University of Illinois and given away for free. Mosaic formed the basis of one of the earliest Internet start-ups, Netscape, which was established in April 1994 by Jim Clark, a former professor at Stanford and a founder of Silicon Graphics. He went to the University of Illinois and hired most of the key people who had designed Mosaic and moved them to Silicon Valley. Less than one and one-half years later, Netscape had an initial stock offering in August 1995 at a valuation of nearly US$1 billion. Netscape's remarkable increase in value alerted every venture capitalist and entrepreneur that the Web was a new opportunity. Given the greater venture capital resources and large numbers of entrepreneurs, the Bay Area quickly became the center for Internet start-ups (Kenney 2003; Zook 2002).

As the number of Internet users exploded, new business ideas and opportunities proliferated. This expansion provided opportunities for still more start-ups to develop new software and Web-based services. Businesses were built around searching and cataloging other sites, providing instant messaging, selling products online, selling software tools, and hosting Web sites, among other activities. Investors were willing to fund entrepreneurs experimenting with an amazing proliferation of business models. As these firms went public or were acquired at large premiums, and as the user base grew, the high stock market valuations for Internet-related firms unleashed a frenzy of investing, thus encouraging even greater speculation.

By mid-1999, full-scale investment panic emerged as public investors drove the price of new issues skyward. By the time the bubble ended in 2000, more than 370 self-identified Internet-related firms had gone public, and their total valuation had reached US$1.5 trillion, though they had only US$40 billion in sales (Perkins 2000). Approximately 50 percent of all new Internet firms were headquartered in the Bay Area. In 1999, the average return for early-stage venture capital funds was 91.2 percent, the highest in history (NVCA 2000b).[9] The returns for the most successful funds were astronomical: many had annual returns of 100 percent, and one even had a 400 percent annualized return. The amount of venture capital invested in Internet-related firms grew from a nearly negligible US$12 million in the first quarter of 1995 to US$31 billion in 1999 (NVCA 2000a). In percentage terms, the increase was equally dramatic, growing from a negligible percentage in 1995 to more than 60 percent of total U.S. venture capital investment in the fourth quarter of 1999 (NVCA 2000a: 31). Faster than anywhere else, Silicon Valley entrepreneurs glimpsed the potential of the Internet as a commercial opportunity and mobilized the resources necessary to realize that future.

Software
The richness and diversity of software firms in Silicon Valley is remarkable. As mentioned earlier, the highly specialized field of semiconductor design software is almost entirely located in Silicon Valley. In 2003, software was the largest employer in Silicon Valley, and despite recent setbacks, it is expected to grow in the longer term (see figure 2.2).

In software, as has been the case with other industries, Silicon Valley pioneered certain software sectors and then lost them. For example, it is no longer a significant producer of PC software, with certain exceptions, such as Intuit's PC financial applications and the PC game software produced by various firms. Microsoft's PC software monopoly resulted in the demise of Silicon Valley firms such as VisiCalc and Borland. Even when new PC software such as the Netscape browser was commercialized

---

9 The three-year compounded average annual return was a more modest 47.9 percent.

in Silicon Valley, Microsoft was able to use its monopoly power to destroy the new firms. The only major survivors have been Intuit, a tax and financial software producer, and Symantec, a utilities and security software firm—and Microsoft threatens them also.

Silicon Valley firms have been far more successful in business productivity software. The most significant is relational database software, which was pioneered roughly contemporaneously at IBM's San Jose Laboratories and the University of California–Berkeley. All of the key independent relational database firms (with the exception of Microsoft, a late entrant) are located in Silicon Valley. The largest of these is Oracle, which is the second-largest independent software firm in the world. Other important firms include Sybase, Informix (purchased by IBM), and IBM. Oracle, in particular, has spawned other important business software firms, including PeopleSoft and Siebel, which pioneered other niches in the business software field.

In entertainment software, Silicon Valley also experienced success. The Silicon Valley pioneer was Atari, which was sold to Warner Brothers in 1976 and then in early 1980s experienced severe difficulties, Because of these difficulties, Japanese firms were able to enter the market, and control over the game boxes moved to Japan. Today, Japanese firms are the major competitors for U.S. game software makers. The largest entertainment software firm in Silicon Valley is Electronic Arts, which is located in Redwood City. Electronic Arts, was originally a developer, but today it not only produces games, but also distributes them for other producers. The company is intimately connected to the cutting-edge PC graphics chipmakers also located in the region, because these graphics capabilities determine software usability. Drawing on a similar expertise base, a number of leading computer-animation film firms, including Pixar and LucasArts, also are located in the Bay Area. Producing special effects, these firms are important for contemporary cinema and computer games.[10]

Though Silicon Valley has not proved to be as dominant in software as it is in some other industries, it is still a key global software center. Today's Silicon Valley start-ups use the Linux operating system and programs such as Java as the basis of their products. In fact, the Finnish developer of Linux moved to Silicon Valley. Open source software, such as Linux, offers these companies a way to outflank Microsoft's grip on

---

10 This situation may be changing because these firms use PC-like computers that are harnessed by sophisticated graphics software, thereby eliminating the need for a dedicated graphics workstation.

software innovation. Moreover, even at the time of this writing, Silicon Valley start-ups are integrating Indian software production capabilities into their business plans, in the same way that semiconductor design firms have integrated fabs from Taiwan (China). In other words, new business models are still being created.

Entrepreneurial Support Networks and Culture

The development of a rich and complicated support infrastructure for entrepreneurs provides important advantages to Bay Area entrepreneurs (Kenney and Patton 2005). The goal of support network actors is to participate in the capital gains that accrue when one of the start-ups is successfully sold either to the public in an initial public stock offering or through an acquisition. The ESN has become so resource laden that the various actors in the network will fund emerging ideas in unrelated new fields, as was the case in biotechnology (see Kenney 1986), superconducting, and, most recently, nanotechnology. If these investments fail, as was the case in superconducting, only a relatively small proportion of the total venture capital resources and perhaps a few venture capitalists will be lost. If the investments succeed, as was the case with biotechnology, a new investment field emerges. Ultimately, the actors are agnostic as to what constitutes a suitable field for investment. They experiment with investments, and the market for the firms they supported informs them by providing capital gains.

The entrepreneurial environment benefits from interaction in many venues that contribute to cross-disciplinary information sharing and synthesis. With so many technologists, investors, and others interacting, there are ample opportunities for recombining existing technologies to create new products (Hargadon 2003). One often-cited example is bioinformatics start-ups, which combine the technologies of computing and gene mapping. Consider another new business area, the storage area network start-ups, whose software allows firms to use the enormous amount of hard disk drive storage space throughout their computer networks, thereby reducing the need to buy more data storage.

The repeated success in establishing new firms and garnering large capital gains on a significant number of them created a culture of entrepreneurship. Interestingly, this culture differs remarkably from entrepreneurial cultures that are based on the idea of establishing, managing, and controlling one's own firm. The Silicon Valley culture is based on establishing the company and then selling it to either the public or a corporate acquirer. In either case, the entrepreneur cedes control of the firm. The objective, then, is the capital gain, which under normal conditions can be secured only by creating a viable firm (though during the last high-technology bubble, many unviable firms were created and foisted on the public). It also bears mentioning that other regions, such as Boston and Israel, have similar cultures.

Though this chapter focuses on identifiable institutions, it is important to note that an entrepreneurial culture developed in Silicon Valley, which, though not unique, can be characterized as *extreme entrepreneurism*. During economic boom periods, changing jobs is a given part of the labor market in Silicon Valley (of course, highly skilled engineers and managers are taking only a minimal risk, because they can always get a job if a start-up fails). Over time, participating in a start-up became a career path. This acceptance of start-ups as normal has reduced the career risk inherent in becoming an entrepreneur. Moreover, whereas 30 years ago entrepreneurs were expected to use credit card debt and even mortgage their homes as part of the process, in the past 20 years such measures are no longer necessary before receiving venture capital. It is not in the venture capitalist's interest to raise the barriers to entrepreneurship and to increase the concerns of the entrepreneur. This lowering of entry barriers has culminated in the mythology that failure will not necessarily prevent an entrepreneur from receiving funding for another start-up.[11] What is clear is that no one has any interest in punishing a failure; it will not return the monies lost and will discourage other ventures. Rather than saying failure is "accepted," it is more accurate to say that failure is not punished. Given that the Silicon Valley economy is based on capital gains, a culture encouraging entrepreneurship is a prerequisite and a logical outcome.

In keeping with the capital gains–driven economy, one of the primary cultural and economic goals is to secure stock options or equity. This goal has led to an environment within which equity is extended to a large number of people in the corporate hierarchy. The ownership of options elicits extraordinary effort from employees and, if the firm is successful,

---

11 It is important to be careful of uncritical acceptance of the myth that failure is accepted. The acceptance depends on many factors, including who is assessed as having caused the failure and why. For example, founders who are bad managers but never accept that fact would be unlikely to receive funding again. Alternatively, if the technology was just too early or advanced for the market, technical people who are founders might not be blamed, particularly if they could demonstrate that they had learned from the first failure. Failure can be forgiven in certain cases. In other cases, it will not be forgiven, and that person will not be funded again. As always, success is appreciated far more than failure.

creates many wealthy managers and engineers. A certain number of these experienced and now wealthy individuals will, in turn, be willing to invest in other entrepreneurs or even launch their own start-ups, thereby perpetuating the entrepreneurial cycle.

Another aspect of the Silicon Valley culture was memorialized in Michael Lewis's (2000) book titled *The New New Thing*, which described Jim Clark's involvement in the creation of Netscape. Clark ruthlessly capitalized on the new Web browser technology and reaped enormous capital gains. Silicon Valley has developed a corporate environment within which new technologies, a great "hack," and huge capital gains are the reigning myths. In this environment, a hot new firm or technology attracts attention and floods of résumés. The opportunity to commercialize the hottest new technologies attracts many of the best engineers in that field. The economic incentives and culture are aligned to encourage high-risk entrepreneurship.

Lessons for Kyushu

It is difficult to compare the environment in Silicon Valley with other regions that have different endowments of universities, entrepreneurial firms, and venture capital. Ultimately, the most important single input is the entrepreneurs themselves. Japan has powerful support networks for existing firms, and entrepreneurship has been relatively discouraged. The last major wave of entrepreneurship in Japan was ignited at the end of World War II, when the economy was collapsing and individuals were forced to create new firms to survive. From the chaos of this period, many major Japanese electronics firms emerged, including Sony, Alps Electric, Taiyo Yuden, and ROHM. However, when industrial order was reestablished, Japanese managers and researchers—particularly those from elite universities and firms—were no longer willing to forsake the security and lifelong tenure offered by established firms and to undertake the risk of establishing new firms. In an environment of few start-ups and even fewer success stories, it is difficult for the culture of entrepreneurship to thrive and for a competent ESN to emerge.

Japan is not without some recent successes of entrepreneurial clusters. For example, entrepreneurship emerged in the Hokkaido area, where a game software cluster of start-ups formed. Unfortunately, more recently, this cluster has ceased to spin off many firms, and few of the firms received venture capital or had successful exits. The cluster never triggered an expanding cascade of start-ups.

During the Internet bubble, there was much entrepreneurship in the Shibuya-ku area of Tokyo that might have continued to expand into an entrepreneurial cluster, though this grouping was based more on design and Web site creation, and was not the hard-core technology that characterizes Silicon Valley and Boston. Also, it had few links with elite Japanese universities and skilled managers and researchers who left major corporations. In other words, these firms did not have the high level of talent that characterizes Silicon Valley firms. This absence of managerial talent is exhibited by the recent collapse of many of these firms and particularly the demise of the Japanese Internet firm livedoor in 2006. Such failures are more than just a loss of investor's money; they also discredit the idea of entrepreneurship and discourage other investors.

There are other ways in which entrepreneurship—or at least successful small or medium-size firms—can be built. For example, small semiconductor equipment suppliers on the island of Kyushu are able to take existing expertise and apply it to other high-technology fields. This process, which Henry Ergas (1987) termed *shifting*, operates almost like entrepreneurship to preserve jobs and firms. This process is fascinating because it treats the firm as an organic, evolving organization and can be a successful economic development strategy if a whole region can continue to evolve. Instead of an ESN, what are necessary in this case may be sensitive local governments able to invest in retraining and assisting firms in repositioning themselves.

In Japan, ESNs have never had an opportunity to emerge and coevolve with start-ups. Thus, Japanese venture capitalists are largely from a financial background, because few entrepreneurs have experienced the entire start-up process. Unfortunately, for this reason, Japanese venture capitalists are ill prepared to assist the entrepreneurs they do invest in. Entrepreneurs are unlikely to get the type of advice that would help them avoid mistakes. The absence of start-ups also retards the development of other members of an ESN that assist U.S. start-ups. Absent a sea change in the organization of the Japanese political economy, this situation is unlikely to change dramatically. Hence, those wishing to encourage behavior that resembles entrepreneurship should probably concentrate their efforts on encouraging Japanese small and medium-size firms to move into more cutting-edge fields that have rapid improvement trajectories or that allow skills to be developed that are not easily imitable in lower-wage environments. Success with this strategy might create "upgrading support networks" that could operate in a fashion similar to an ESN.

Reflections

An evolutionary and systemic perspective provides an appropriate perspective for understanding Silicon Valley and, by extension, other industrial regions (Avnimelech, Kenney, and Teubal 2003). Often discussions omit or elide the technological trajectories that underpin such regional industries and overemphasize cultural aspects; this chapter explicitly argues against doing so. The basis of much of this romanticizing of the entrepreneur is a belief that the culture is sui generis. A more appropriate model would treat culture as a constructed and evolving social artifact. Entrepreneurs that have benefited from the system and actors in the support infrastructure have every reason to support a specific set of cultural beliefs. The environment evolved, though not in a consciously directed manner, as a result of individuals pursuing various goals, one of the most important of which was the capture of capital gains. In Japan, capital gains may not be an appropriate goal, so those interested in improving the economy of regions in Japan must ask, "What is the appropriate goal?"

Viewed from a longer-term historical perspective, it is striking how a number of the technologies exploited in Silicon Valley, such as semiconductors, magnetic storage, and computer networking, have had trajectories that unfolded in a way that enables yet further opportunities to establish new firms. In a number of sectors, the potential for future start-ups appeared stymied by burdensome requirements, such as the enormous capital investments needed to create semiconductor fabrication facilities. Yet new business models were developed to circumvent the entry barriers. An evolutionary perspective highlights the region's remarkable success in redirecting its intellectual assets and attracting new talent from around the world. This extraordinary feature may be difficult for Kyushu and other regions to duplicate.

The constituents of the support network created their own niches and were able to draw resources from the environment. They became actors trying to improve their processes, which, by definition, meant supporting and assisting the entrepreneurs. They also changed the environment by creating more demand for entrepreneurs, thus reinforcing the cultural valuation of the entrepreneur and routinizing the start-up process. These actions explicitly recognized that the entry barriers for entrepreneurship are not only financial but also social and psychological. The literature has treated Silicon Valley's willingness to take a chance as an innate characteristic; however, it is actually a communally created social norm that aligns with the goal of creating capital gains. The support network assists in a wide variety of ways, from developing an understanding that it is not necessary for entrepreneurs invest their entire net worth in the firm, to allowing entrepreneurs to receive the greatest attention from financiers and other providers of business and legal services. In other words, agents in the support infrastructure changed the environment to make it more favorable.

Institutions and routines developed in the Bay Area ensure that the region can attract the entrepreneurs of the future. Its global-class universities and corporate research laboratories continue to attract many of the best and brightest students, researchers, and faculty members. The many successful high-technology firms attract thousands more engineers and managers, some of whom will become entrepreneurs and still more of whom are willing to join start-ups. These individuals join a munificent environment that places the resources for attempting a start-up within reach. It is little wonder that "new" new things emerge and attract seed funding in an environment where venture capitalists and a large community of angel investors are willing to invest to explore their business potential.

This evolutionary treatment of organizations and technologies presents Silicon Valley as a complex tapestry replete with commensurate coevolution within which the organizations and actors mutually monitor and respond to each other, creating routines and a cultural gestalt that is self-reinforcing. Organizations in the support infrastructure function as an initial selection mechanism. Firms without the perceived requisite potential for outsized capital gains are not funded, while ideas that appear to be sound by the standards of the support network receive funding, thereby ensuring their survival. In this ecosystem, actor incentives, technological trajectories, and business models are mutually reinforcing. The creation of a more entrepreneurial ecosystem should be possible in Kyushu, but the primary impetus must come from entrepreneurs.

References

Abbate, Janet. 1999. *Inventing the Internet*. Cambridge, MA: MIT Press.

Abernathy, William J. 1978. *The Productivity Dilemma*. Baltimore, MD: Johns Hopkins University Press.

Abernathy, William J., and J. M. Utterback. 1978. "Patterns of Industrial Innovation." *Technology Review* 80 (7): 40–47.

Angel, David, and James Engstrom. 1995. "Manufacturing Systems and Technological Change: The U.S. Personal Computer Industry." *Economic Geography* 71 (1): 79–102.

Avnimelech, Gil, Martin Kenney, and Morris Teubal. 2003. "Building Venture Capital Industries: Understanding the U.S. and Israeli Experiences." BRIE Working Paper 160, Berkeley Roundtable on the International Economy, University of California–Berkeley, August 18.

Dosi, Giovanni. 1984. *Technical Change and Economic Transformation*. London: Macmillan.

Ergas, Henry. 1987. "Does Technology Policy Matter?" In *Technology and Global Industry: Companies and Nations in the World Economy*, ed. Bruce R. Guile and Harvey Brooks, 191–245. Washington, DC: National Academies Press.

Feldman, Maryann P. 2001. "The Entrepreneurial Event Revisited: An Examination of New Firm Formation in the Regional Context." *Industrial and Corporate Change* 10 (4): 861–91.

Ferguson, C. H. 1999. *High Stakes, No Prisoners*. New York: Times Books.

Freiberger, Paul, and Michael Swaine. 1984. *Fire in the Valley*. Berkeley, CA: Osborne/McGraw-Hill.

Garud, Raghu, and Peter Karnøe. 2003. "Bricolage versus Breakthrough: Distributed and Embedded Agency in Technology Entrepreneurship." *Research Policy* 32 (2): 277–300.

Gompers, Paul, Josh Lerner, and David Scharfstein. 2003. "Entrepreneurial Spawning: Public Corporations and the Genesis of New Ventures, 1986–1999." NBER Working Paper 9816, National Bureau of Economic Research, Cambridge, MA.

Hargadon, Andrew B. 2003. *How Breakthroughs Happen: The Surprising Truth about How Companies Innovate*. Cambridge, MA: Harvard Business School Press.

Hargadon, Andrew B., and Yellowlees Douglas. 2001. "When Innovations Meet Institutions: Edison and the Design of the Electric Light." *Administrative Science Quarterly* 46 (3): 476–501.

Hsu, David H., and Martin Kenney. 2005. "Organizing Venture Capital: The Rise and Demise of American Research and Development, 1946–1973." *Industrial and Corporate Change* 14 (4): 579–616.

Kenney, Martin. 1986. *Biotechnology: The University-Industrial Complex*. New Haven, CT: Yale University Press.

———, ed. 2000. *Understanding Silicon Valley: Anatomy of an Entrepreneurial Region*. Stanford, CA: Stanford University Press.

———. 2003. "The Growth and Development of the Internet in the United States." In *The Global Internet Economy*, ed. Bruce Kogut, 69–108. Cambridge, MA: MIT Press.

Kenney, Martin, and W. Richard Goe. 2004. "The Role of Social Embeddedness in Professorial Entrepreneurship: A Comparison of Electrical Engineering and Computer Science at UC Berkeley and Stanford." *Research Policy* 33 (5): 691–707.

Kenney, Martin, and Donald Patton. 2005. "Entrepreneurial Geographies: Support Networks in Three High-Tech Industries." *Economic Geography* 81 (2): 201–28.

Kenney, Martin, and Urs von Burg. 1999. "Technology and Path Dependence: The Divergence between Silicon Valley and Route 128." *Industrial and Corporate Change* 8 (1): 67–103.

Klepper, Steven. 1996. "Entry, Exit, Growth, and Innovation over the Product Life Cycle." *American Economic Review* 86 (3): 562–83.

Lampel, Joseph. 2001. "Show-and-Tell: Product Demonstrations and Path Creation of Technological Change." In *Path Dependence and Creation*, ed. Raghu Garud and Peter Karnoe, 303–27. New York: Lawrence Erlbaum Associates.

Langlois, Richard. 1990. "Creating External Capabilities: Innovation and Vertical Disintegration in the Microcomputer Industry." *Business and Economic History* 19: 93–102.

Leachman, Robert C., and Chien H. Leachman. 2004. "Globalization of Semiconductors: Do Real Men Have Fabs, or Virtual Fabs?" In *Locating Global Advantage: Industry Dynamics in a Globalizing Economy*, ed. Martin Kenney with Richard Florida, 203–31. Stanford, CA: Stanford University Press.

Lécuyer, Christophe. 2006. *Making Silicon Valley: Innovation and the Growth of High Tech, 1930–1970*. Cambridge, MA: MIT Press.

Leslie, Stuart. 2000. "The Biggest 'Angel' of Them All." In *Understanding Silicon Valley: The Anatomy of an Innovative Region*, ed. Martin Kenney, 48–70. Stanford, CA: Stanford University Press.

Lewis, Michael. 2000. *The New New Thing*. New York: W. W. Norton & Company.

Mayer, David, and Martin Kenney. 2004. "Ecosystems and Acquisition Management: Understanding Cisco's Strategy." *Industry and Innovation* 11 (4): 299–326.

McKendrick, David G., Richard F. Doner, and Stephan Haggard. 2000. *From Silicon Valley to Singapore: Location and Competitive Advantage in the Hard Disk Drive Industry*. Stanford, CA: Stanford University Press.

Moore, Gordon, and Kevin Davis. 2001. "Learning the Silicon Valley Way." SIEPR Discussion Paper 00–45, Stanford Institute for Economic Policy Research, Stanford University, Stanford, CA.

National Research Council. 1999. *Funding a Revolution: Government Support and Computing Research*. Washington, DC: National Academies Press.

Nelson, Richard R., and Sidney G. Winter. 1982. *An Evolutionary Theory of Economic Change*. Cambridge, MA: Harvard University Press.

NVCA (National Venture Capital Association). 2000a. *2000 National Venture Capital Association Yearbook*. Washington, DC: NVCA.

———. 2000b. "Venture Capital Funds Raise a Record $46.55 Billion in 1999." Press release, March 27.

ÓhUallacháin, Breandán. 1997. "Restructuring the American Semiconductor Industry: Vertical Integration of Design Houses and Wafer Fabricators." *Annals of the Association of American Geographers* 87 (2): 217–37.

Perkins, Anthony. 2000. "Investors: Brace Yourselves for the Next Bubble Bath." *Red Herring* (November 13): 21–22.

Porter, Michael. 1998. "Clusters and the New Economics of Competition." *Harvard Business Review* 76 (6): 77–90.

Rowen, Henry S., Marguerite Gong Hancock, and William F. Miller. 2007. *Making IT: The Rise of Asia in High Tech*. Stanford, CA: Stanford University Press.

SEMI (Semiconductor Equipment and Materials International). 1986. "Semiconductor Industry Genealogy." SEMI, San Jose.

Spender, J.-C. 1989. *Industry Recipes: Nature and Sources of Managerial Judgement*. Oxford, U.K.: Basil Blackwell.

Stinchcombe, Arthur L. 1965. "Social Structures and Organizations." In *Handbook of Organizations*, ed. James G. March, 142–93. Chicago: Rand McNally.

Sturgeon, Timothy J. 2000. "How Silicon Valley Came to Be." In *Understanding Silicon Valley: Anatomy of an Entrepreneurial Region*, ed. Martin Kenney, 15–47. Stanford, CA: Stanford University Press.

von Burg, Urs. 2001. *The Triumph of Ethernet: Technological Communities and the Battle for the LAN Stand*. Stanford, CA: Stanford University Press.

von Burg, Urs, and Martin Kenney. 2000. "There at the Beginning: Venture Capital and the Creation of the Local Area Networking Industry." *Research Policy* 29 (9): 1135–55.

———. 2003. "Sponsors, Communities, and Standards: Ethernet vs. Token Ring in the Local Area Networking Business." *Industry and Innovation* 10 (4): 351–75.

von Hippel, Eric. 1988. *The Sources of Innovation*. Oxford, U.K.: Oxford University Press.

Walker, Rob. 1998. "Interview with Rob Walker." Interview by Susan Ayers Walker, July 9 Atherton, CA in *Silicon Genesis: An Oral History of Semiconductor Technology*. Stanford, CA: Stanford University. http://silicongenesis.stanford.edu/transcripts/walker.htm.

Young, Jeffrey. 1988. *Steve Jobs: The Journey Is the Reward*. Glenview, IL: Scott, Foresman.

Zhang, Junfu. 2003. *High-Tech Start-Ups and Industry Dynamics in Silicon Valley*. San Francisco: Public Policy Institute of California.

Zook, Matthew A. 2002. "Grounded Capital: Venture Financing and the Geography of the Internet Industry, 1994–2000." *Journal of Economic Geography*. 2 (2): 151–77.

CHAPTER 3

The Emergence of Hsinchu Science Park as an IT Cluster

Tain-Jy Chen

Although the success story of Hsinchu Science Park (HSP) as a high-tech cluster is well known, the factors that contributed to its success have not been examined in detail. After studying HSP, along with other successful clusters, such as those in Cambridge, United Kingdom, and Bangalore, India, Bresnahan, Gambardella, and Saxenian (2001) concluded that entrepreneurship, links to a growing market, and a supply of skilled labor are three key ingredients to successfully starting a high-tech cluster. In other studies, the human connections to the high-tech community in Silicon Valley are seen as providing the key impetus to Hsinchu's emergence and growth, but the development of the cluster is essentially led by entrepreneurs (Saxenian 2002; Saxenian and Hsu 2001). Other authors credit the government of Taiwan (China) for providing the infrastructures and institutions that paved the way for HSP's success (Amsden and Chu 2003; Hobday 1995; Mathews 1997). They assign a strong role to the state.

The purpose of this chapter is to review the development history of HSP and to examine the role of the government in developing the personal computer (PC) and integrated circuits (IC) industries. The chapter concludes that the PC cluster in Taiwan (China) was essentially entrepreneur led, whereas the state had a strong role in the development of the

IC cluster. Moreover, it is the IC industry that drove the agglomeration process, with a geographic locus on HSP. The government not only was involved in building infrastructure and in providing key technologies to the IC industry, but also contributed to firm building and market building. Scale economies and innovations are two key elements in the success of a high-tech cluster such as HSP, but these two elements cannot be brought about by the government alone. The chapter discusses how the scale economies and innovation capability were achieved.

The History of HSP

HSP was established in 1980 by the government of Taiwan (China) to jump-start the high-tech industry and to upgrade the economy's labor-intensive production base. The park was located in northern Hsinchu, about 70 kilometers from the capital city of Taipei, in an area dominated by tea plantations. The government chose Hsinchu because it hosts two premier universities, Tsinghua and Chiaotung, plus a government-sponsored research institute, the Industrial Technology Research Institute (ITRI).[1] The park was apparently modeled after Silicon Valley in many aspects of land-use design: (a) the ratio of building space on each unit of land was much more restricted than that found in the rest of Taiwan (China), (b) more space was allowed between buildings, (c) more green areas were reserved, and (d) commercial billboards were prohibited. A bilingual high school was established in the park to accommodate the children of experienced engineers returning from Silicon Valley.[2] Generous fiscal incentives have been offered to enterprises located in the park, including a five-year tax holiday on business income tax; the exemption of tariffs on imported machinery and imported materials, provided that the final goods produced out of these materials are exported; and a subsidized rent for land lease.[3] Standard buildings were also provided for small start-ups that were not big enough to invest in their own buildings.

---

1 According to Kwoh-ting Li, who was the architect of the high-tech policy of Taiwan (China) in the 1970s and 1980s, the decision to inaugurate HSP was made in 1977 (Li 1997).
2 The migratory behavior and lifestyles of the engineering elite in Taiwan (China), some of whom crisscross the Pacific and maintain two homes—one in the United States and one in Taiwan (China)—are described by Saxenian (2006).
3 Unlike the other industrial estates in Taiwan (China), land in HSP is available only for lease, not for sale.

As can be seen from the policy setting, the park envisaged by the policy makers was to be similar to an export processing zone (EPZ), which provided the same incentives. Between 1960 and 1971, Taiwan (China) established EPZs in Kaohsiung and Taichung. These EPZs were instrumental in incubating labor-intensive industries for exports. The fact that the policy package for HSP was modeled after that offered by the EPZs means that the industry cultivated was to be export oriented; therefore, trade protection measures have never been a consideration for policy makers. To signal HSP's high-tech status, a corporate income tax rate of no more that 22 percent would be assessed on the companies located in HSP instead of the regular 35 percent rate that applied elsewhere, should the tax holiday expire.[4]

Unlike some other East Asian export processing zones in the 1960s, HSP was not an immediate success. In fact, it had a very slow start. The park was not large to begin with—only 210 hectares were developed in the first phase of operation—but it took almost 10 years to fill up the space. In contrast, the first EPZ was filled up a couple of years after it was inaugurated in Kaohsiung in 1966. EPZs were intended to accommodate the competitive advantage of Taiwan (China) at the time: labor-intensive production. HSP tried to create a competitive advantage that had not existed before (Mathews 1997). In the first 10 years of HSP, PCs and their peripheral products dominated the park. In fact, the first companies to use the park were not new start-ups, but companies that were already established in Taiwan (China), such as Acer and Mitac. These companies relocated to the park to take advantage of fiscal incentives. They served mainly as subcontractors for international brands and spent little on research and development (R&D). The government also lured a U.S.-based major computer terminal producer, Wyse, to the park, but it was hardly an innovative company and folded in a few years.[5]

Because the firms were mainly contract manufacturers, innovations among these companies were limited and did not generate any of the

---

4 The maximum marginal tax rate on corporate income in Taiwan (China) was 35 percent at the time HSP was established, and it was later reduced to 30 and 25 percent successively. When the marginal tax was cut to 25 percent, the rate that applied in HSP was brought in line with that applied in the rest of the economy, thereby ending the preferential treatment. The tariff exemption on imported machinery was also repealed when a zero tariff was applied universally to any imported machinery that was unavailable in Taiwan (China).

5 Wyse was acquired by a consortium comprising a government investment fund and a group of private companies in 1989. As a result of acquisition, Wyse was delisted on the New York Stock Exchange and relisted on the Taipei Stock Exchange.

visible knowledge spillover effects that characterize a high-tech cluster. The government jump-started a venture capital industry by providing tax incentives to investors in venture funds and even invested public money in several funds. However, all these efforts produced only a few start-up companies established by scientists and engineers who had returned from Silicon Valley. One such company, named Microtek, did generate a mini-agglomeration effect in HSP. Established in 1984 by Dr. Bo-bo Wang, who previously worked for Xerox, Microtek developed the first computer-affiliated scanner in the world. The innovation attracted at least 20 similar companies to join the industry, making Taiwan (China) the leading provider of scanners in the world. However, the technological edge of these companies was not strong enough to protect their market-leading positions. When major players in the field of image processing, such as Hewlett-Packard and Canon, joined the industry in later years, producers in Taiwan (China) quickly lost their market shares (Ma 1999). Scanner producers failed to produce the kind of agglomeration effects that HSP was seeking because the value of the products was too small. In fact, major players like Hewlett-Packard and Canon waited until the market had grown to a viable size and then intervened.

By 1990, 121 companies were located in HSP, with 22,356 employees and a total turnover of NT$65.6 billion (table 3.1). Computer and peripherals accounted for 56.5 percent of the sales value, but HSP was nothing but a congregation of subcontractors that had little influence on the world's high-tech industry. It was hardly the "Silicon Valley of the East."

If products in HSP are categorized according to stages in the product life cycle, only a small proportion can be called innovative products. According to a study by the Chung-Hua Institution for Economic Research (CIER 1990), only 21.8 percent of HSP companies surveyed considered their products to be in the innovative stage. In contrast, 29.4 percent of them characterized their products as in the growth stage, and 47.7 percent considered their products already mature. When HSP celebrated its 10th anniversary in 1990, the director of HSP administration spoke of attracting new industries, such as telecommunications and photoelectronics, to HSP rather than enlarging the existing base of computer and IC industries. He alluded to the need for diversification, because "there are already many companies in the computer and IC industries" (*Economic Daily News* 1990). Evidently, he did not envisage any agglomeration effects at that time.

A miraculous change occurred when semiconductor manufacturing came onto the scene and began to dominate the park. In 1993, the value of

Table 3.1. Statistics of Hsinchu Science Park, 1981–2004

Year	Number of companies	Number of employees	Paid-in capital (NT$ hundred million)	Sales (NT$ hundred million)
1981	17	—	7.2	—
1982	26	—	11.6	—
1983	37	3,583	19.6	30
1984	44	6,490	32.3	95
1985	50	6,670	40.6	105
1986	59	8,275	57.1	170
1987	77	12,201	105.6	275
1988	94	16,445	158.3	490
1989	105	19,071	282.2	559
1990	121	22,356	426.9	656
1991	137	23,297	551.1	777
1992	140	25,148	628.3	870
1993	150	28,416	668.9	1,290
1994	165	33,538	935.0	1,778
1995	180	42,257	1,477.0	2,992
1996	203	54,806	2,585.0	3,181
1997	245	68,410	3,756.5	3,997
1998	272	72,623	5,106.3	4,550
1999	292	82,822	5,660.2	6,509
2000	289	96,642	6,944.8	9,293
2001	312	96,293	8,588.2	6,625
2002	334	98,616	9,099.9	7,054
2003	369	101,763	9,924.5	8,578
2004	384	115,477	—	10,859

Source: Hsinchu Science Park Administration, yearly statistics.
Note: — = not available.

IC production and IC design surpassed that of computers and peripherals (see figure 3.1). In that year, the total sales revenue of HSP reached NT$129.0 billion, almost double the value in 1990 (see table 3.2). Ten years later, in 2003, sales revenue reached NT$856.5 billion, nearly a sevenfold increase. The number of companies operating in HSP also mushroomed from 150 in 1993 to 384 in 2004. The park went through two phases of expansion during that period, enlarging it to 632 hectares, and the expansion was halted only because the land in the adjacent region was not available.[6] More important, the influence of HSP on the world's high-tech industry was keenly felt, beginning in the mid-1990s.

---

6 Beginning in late 1990s, two new science parks were established, in Tainan and Taichung, as a means of branching out and to offer an alternative to HSP.

Figure 3.1. Percentages of Sales of Integrated Circuits and Computers and Peripherals in Hsinchu Science Park, 1984–2003

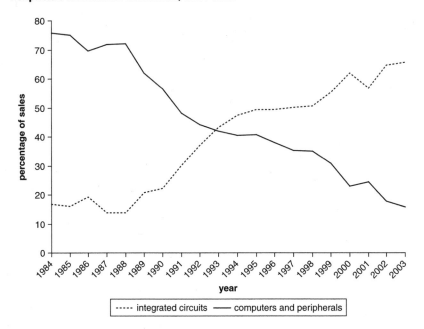

Source: Hsinchu Science Park Administration, yearly statistics.

As a manifestation of this influence, when a 7.3 Richter-scale earthquake hit Taiwan (China) in September 1999, the spot price of semiconductor products shot up on world markets immediately following the news, because investors were wary that damage from the earthquake would disrupt production. HSP had become a core manufacturing base for the world's semiconductor chips.

Compared with the PC industry—in which the government seldom intervened, except in the area of technology development—the government was deeply involved in nurturing the semiconductor industry. Such intervention included grassroots firm building and market building. It is in the semiconductor industry that the agglomeration effect is most evident in HSP. In fact, today the majority of the PC and peripheral firms of Taiwan (China) are located outside HSP, although they are in the corridor stretching from Taipei to Hsinchu.[7] HSP can hardly take credit

---

7 Recently, many firms have relocated to Shanghai as a result of rising labor costs in Taiwan (China).

Table 3.2. Growth of Combined Sales by Industry, 1984–2004

Year	Industry (NT$ hundred million)						Sales (NT$ hundred million)
	Integrated circuits	Computers and peripherals	Telecommunications	Optoelectronics	Precision machinery and materials	Biotechnology	
1984	16.00	72.00	5.00	0.70	1.30	0.00	95.00
1985	17.00	79.00	6.00	1.50	1.80	0.03	105.33
1986	32.91	118.66	9.65	6.05	2.72	0.44	170.43
1987	38.09	199.06	23.48	12.18	2.69	1.85	277.35
1988	68.08	353.26	45.00	15.99	3.00	4.53	489.86
1989	116.57	345.92	69.85	13.90	5.81	7.13	559.18
1990	146.49	370.34	113.60	11.43	8.18	5.58	655.65
1991	233.17	373.44	135.65	18.21	10.46	5.78	776.71
1992	322.14	385.71	124.48	20.18	13.28	4.59	870.38
1993	558.39	541.77	134.70	35.64	16.22	2.87	1,289.59
1994	840.85	719.08	147.29	47.24	19.46	3.72	1,777.64
1995	1,479.50	1,215.44	170.02	100.29	24.92	2.01	2,992.18
1996	1,570.53	1,212.37	192.63	175.34	27.68	2.47	3,181.47
1997	1,998.84	1,409.62	271.32	278.49	34.14	4.04	3,996.46
1998	2,308.29	1,598.94	264.48	297.60	75.02	5.69	4,550.02
1999	3,608.01	2,008.96	323.99	513.88	47.95	6.65	6,509.44
2000	5,757.11	2,124.89	507.70	809.22	72.58	11.34	9,292.65
2001	3,757.19	1,610.71	561.23	623.55	47.97	13.35	6,613.99
2002	4,562.59	1,245.28	565.58	600.35	53.89	14.16	7,041.88
2003	5,632.75	1,347.71	564.59	943.35	57.89	18.41	8,564.71
2004	7,427.38	1,382.45	605.30	1,312.63	92.47	25.39	10,859.22

Source: Hsinchu Science Park Administration, yearly statistics.

for the agglomeration of the PC industry. In contrast, HSP houses the mainstay of semiconductor manufacturers and IC design houses. The following section will describe the development and agglomeration processes of the semiconductor industry and the role of the government of Taiwan (China).

The Role of the Government in the Semiconductor Industry

The semiconductor industry in Taiwan (China) started with a government-sponsored project to transfer complementary metal oxide semiconductor technology from RCA, a U.S. firm, in 1976. The project team was then spun off from ITRI to set up a semiconductor company named United Microelectronics Corporation (UMC). The new company established its first fabrication plant at HSP in 1982. UMC was mainly funded by government money and state-owned banks. UMC produced some low-end niche IC products, such as electronic watches and IC chips for telephones. These products, which mainly served the regional markets in Southeast Asia, were consumer oriented rather than built on the strength of booming computer industry of Taiwan (China). In the same year, ITRI also spun off the first IC design house in Taiwan (China), Syntek. Subsequently, two IC design houses, Mosel and Vitelic, were established in HSP by some engineers who had returned from Silicon Valley. Because of the lack of foundry capacity, they had to source foundry services from Japanese semiconductor manufacturers such as Oki, while cooperating with ITRI in building their design capabilities. Local industry was segmented and failed to generate any synergy. Mosel successfully designed the 256K DRAM (dynamic random access memory) but decided to sell the technology to the Republic of Korea's Hyundai instead of manufacturing it in Taiwan (China).

The government soon recognized the need for a major semiconductor manufacturing company in Taiwan (China) to provide foundry capacity. It initiated a five-year project, called the Very-Large-Scale IC (VLSI) project, to develop a new generation of processing technologies. The VLSI project ended in 1987 with the establishment of Taiwan Semiconductor Manufacturing Corporation (TSMC). TSMC was intended to be a private company, but the government had to coerce some major private enterprises to take stakes in the new venture. Although the government persuaded the Dutch company Philips to take a significant share (27.5 percent) in TSMC under very favorable terms, in the end the government was still the largest shareholder. At the time of TSMC's inauguration, the government closed the experimental foundry at ITRI. Consequently, the ITRI team spun off another company, named Winbond, with the support of a private business conglomerate. For the first time, a private investor voluntarily took a major stake in IC manufacturing.

The establishment of TSMC, which strategically decided to devote itself to foundry services without offering its own products, was the starting point of a visible agglomeration process in HSP. Following the creation of TSMC, 27 engineers returned to Taiwan (China) from the United States to establish a semiconductor company named Macronix International. The company was founded in 1989 with the support of a government-sponsored venture fund, together with a group of private investors. A former vice president of ITRI, Tinghua Hu, served as the chairman. Macronix was devoted to producing nonvolatile semiconductor devices such as mask ROM (a type of read-only memory) and flash EPROM (erasable programmable read-only memory).

With the provision of foundry services by TSMC, which turned out to be the first company of its type in the world, 37 IC design houses were established between 1987 and 1990.[8] These companies included some of today's major design houses, such as Silicon Integrated Systems (SiS), Realtek, and Sunplus. The capital requirement for IC design houses is minimal, and with a foundry service provider close by, such companies can offer the most innovative and competitive products. Hence, TSMC generated an obvious external benefit.

Observing TSMC's success as a foundry service provider, UMC changed its own strategy. It spun off its design department into an independent design house and became a foundry service provider itself. The rivalry between TSMC and UMC produced one of the most competitive foundry service industries in the world, allowing Taiwan (China) to dominate the business even until today. TSMC and UMC's race in the foundry capacity and processing technology business produced a rapidly growing industry with advancing technologies. Along with the growing foundry capacity in HSP, assembly and testing companies also mushroomed. Companies such as Advanced Semiconductor Engineering (ASE) and Silicon Precision Industries Limited (SPIL) quickly became the world's leading IC assembly and testing firms.

---

8 There were already 18 design houses at the end of 1986, and the number increased to 55 at the end of 1990. The sales revenue of IC design houses increased from NT$560 million in 1986 to NT$5.9 billion in 1990.

On the upstream side, the government spun off the photomask service team at ITRI to establish Taiwan Mask Corporation in 1988. Taiwan Mask Corporation would provide locally made photomasks for IC processing, reducing the need for companies to outsource masking services to the United States. As the industry boomed, a private mask-making company, Hsin-Tai, was established in 1991, and TSMC established its own mask-making facility that same year. Some foreign affiliates, such as DuPont and Toppan, joined the photomask industry only much later, in 1998. The world's leading semiconductor equipment producer, Applied Materials, set up a subsidiary in HSP in 1993 to provide hands-on services.

Capping the stream of vertical integration was the establishment of Taisel in 1994 to provide polished and epitaxial wafers for IC fabrication. Taisel was a joint venture between the U.S. company MEMC and China Steel Corporation, which is owned by the government of Taiwan (China). Again the government's effort to create a vertically integrated industry was evident. Following Taisel, two joint venture companies involving the Japanese companies Shin-Etsu and Komatsu began to offer similar products in 1996 and 1999, respectively. The Shin-Etsu subsidiary was located in HSP, but because the park had already run out of space, the Komatsu subsidiary was located in the Yunlin county in central Taiwan (China). The vertical integration of the semiconductor industry in HSP was largely completed by 1995.

It had been 13 years since UMC was founded in 1982 to jump-start the IC industry in Taiwan (China), and the government's fingerprints were visible in every step of the process. The government not only provided infrastructure, technology inputs, and fiscal incentives, but also was deeply involved in firm building and market building. The government went beyond "market augmentation," as Wade (1990) has described the pre-1990 industrialization process. The government was effectively making a market for the development of the industry. Two major semiconductor manufacturing companies that were purely privately owned—Powerchip Semiconductor Corporation and Nanya Technology—were established in 1994 and 1995, respectively, to join the ranks of IC fabrication. Both concentrated on the production of DRAMs. Powerchip serves as a subcontractor for Japanese clients such as Renesas and Elpida, and Nanya Technology sells under its own brand. In 1995, the sales revenue of the semiconductor industry in HSP was NT$148.0 billion, and it accounted for 49.5 percent of the total revenue in HSP. The sales revenue of the semiconductor industry further grew to NT$563.3 billion in 2003, accounting for 74.5 percent of the total revenue growth in HSP during that period. It is quite clear that the chief engine for growth since 1995 was the IC industry, although a prominent liquid crystal display industry began to emerge around the same time.

Innovations and Scale Economies

It is essential that major innovations take place within a high-tech cluster to drive the agglomeration process. These innovations have some externality effects in that they provide new opportunities for other business concerns and create economic rents to attract new investment. In Silicon Valley, innovations led to other innovations, which drove the agglomeration process. In HSP, the technological depth was not enough to produce such a positive cumulative effect. After all, HSP is only an imitation of Silicon Valley (Saxenian 2001), and imitations do not produce the kind of positive externality that genuine innovations like those in Silicon Valley do. Imitations, even if they are achieved in an innovative way, are not likely to induce second-generation innovations. A study conducted in 1993 (Ma 1996) indicated that HSP firms spent an average of 4.95 percent of sales on R&D, which was five times the national average, and 48.5 percent of the firms indicated that their major technologies were self-owned and self-created. The returning engineers from Silicon Valley provided the most important source for self-owned technologies. Another study showed that HSP firms that hired returning overseas engineers spent more on R&D (San 2004). This finding suggests that returning engineers increased the efficiency of R&D investment because of their knowledge and management experience in technology companies, which, in turn, encouraged the relevant firms to invest more on R&D. However, most innovations generated through local R&D or brought back by the returning engineers were peripheral technologies, which only enhanced the value of products and strengthened ties to Silicon Valley but were unable to generate the kind of positive externality that drives the agglomeration process.

It is the foundry service model pioneered by TSMC in response to the growing demand from design houses in Silicon Valley (as noted by Kenney in chapter 2) and later followed by UMC that created an important externality to drive the agglomeration process in HSP. The emergence of TSMC and UMC as capable foundry service providers changed the rules of the game for the world's semiconductor industry. Before the emergence of this service, the world's semiconductor production was ubiquitously vertically integrated, with rising entry barriers embodied in technological and capital requirements. With the availability of a foundry service, "fabless" design houses without their own factories were able to challenge the well-established integrated device makers by offering innovative products.

With TSMC serving as a virtual "fab" for them, these design houses did not need to invest in modern equipment that is often in the magnitude of billions of U.S. dollars. TSMC also helped design houses circumvent intellectual property rights protection in the IC fabrication process. In return, TSMC was able to leverage the technologies of these innovation-oriented designers to advance its own technologies. The platform provided by TSMC and UMC allowed engineers returning from Silicon Valley to put their knowledge and innovations to work with a small investment, which was often rewarded with big returns in a short span of time. Many of the local start-up design houses, such as Realtek, Sunplus, VIA Technologies, and MediaTek, enjoyed an enormous price-to-earnings ratio after their stocks went public, and the engineers-turned-entrepreneurs became billionaires overnight. It is this HSP dream that induced the repatriation of seasoned engineers from Silicon Valley. In 2001, an estimated 4,292 engineers who came back from overseas were working in HSP (Jou 2004).

Proximity provides an important edge to design houses in HSP compared to their competitors in the United States. As argued by Pavitt (1999: xi), physical proximity is advantageous for innovative activities that involve highly complex technological knowledge and uncertainty, and require coordinated experimentation across functional and disciplinary boundaries. Audretsch and Feldman (1996) developed a theory showing that location mitigates the inherent uncertainty of innovative activity because proximity allows firms to exchange ideas and be cognizant of incipient knowledge. Their empirical evidence substantiates the proposition that the more innovative an industry is, the more it tends to be geographically concentrated. The IC design houses of Taiwan (China) also attest to this proposition. Design houses in HSP can work closely with the teams in TSMC and UMC to solve any technological problems involved in designing or manufacturing their products. The manufacturing knowledge of TSMC and UMC enables design houses to design products that can be fabricated in the most efficient way. TSMC and UMC provide verification and testing services that are key to the design of new functions. They also provide their own intellectual property (IP) or arrange an IP trade to shelter the design houses from the risks of IP infringement. In return, the knowledge and newly created functional objectives of the design houses have allowed TSMC and UMC to experiment with the frontiers of processing technologies. If clients allow TSMC and UMC to experiment with new processing technologies, they are willing to undertake even a very small batch of orders (Hsu 2000).

IC design houses are the most dynamic sector in the local semiconductor industry. In 2000, Taiwan (China) had 140 IC design houses (57 located in HSP) compared with 16 IC manufacturers (15 located in HSP). By 2003, the number of design houses mushroomed to 250. Taiwan (China) ranked second only to the U.S. in terms of the output value of the IC design sector. In fact, there has been a boom of fabless design houses since 1990, not only locally, but in the United States as well, driven by the widening technology gap between IC design capability and IC fabrication. Although the productivity of IC fabrication has been increasing at a 58 percent compound annual growth rate over the past 20 years, the productivity of chip design has lagged (Ernst 2004). The gap opens up a great opportunity for start-up design houses to explore the advantages of the IC fabrication technology and capacity located in HSP. The chip designers of Taiwan (China), like their counterparts in the United States, focus on niche products, but they are blessed with proximity to foundry services as well as lower labor costs.

The key to success in chip design is a capacity to design differentiated performance features that meet the needs of the industry, in addition to being able to use leading-edge process technology to produce the low-cost devices containing these features (Ernst 2003). In this regard, the vibrant PC industry of Taiwan (China) provides a fertile ground for product differentiation. The most notable players that developed out of this cozy environment are the chipset designers. These designers take the central processing units (CPUs) offered by Intel and other makers and complement them with auxiliary functions, embodied in logical and memory devices, to come up with a single chip that can be adopted by motherboard producers as a module to speed up the introduction of new-generation computers. Chipset makers serve as specialized suppliers in the vertical value chain linking the CPU makers with the computer makers. They have helped CPU makers like Intel and Advanced Micro Devices (AMD) to quickly transform a new CPU into a new fleet of computers. Because of their close interactions with CPU makers, they are able to access the latest technologies in Silicon Valley. Their role in the value chain is backed up by the formidable foundry service capacity in HSP. Major chipset makers like VIA Technologies and SiS became important allies of Intel and AMD, thus benefiting from the innovations in Silicon Valley.

One important reason design houses are more innovative than the rest of the local industry is that they own their products rather than making products for their clients. Most IC design houses design their products, have their products manufactured by TSMC or UMC, and then sell their products to device makers, such as makers of motherboards, DVD players, and handsets. Their products are mostly application-specific standard products (ASSPs) that provide integrated functions in a module that can be quickly adopted into a large system. In 2003, a survey by CIER (2004) indicated that 96.1 percent of the design houses of Taiwan (China) considered themselves fabless and offered ASSPs under their own brand names, while only 3.9 percent served as contract designers for integrated device makers or other design houses. Such design houses thus stand in sharp contrast to other sectors of the information industry, where most firms serve as subcontractors for multinational corporations. The fabless design houses take strong initiatives in R&D to explore niches for new products, while subcontractors stand passively to respond to the demands of their clients. The downstream information industry in Taiwan (China) and mainland China form the customer base of these fabless designers. In 2003, 45.4 percent of their products were sold in Taiwan (China), 33.5 percent were exported to China, and the rest were consumed in Korea, the United States, and other countries (CIER 2004). The rising demand from China for chipsets used in personal computers, DVD players, caller ID devices, and other audio and video devices has made China the second-largest market for ASSPs from Taiwan (China) (CIER 2004).

Innovations have generated economic rents. Rents accrue not only to entrepreneurs, but also to skilled workers. In a typical practice in HSP, initiated by UMC and later followed by other firms, skilled workers are awarded company shares at the end of each year in a profit-sharing scheme. The stock bonus helps bond the workers' loyalty to the company and rewards them for their contribution to the company's growth. It encourages skilled workers to devote extra effort to their employer. As a result, the most prominent engineering graduates from the premier universities of Taiwan (China) have flocked to HSP to work.[9] Although expatriate engineers played a key role in the early development of HSP,

---

9 A popular saying on university campuses in the 1960s and 1970s was "Come, come, come to Taita [National Taiwan University]; go, go, go to the U.S.A." Recently, this saying has changed to "Come, come, come to Tai-Tsing-Chiao [National Taiwan University, Tsinghua University, and Chiao Tung University]; go, go, go to Hsinchu."

local graduates formed the mainstay of the R&D force in later years (Jou 2004). Without them, HSP could not have grown to its current size. In December 2003, a total of 101,763 people were employed in HSP. Their average age was 31.72 years, and 21.4 percent of them held a master's degree or Ph.D. They must represent one of the most educated labor forces in the world.

Because the agglomeration process in HSP is manufacturing based, most innovations taking place in the park are related to processing technologies. In 2006, firms from Taiwan (China) were granted 6,360 patents by the U.S. Patent Office, making Taiwan (China) the third-ranked patent receiver in the United States. The majority of these patents are semiconductor related, and most are process technologies, with TSMC and UMC among the leading contributors of these patents. To make these process technologies work, IC manufacturers from Taiwan (China) invest a large proportion of sales revenue (sometimes over 100 percent) in new equipment year after year. Such capital investment is possible only if production is highly profitable. A normal return is not able to sustain this kind of speed.

Rapid capital accumulation did, however, lead to diminishing returns, and the profitability of IC fabrication has declined drastically in recent years. In 2003, the rate of return on investment realized by IC manufacturers in Taiwan (China)—for the entire industry, including firms located outside of HSP—was only 6.9 percent. Conversely, the IC design industry continued its high-flying path of prosperity, manifested by a 40.2 percent return on investment in the same year (Shih 2004). The design industry is also characterized by rapid entry and exit; however, turnover ensures that innovative power is regularly refreshed.

One important element in the agglomeration process is scale economies. A cluster must be able to grow in terms of both the size and the number of firms. Some firms in the cluster must grow to a commanding size before backward or forward links start to multiply—particularly when vertical integration requires the participation of some innovative firms that possess significant market power in the world market. A large number of small firms may not be powerful enough to prompt suppliers or service providers to co-locate with them.

The two major IC manufacturers, TSMC and UMC, have undertaken aggressive investments as well as mergers and acquisitions to increase their size over the years. As a result of this aggressive strategy, they have maintained their position as the leading foundry service providers in the world ever since the business was created in 1987, and they command over 70 percent of the world market share in foundry services.[10] In sharp contrast, the IC design houses kept expanding in number instead of size. There have never been any significant instances of mergers between design houses, and even acquisitions are rare. Instead spinoffs and spin-outs have been numerous. Each design house is very narrowly specialized and clearly focused. For example, there are two major UMC-spunoff IC design houses: MediaTek and Novatek. MediaTek specializes in DVD drivers, and Novatek in liquid crystal display drivers. Another major design house, SiS spun out its consumer device department to become a new company named Sunplus, which focused on consumer-related IC designs. Each IC design house explores its own niches for profits. The growth in the number of design houses provides needed scale and stability for the foundry service companies.

The experience of the computer industry contrasts with that of the semiconductor industry. Although, by the end of the 1980s, Taiwan (China) dominated the production of the world's personal computers, no major semiconductor companies had ever decided to manufacture chips in Taiwan (China) to serve those important customers. Even the providers of cathode ray tube (CRT) or flat panel displays did not care to locate a plant in Taiwan (China). When Philips opened its first CRT plant in HSP in 1993 to provide 15-inch tubes for the economy's world-leading computer monitor industry, it was greeted with great enthusiasm. Philips opened the plant only after one local producer, Chunghwa Picture Tubes, had threatened its market position in CRTs; Philips had previously decided to relocate its TV production lines from Taiwan (China) to Mexico. The computer industry in Taiwan (China) had a large number of firms, which together accounted for a large share in the world market, but the economy lacked dominant firms to orchestrate a vertical integration process involving key technologies. The computer industry was unable to form a high-tech cluster.

The agglomeration phenomenon suggests that firms cannot grow continuously without constantly enhancing their competitiveness, and enhancing competitiveness often has to be aided by vertically connected operations in proximity to each other. Therefore, a cluster is caught in a Catch-22 if there are no major players in the industry. To resolve this problem, the government can give a helping hand. Some countries choose to provide resources to create national champions so that they can

---

10 Others include Chartered Semiconductor Manufacturing, SMIC (Semiconductor Manufacturing International Corporation), and Silterra.

orchestrate vertical integration within the firm boundary. The government in Taiwan (China) chose to invest in vertically related companies before the market conditions were mature. Therefore, it invested in Taiwan Mask Corporation, Taisel, and the like to complete the vertical chain before private investors were willing to assume the risks in establishing similar ventures. Had TSMC and UMC not grown to a commanding size as foundry service providers, thereby generating significant demand for semiconductor equipment, Applied Materials would not have set up a shop in HSP to provide hands-on service. When TSMC established one of the first 12-inch wafer fabrication lines in the park to embark on leading-edge wafer processing, Applied Materials had the chance to experiment with its newest equipment. Being adopted by TSMC with enviable yield rates boosted the reputation of Applied Materials and allowed it to sell the same equipment to TSMC's competitors.

A cluster must also grow in terms of the number of firms to facilitate the horizontal integration of the industry. Horizontal integration is important for two reasons. One is that it allows local rivalry, and the other is that it generates a knowledge spillover effect in a closely related technology field. Porter (1998) listed local rivalry as an important feature of a successful cluster. International competition is not irrelevant, but local competition brings a stronger impetus for progress.

Working in similar environments and facing similar constraints, local rivals exert stronger pressure than international rivals. If TSMC is more profitable, then UMC will lose skilled workers to its neighbor, which offers more attractive stock bonuses. If TSMC invests in a new-generation processing line, then UMC has to assess the effect of this investment and respond. Peer pressure amplifies competitive pressure within a cluster, even among noncompeting firms. Difficulties arising from local competition provide no justification for government assistance. The rivalry between TSMC and UMC has prompted many innovations, not only in the technology field, but also in business models. Recently, when TSMC decided to switch its stock bonus scheme to an American-style stock option program, UMC defended its scheme and pledged to offer the old-style incentives to skilled workers.

Growth in the number of firms also means that a greater variety of products are provided in the same region. In addition to TSMC and UMC, which offer foundry services mostly for logic devices and serve a large pool of clients, there is Powerchip Semiconductor Corporation, which offers foundry services for memory devices and serves a small, exclusive group of clients. There is also Macronix International, which produces nonvolatile memory products such as mask ROMs. Nanya Technology produces DRAMs under its own brand and, in 2003, entered a joint venture with Germany's Infineon Technologies to produce high-end memory products. Product differentiation attenuates the business cycle, which is notoriously severe in the semiconductor industry, and gives some stability to employment in HSP, a benefit of industry clustering that was recognized long ago by Alfred Marshall (1890).

As the industry has grown, an increasing number of specialized suppliers have appeared in the park. Some provide auxiliary services that may not be critical to production but are nevertheless useful. For example, there are construction companies that specialize in building clean rooms, laundry services that specialize in clean-room robes and gear, and health clubs that make sure that the high-tech employees stay fit. Many suppliers of legal, financial, and business services also have a vital role to play, as noted by Kenney in chapter 2 (see also Bresnahan, Gambardella and Saxenian 2001).

Some scholars tend to attribute HSP's success to its link to Silicon Valley (Saxenian 2001, 2002). This link is important in terms of access to a growing market that provides the impetus for output growth in the cluster. Output growth, in turn, is essential to the division of labor within a cluster (Amsden 1977). Linking to a growing market is important for creating the scale economies that help start a cluster, but such links probably will not be strong enough to sustain the cluster, which requires local technological capabilities. In the end, innovations have sustained the growth of HSP, not the U.S. market, and innovations are manifested in an IC design industry that is underpinned by local technological capabilities. Beginning around 2000, an SoC (system-on-a-chip) design industry began to cluster in HSP, and this time the growth of the industry was not caused by the transfer of technologies from Silicon Valley, but by the deepening of local capabilities.

Conclusions

This chapter argues that scale economies and innovation are two key elements in the success of a high-tech cluster like Hsinchu Science Park. Although scale economies are critical to the inauguration of a cluster, innovation is critical to the growth of a cluster. When HSP was first conceived, it was intended to be a high-tech park, in the sense that most employees would engage in R&D work. The fact that HSP turned out to be a manufacturing-based high-tech park disappointed many

R&D-minded people in Taiwan (China). The reality is, were it not for the manufacturing activities, HSP could not have achieved scale economies needed to set the agglomeration process in motion, because even today the intrinsic comparative advantage of Taiwan (China) still lies in manufacturing.

Scale economies provide a foundation for backward and forward links and for the horizontal differentiation of products as well. Backward and forward links drive vertical integration, which gives a competitive edge to firms located in geographically proximate areas. Horizontal differentiation creates a competitive environment that is conducive to innovation. Because Taiwan (China) is a small economy, the domestic market cannot provide the scale economies that engender the agglomeration process, and it has to link to major external markets to realize such scale economies. Hence, links to the growing information technology market in the United States have played an important role in the takeoff of HSP.

The experience of HSP indicates that even if the link to a growing major market like the United States is successful, there is no guarantee that backward and forward integration will take place automatically. There are always technological barriers that prevent potential local firms from participating and benefiting from the advantage of vertical integration, and market power arising from technological advantages allows foreign firms to remain distant from local industry. The government had to take the initiative in acquiring technologies and in establishing relevant companies to take up the slack in the vertical integration process. It is also important that some major players in the industry emerged from HSP to allow the late-coming cluster to leverage the critical resources of an established cluster like Silicon Valley. Without such major players, the leverage would have been too weak to make HSP technologically sustainable.

HSP achieved links to the major markets by its innovation of a new business model whereby IC firms from Taiwan (China) provide foundry services to the world's integrated device makers and fabless design houses. The innovation has forced a new division of labor in the industry, from which firms from Taiwan (China) attained a strategic position in the value chain. This innovation was the beginning of the agglomeration process in HSP. It created two of the world's premier foundry service providers in HSP, attracting a fleet of fabless IC designers to the park to take advantage of the proximity of the foundries and their leading-edge process technologies. Although the co-location of assembly and testing facilities, photomask providers, and wafer suppliers is important in lowering the overall cost of foundry services and in enhancing flexibility, the interactions between foundries and design houses are the core source of positive externalities generated by proximity. Because both process technologies and design capabilities involve tacit knowledge, proximity provides the opportunity for them to reinforce each other and to create synergy. This environment has produced some of the world's most prominent IC design houses, along with two premier foundry service providers.

In the end, it is innovations that underlie the evolution of HSP from an imitator of Silicon Valley to a major partner of Silicon Valley. Because scale economies are manufacturing based, most innovations in HSP are process technologies rather than product innovations. Implementing these innovations requires continued capital investment, and that investment has to be supported by large-scale production. Therefore, scale provides the base for innovations. These innovations reinforce the capability of fabless design houses, which use this production advantage to create new features and new functions in IC chips. The innovations of these design houses are often peripheral and complementary, with some fundamental technologies originating from Silicon Valley. However, the design houses are able to succeed in the market because of their superior speed in terms of time to market, which is ultimately built on the readily accessible foundry capacity located in the neighborhood. The most dynamic and prosperous industry in HSP is IC design rather than IC manufacturing itself (Ernst 2004).

HSP's link to Silicon Valley's technology community is not the main force behind HSP's innovations. One reason HSP has been able to obtain key technologies from Silicon Valley is the change in global production in recent years. The reorganization of IC production from a vertically integrated, geographically concentrated, closed system to a vertically disintegrated, geographically dispersed, open system forces the flagship companies in the global production system to share their knowledge more aggressively with distant network partners, because they are under constant pressure to deliver products faster and at lower costs (Ernst and Kim 2002). Such a system provides opportunities for local producers to leverage their knowledge with those in Silicon Valley. However, the ability to leverage depends on local technological capability. Although returning engineers from Silicon Valley were critical in transferring technologies to HSP in the early stage of its development, locally educated engineers have become the mainstay of R&D activity in recent years. Process technology is the core of innovations in HSP, and it can hardly be transferred in piecemeal through an uncoordinated, reverse brain drain. When Taiwan (China) first obtained complementary metal oxide semiconductor technology from RCA, it adopted a carefully coordinated transfer apparatus with the wholehearted cooperation of RCA. Although the link to the technology community in Silicon Valley was helpful, it was not sufficient for innovation.

The local government played an important role in the micromanagement of HSP. It was deeply involved in firm building and market building. In addition, it played a macromanagement role by providing infrastructure and environment. However, the government's role in creating scale economies was limited. No protective measures were ever used to create a market for the budding IC industry. The penetration into the global market was mainly a private effort, although private firms may have been created by the government. UMC chose to attack niche markets that were largely ignored by major integrated device makers, and TSMC chose to offer a unique service to the industry. Unlike the strategy that the Taiwan (China) government undertook to develop the steel and petrochemical industries in the 1970s, where market entry was controlled to ensure scale economies for national champions, no entry restrictions have ever been imposed on the IC industry.

The government was actively involved in innovations through state-sponsored research agencies such as ITRI and the Institute for Information Industry. Government-funded research projects have accounted for more than half of local R&D until recent years, but critics often question the effectiveness of these research projects. However, there have been many undisputedly successful spinoff companies originating from government research projects—notably UMC and TSMC. For this part of the firm-building process, technology acquisition was a prerequisite. Many researchers at ITRI and other government-sponsored research institutions left government service to establish or join the private companies that gave new life to HSP. Hence, government-funded research projects appear to serve the purpose of training personnel and allowing them to accumulate skills rather than contributing actual innovations. It is private enterprises that contribute critical inputs to innovations, not the government.

References

Amsden, Alice. 1977. "The Division of Labor Is Limited by the Type of the Market: The Case of Taiwanese Machine Tool Industry." *World Development* 5 (3): 217–33.

Amsden, Alice, and Wan-Wen Chu. 2003. *Beyond Late Development: Taiwan's Upgrading Policy*. Cambridge, MA: MIT Press.

Audretsch, David B., and Maryann P. Feldman. 1996. "R&D Spillovers and the Geography of Innovation and Production." *American Economic Review* 86 (4): 253–73.

Bresnahan, Timothy, Alfonso Gambardella, and AnnaLee Saxenian. 2001. "'Old Economy' Inputs for 'New Economy' Outcomes: Cluster Formation in the New Silicon Valleys." *Industrial and Corporate Change* 10 (4): 835–60.

CIER (Chung-Hua Institution for Economic Research). 1990. "The Strategy to Attract High-Tech Businesses and Amendments to the Statute of Science-Based Industrial Park." [In Chinese.] Project report, CIER, Taipei.

———. 2004. "Survey on the Roles of Design Houses in the Development of Semiconductor Industry in Taiwan." [In Chinese.] Project report, CIER, Taipei.

Economic Daily News. 1990. "Taiwan Silicon Valley's Yesterday, Today, and Tomorrow." November 25.

Ernst, Dieter. 2003. "Internationalisation of Innovation: Why Is Chip Design Moving to Asia?" Economics Series 64, East-West Center, Honolulu.

———. 2004. "Late Innovation Strategies in Asian Electronics Industries: A Conceptual Framework and Illustrative Evidence." Economics Series 66, East-West Center, Honolulu.

Ernst, Dieter, and Linsu Kim. 2002. "Global Production Networks, Knowledge Diffusion, and Local Capability Formation." *Research Policy* 31 (8): 1417–29.

Hobday, Michael. 1995. *Innovation in East Asia: The Challenge to Japan.* Aldershot, U.K.: Edward Elgar.

Hsu, Ching-Yu. 2000. "The Spatial Strategy and Dynamic Learning: The Case of IC Industry in Hsinchu Science Park." [In Chinese.] *Cities and Design* (March): 67–96.

Jou, Su-Ching. 2004. "Cluster and Labor Force Dynamics: Human Resources and Structural Change of the Labor Force in the HSP." Project report, Chung-Hua Institution for Economic Research, Taipei.

Li, Kwoh-ting. 1997. *My Taiwan Experience: Selected Essays of Dr. Kwoh-ting Li.* [In Chinese.] Taipei: Commonwealth Publishing.

Ma, Wei-Yang. 1996. "An Assessment of Hi-Tech Industry Development in Hsinchu Science Park." [In Chinese.] *Taiwan Finance Monthly* (October): 36–47.

———. 1999. "The Development of Hsinchu Science Park from the Viewpoint of Industrial Economics." [In Chinese.] *Taipei Bank Monthly* 29 (6): 193–213.

Marshall, Alfred. 1890. *Principles of Economics.* London: Macmillan.

Mathews, John. 1997. "A Silicon Valley of the East: Creating Taiwan's Semiconductor Industry." *California Management Review* 39 (4): 26–54.

Pavitt, K. 1999. *Technology, Management, and Systems of Innovation.* Cheltenham, U.K.: Edward Elgar.

Porter, Michael. 1998. "Clusters and the New Economics of Competition." *Harvard Business Review* 76 (6): 77–90.

San, Gee. 2004. "The Movement of High-Tech Manpower between Industrial Clusters in Silicon Valley, Hsinchu, and Shanghai." Chung-Hua Institution for Economic Research, Taipei.

Saxenian, AnnaLee. 2001. "Taiwan's Hsinchu Region: Imitator and Partner for Silicon Valley." Working Paper 00–44, Stanford Institute for Policy Research, Stanford University, Palo Alto, CA.

———. 2002. "Transnational Communities and the Evolution of Global Production Networks: The Case of Taiwan, China, and India." *Industry and Innovation* 9 (3): 183–203.

———. 2006. *The New Argonauts*. Cambridge, MA: Harvard University Press.

Saxenian, AnnaLee, and Jinn-Yuh Hsu. 2001. "The Silicon Valley-Hsinchu Connection: Technical Communities and Industrial Upgrading." *Industrial and Corporate Change* 10 (4): 893–920.

Shih, Chin-Tai. 2004. "The Challenges to the Competitiveness of Taiwan's Electronics Industry: Examining the Development of Tri-trillion Industries." [In Chinese.] Industrial Technology Research Institute, Taipei.

Wade, Robert. 1990. *Governing the Market*. Princeton, NJ: Princeton University Press.

CHAPTER 4

Coping with Globalization of Production Networks and Digital Convergence

The Challenge of ICT Cluster Development in Singapore

Poh-Kam Wong

Since the early 1980s, Singapore has emerged as a major regional industrial hub for information and communication technology (ICT) in East Asia by leveraging its strategic geographic position, its heavy public investment in telecommunication and transport infrastructure, its public investment in ICT human resource development, and its active policy of attracting foreign ICT multinational corporations (MNCs) (Wong 2001b, 2001c). However, since the late 1990s, the ICT industrial landscape in Asia has undergone rapid transformation, driven by the increasing globalization of production networks in general and the rapid rise of China and India in particular—the former as the world's leading electronics manufacturing platform and the latter as a global hub for outsourced software development and IT-enabled business services. In addition, the acceleration of digital convergence in recent years has caused dramatic disruptions to the traditional ICT industrial structure, resulting in significant blurring of industry boundaries between the traditional "4C" industries (computer, communications, consumer electronics, and media contents) and the rapid rise of new ICT firms that threaten to bring Schumpeterian destruction to many incumbent ICT firms.

This chapter examines the development dynamics of Singapore's ICT industrial cluster in recent years. It highlights the island state's future challenges in developing ICT clusters in the face of the two growing trends of production network globalization and digital convergence, as well as its future policy options for remaining a viable node in the globalized production network. In particular, the chapter argues for giving greater priority to a number of emerging subclusters, including computer games and animation, mobile content, and specialized applications such as sensor networks and security in logistics. In addition, it highlights the need for greater public investment in key supporting infrastructure, including the deployment of broadband to the home, the development of personnel specializing in intellectual property (IP), and seed funding for the commercialization of home-grown technology. Greater policy coordination and coherence is also needed in dealing with ICT clusters that are characterized by a high degree of digital convergence, particularly digital media.

Conceptual Framework for an Information Economy

The ICT industry has been variously defined in the research literature, ranging from narrow coverage of computer and telecommunication equipment manufacturing to broader definitions that encompass not only hardware equipment manufacturing but also software production, information technology (IT) and telecommunication services, and the emerging digital media industries (electronic games, mobile content, and the like). Other researchers have argued for the need to incorporate all forms of activities involved in the production and distribution of information content.

There is by now a vast popular literature on the information economy (often referred to as the *digital economy*) and the information society. Although there is no uniform definition of *information economy* in the literature (see, for example, OECD 2002; U.S. Department of Commerce 2003), the proposed conceptualization in Wong (1998) serves as a useful reference framework (figure 4.1). In essence, an information economy can be conceptualized as consisting of four components: (a) the ICT goods production sector that creates, makes, and distributes ICT appliances and equipment; (b) the information content production sector

Figure 4.1. Conceptual Framework of Information Economy

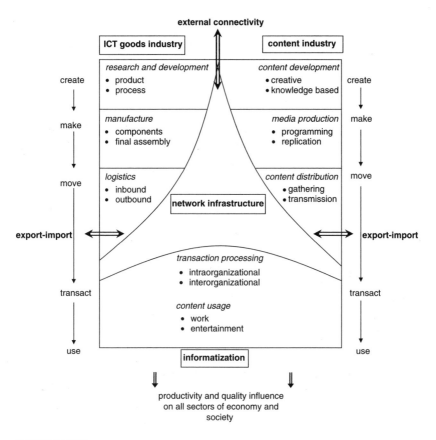

Source: Wong 1998.

that creates, makes, and distributes information content and services; (c) the ICT network infrastructure sector that provides the connectivity between people and ICT equipment to enable the flow and exchange of information content; and (d) the informatization component, in which ICT goods and network infrastructure are used to access and consume information content, whether in households or businesses.

As depicted in figure 4.1, these four components of a national information economy are linked to one another as well as to the external regional and global economic environments through either physical movement of ICT goods and content or electronic transmission of digital content over network infrastructure. For instance, both ICT goods and content can be produced for domestic use or for export, whereas informatization may draw on domestic supply or import of ICT appliances and content. Thus, although the conceptual framework suggests a close link between the production and consumption (*informatization*) of ICT goods and services in an information economy, the two sets of activities need not be co-located.

From the perspective of an economic development strategy, the first two components (ICT goods and content production) represent major new industrial growth opportunities to create jobs and wealth. Hence, they are natural targets for policies that promote industry development. The fourth component (informatization) represents opportunities to improve the productivity and competitiveness of existing economic activities as well as the overall quality of life of the population through diffusion policies. Hence, it relates directly to the goals of both economic development and more general development of an information society. The third component (network infrastructure) is really an enabler for both production and informatization. Hence, the regulatory and promotional policies that affect its development need to be coordinated and synergized with the policy goals for industry development and diffusion.

Two major implications emerge from this integrative framework. First, with the trend toward globalization of economic activities, the value chain of create-make-move-use will be increasingly decoupled in space. This spatial decoupling will affect the value chains for both physical goods and information content. In particular, the manufacturing and assembly activities for physical ICT goods and the programming and replication activities for information goods are the easiest to outsource to lower-cost locations. High-cost regions will thus need either to shift their competitive competence toward creation activities (product and process research and development and innovation in the case of physical goods; new creative content and knowledge-based development in the case of digital goods) or to position themselves to become regional distribution hubs (a logistics and supply chain hub for physical goods; a content hosting, broadcasting, and publishing hub for information goods).

Second, with the trend toward digital convergence, traditional industry boundaries separating physical ICT goods (consumer electronics, computer devices, and communications devices) are rapidly dissolving, as players from each industry increasingly enter each other's territories. Likewise, traditional boundaries separating the computer game, music, video, and print publishing industries are blurring with the rise of Web-based services and interactivity. The traditionally separate network infrastructures (the public switched telephone network; over-the-air, cable, and satellite broadcasting networks; and computer networks) for voice, video, and data services are also rapidly converging into a ubiquitous Web connectivity. Together they drive digital convergence. Because of the growing integration of ICT goods, information content, networks, and informatization processes through digital convergence, it is increasingly difficult to examine the growth of a particular component (such as the ICT goods manufacturing cluster) without taking into account the growth of related components (software, networks, and applications deployment, for example).

In view of this difficulty, this chapter will attempt to cover both the ICT goods and the content clusters and their relationship with the national network infrastructure and informatization pattern. In particular, it examines the extent to which underdevelopment of network deployment and lack of sophistication by users of applications may limit the growth and development of innovation in ICT goods and the development of creative content.

ICT Industrial Cluster Development in Singapore: Features

Wong (1998) documented in detail the progress that Singapore made in growing its ICT industries as well as in diffusing the use of ICT in the economy and in society from the early 1980s to the mid-1990s. Some updates on developments in the late 1990s are provided in Wong (2002a, 2003, 2004, 2006). Synthesizing from these earlier analyses and from new data that were compiled to extend the statistical time series to the early 2000s allows features of Singapore's ICT development to be highlighted. These features are described in the following sections.

ICT Manufacturing Industry

As highlighted in Wong (1998, 2006), the manufacturing of electronics goods in general and ICT goods in particular has been a major source of economic growth for Singapore since the early 1980s. As table 4.1 shows, the share of electronics manufacturing in total manufacturing has been expanding over the past four decades, reaching more than half of total output and 44 percent of value added in 2000. Moreover, the growth rate of labor productivity and capital intensity in the sector has consistently exceeded the overall manufacturing average.

However, ICT manufacturing in Singapore appears to have experienced a considerable slowdown since 2000, owing both to the relocation of manufacturing activities to China and the region and to a global slowdown

Table 4.1. Electronics Manufacturing Industry Growth in Singapore, 1960–2004

Year	Output (S$ million)	Number of workers	Value added (S$ million)	Fixed assets (S$ million)	Value added/labor (S$ thousands)	Value added/output (%)	Capital/labor (S$ thousands)
1960	17.1	1,252	7.9	—	6.3	46.2	—
1970	212.9	11,251	99.1	—	8.8	46.5	—
1980	5,344.0	71,727	1,668.9	585.1	23.3	31.2	8.2
1990	27,878.1	122,797	7,716.6	3,757.3	62.8	27.7	30.6
2000	83,950.7	102,320	17,228.3	14,885.9	168.4	20.5	145.5
2004	74,026.2	92,446	14,511.0	17,277.8	157.0	19.6	186.9

Average per annum growth (%)

Period	Output	Number of workers	Value added	Fixed assets	Value added/labor	Value added/output	Capital/labor
1960–70	32.4	26.9	32.1	—	3.4	—	—
1970–80	34.2	18.1	29.3	—	10.2	—	—
1980–90	18.0	5.5	16.5	—	10.4	—	14.1
1990–2000	11.7	-1.8	8.4	—	10.4	—	16.9
2000–04	-3.1	-2.5	-4.2	—	-1.7	—	6.5

Share of total manufacturing (%)

Year	Output	Number of workers	Value added	Fixed assets	Value added/labor	Value added/output	Capital/labor
1960	3.7	4.6	5.6	—	121.2	—	—
1970	5.5	9.3	9.1	—	96.7	—	—
1980	16.9	25.1	19.6	7.8	77.9	—	31.3
1990	39.1	34.9	35.7	20.8	102.3	—	59.6
2000	51.3	29.7	44.2	35.1	165.4	—	118.4
2004	38.6	25.8	31.3	36.2	121.3	—	140.0

Sources: EDB various years b, various years c.
Note: — = not available.

in market demand for ICT goods in 2001 to 2002. As can be seen from table 4.1, total employment, output, and value added by ICT manufacturing all declined absolutely between 2000 and 2004; by 2004, the share of the ICT manufacturing cluster in total manufacturing output declined to 39 percent, the same level as in 1990. The sharp relative decline has been partly caused by a rapid rise in pharmaceutical production output in recent years, driven by a new government thrust to promote the biomedical industry. Thus, although the ICT manufacturing cluster still remains the largest manufacturing cluster in Singapore today, its significance has diminished in both absolute and relative terms.

Tables 4.2 and 4.3, which are based on different international data sources that use somewhat different coverage of ICT, further confirm the trend derived from the official industrial statistics in Singapore. Using data from the *Yearbook of World Electronics Data* (Elsevier various years) that provide broad coverage of electronics goods (including defense and aerospace electronics), table 4.2 shows that Singapore's share of global ICT goods production increased steadily from 0.8 percent in 1985 to 3.8 percent in 1995 but dropped to 3.0 percent by 2003. A similar pattern is shown in table 4.3, which uses ICT trade data from the World Trade Organization. Singapore's share of total world ICT exports (which covers electronic data processing and office equipment, telecommunication equipment, and electronic components) nearly doubled, growing from 2.5 percent in 1980 to 4.9 percent in 1990, but then fell to 4.3 percent by 2000 and declined further to 3.3 percent by 2004.

Like other newly industrialized economies in Asia, Singapore's electronics manufacturing started in the early 1970s with the labor-intensive assembly of consumer electronics goods, but it quickly moved into electronic components assembly by the late 1970s, and subsequently into the manufacturing of computer and peripheral products (particularly magnetic hard disk drives) from the mid-1980s to the 1990s (table 4.4). However, since the mid-1990s, the focus has shifted more strongly into electronic components again, this time in the form of capital-intensive wafer fabrication activities as well as a growing range of component manufacturing activities for key modules. Meanwhile, some of the more labor-intensive computer and peripheral assembly activities began, like consumer electronics assembly, to relocate to lower-cost countries in the region. By 2000, electronics components had emerged as the largest subsector in the ICT manufacturing cluster. The manufacturing of telecommunication equipment and devices, particularly wireless devices, has also increased in

Table 4.2. Singapore's Share of World Electronics Production, 1985–2004

Subsector	Amount of production (US$ million)				
	1985	1990	1995	2004
Electronic data processing	1,345	6,974	21,127	19,412
Office equipment	—	313	337	212
Control and instrument electronics	119	197	514	706
Medical and industrial electronics	—	59	116	321
Radio communications (including mobile) and radar	119	276	1,127	1,471
Telecommunications	—	233	570	547
Consumer electronics	846	2,155	3,322	1,186
Components	2,029	4,785	12,670	20,749
Total	4,458	14,992	39,783	44,604

Subsector	Singapore as a % of world total			
	1985[a]	1990	1995	2004
Electronic data processing	0.96	3.89	7.36	—
Office equipment	—	1.81	1.68	—
Control and instrument electronics	0.24	0.31	0.64	—
Medical and industrial electronics	—	0.25	0.33	—
Radio communications (including mobile) and radar	0.16	0.31	1.00	—
Telecommunications	—	0.33	0.60	—
Consumer electronics	1.25	2.61	3.23	—
Components	1.51	2.75	4.12	—
Total	0.80	2.14	3.83	2.97[b]

Source: Elsevier various years.

Note: — = not available. The 1985 figures for electronic data processing include office equipment production. The 1985 figures for control and instrument electronics include medical and industrial electronics production. The 1985 figures for radio communications and radar include telecommunication production.

a. 1987 for world figures.

b. 2003 figure.

Table 4.3. Singapore Electronics Domestic Exports, 1980–2004

Subsector	1980	1990	2000	2004
Amount of exports (US$ million current)				
Office and telecommunication equipment	2,107	14,686	41,523	36,979
Electronic data processing and office equipment	—	8,022	22,320	19,068
Telecommunication equipment	—	3,820	3,770	4,268
Integrated circuits and electronic components	—	2,844	15,433	13,643
Singapore as a % of world total				
Office and telecommunication equipment	2.5	4.9	4.3	3.3
Electronic data processing and office equipment	—	—	6.0	4.5
Telecommunication equipment	—	—	1.3	1.1
Integrated circuits and electronic components	—	—	5.0	4.1

Source: WTO 2005.
Note: — = not available. Singapore figures include domestic exports only.

Table 4.4. Sectoral Composition of Value Added in Singapore's Electronics Industry, 1970–2004

Subsector	1970	1980	1990	2000	2004
Amount (S$ million)					
Consumer electronics	99	555	935	324	168
Electronics components	0	836	2,153	9,430	8,901
Computers and peripherals	0	132	3,544	3,194	4,489
Telecommunication equipment and others	0	145	1,085	4,280	953
Telecommunication equipment alone	0	26	493	751	806
Total	99	1,668	7,717	17,228	14,511
Share of total sector (%)					
Consumer electronics	100	33.3	12.1	1.9	1.2
Electronics components	0	50.1	27.9	54.7	61.3
Computers and peripherals	0	7.9	45.9	18.5	30.9
Telecommunication and other equipment	0	8.7	14.1	24.8	6.6
Telecommunication equipment alone	0	1.6	6.4	4.4	5.6
Total[a]	100	100.0	100.0	100.0	100.0

Sources: Calculated from EDB various years b, various years c.
Note: For 1970, 1980, and 1990, *consumer electronics* include television sets and other audio and video equipment; *electronics components* include semiconductor devices, capacitors and resistors, and printed circuit boards; *computers and peripherals* include computers and data processing equipment, disk drives, and computer peripherals; and *telecommunication and other equipment* includes communication equipment and other electronic products and components. For 2000 and 2004, *consumer electronics* include television sets and other audio and video equipment; *electronics components* include wafer fabrication, other semiconductor devices, capacitors and resistors, printed circuit boards, and contract manufacturers; *computers and peripherals* include computers and data processing equipment and disk drives; and *telecommunication and other equipment* includes communication equipment, electronic security system, and other electronic products and components.
a. Percentages may not add up to 100 percent because of rounding.

importance since the late 1990s, in line with the global growth in demand for mobile communications in recent years.

The subsector compositional change in ICT production is reflected in data on the composition of Singapore's ICT exports. As can be seen in table 4.3, exports of integrated circuits and electronic components expanded the fastest between 1990 and 2000, followed by electronic data processing and office equipment; however, both declined between 2000 and 2004. Only exports of telecommunication equipment grew between 2000 and 2004.

Unlike in the United States and Japan, where many global leaders in the ICT goods industry originate, and unlike in the Republic of Korea and Taiwan (China), where indigenous firms play a dominant role, the subsidiaries of foreign MNCs in Singapore have been the dominant players in the country's ICT manufacturing industry. As documented in Wong (2006), foreign firms accounted for more than 80 percent of the equity investment in electronics manufacturing firms in Singapore in the 1990s, and more than 90 percent of its value added. As can be seen from tables 4.5 and 4.6, foreign firms accounted for 100 percent of the top 20 electronics manufacturing firms in Singapore by sales in 1991; by 2003, four indigenous firms managed to enter the top 20, but their joint share of total sales was only 10 percent.

This high dependence on foreign firms in ICT production stands in strong contrast to the situation not only in the United States and Japan but also in Taiwan (China) and Korea, which have developed their ICT manufacturing industries into significant global exporters, primarily by nurturing indigenous enterprises.

Many MNCs have set up research and development (R&D) operations in Singapore, and investment in R&D by indigenous firms and public research institutes and universities is rising rapidly (Wong 2001b). Yet Singapore's ICT manufacturing industry is still highly dependent on technology transfer from parent headquarters of foreign firms, and few local firms are able to pioneer product innovations that enjoy significant global market presence and attract global brand recognition. With the exception of Creative Technology, a global leader in sound cards for personal computers (PCs), one is hard pressed to think of a Singaporean firm with global reach and branding.

As can be seen in table 4.7, patenting by local ICT manufacturing firms has increased steadily in recent years; by the end of 2004, among patents granted by the U.S. Patent and Trademark Office to Singapore-based inventors, the share going to local ICT firms exceeded that going

Table 4.5. Top 20 Electronics Manufacturing Companies in Singapore, 1991–92

Rank	Company	Nationality	1991–92 sales (S$ million)	Electronics manufacturing sector
1	Asia Matsushita Electric	Japan	3,833	Electronic components
2	Seagate	United States	2,677	Disk drives
3	Conner Peripherals	United States	1,936	Disk drives
4	Thomson Consumer Electronics Asia	France	1,798	Electronic products
5	Philips	Netherlands	1,504	Electronic products
6	Texas Instruments	United States	1,298	Electronic components
7	SGS-Thomson MicroElectronics	Italy/France	1,295	Electronic components
8	Toshiba Electronics Asia	Japan	1,115	Electronic components
9	Western Digital	United States	1,030	Disk drives
10	Hewlett-Packard	United States	1,015	Computers
11	Motorola Electronics	United States	919	Electronic products
12	National Semiconductor	United States	847	Electronic components
13	Toshiba	Japan	751	Electronic products
14	Maxtor Peripherals	United States	732	Disk drives
15	Sanyo Electronics	Japan	653	Electronic products
16	Compaq Asia	United States	639	Computers
17	Aiwa	Japan	625	Electronic products
18	Matsushita Electronics	Japan	594	Electronic products
19	Siemens Components	Germany	584	Electronic components
20	Hitachi Electronic Devices	Japan	570	Electronic components
	Total revenue for top 20 companies		24,415	

Source: DP Information Network 1994.

Table 4.6. Top 20 Electronics Manufacturing Companies in Singapore, 2003

Rank	Company	Nationality	2003 sales ($S million)	Electronics manufacturing sector
1	Hewlett-Packard Singapore	United States	10,230.6	Computers
2	IBM Singapore	United States	9,795.5	Computers
3	Seagate Technology International	United States	8,848.3[a]	Disk drives
4	Infineon Technologies Asia Pacific	Germany	4,786.5	Electronic components
5	STMicroelectronics	Italy and France	3,858.5	Electronic components
6	Sony Electronics	Japan	3,255.3	Electronic products
7	Venture Corporation	Singapore	3,170.0	Contract manufacturing
8	Agere Systems	United States	2,977.8	Electronic components
9	Micron Semiconductor Asia	United States	2,847.2	Electronic products
10	Motorola Electronics	United States	2,679.0	Electronic products
11	Philips Electronics	Netherlands	2,496.2	Electronic products
12	Sanyo Asia	Japan	1,644.9	Electronic products
13	Marvell Asia	Bermuda	1,325.9	Electronic components
14	Agilent Technologies Singapore	United States	1,254.0	Electronic components
15	Creative Technology	Singapore	1,207.0	Computers
16	TECH Semiconductor Singapore	Singapore	1,044.3	Electronic components
17	Chartered Semiconductor Manufacturing	Singapore	949.3	Electronic components
18	Toshiba Singapore	Japan	890.8	Electronic products
19	Eastern Asia Technology Limited	Taiwan (China)	837.2	Electronic products
20	Murata Electronics Singapore	Japan	825.1	Electronic components
	Total revenue for top 20 companies		64,923.4	

Source: DP Information Network 2005.
a. 2001 figure.

Table 4.7. U.S. Patent and Trademark Office Patents in ICT and Electronics Granted to Singapore-Based Inventors by Nationality of Assignee, 1976–2004

	Singapore assignees	Foreign assignees	Total	Singapore assignees as a % of total
Communications	78	116	194	40.2
Computer hardware and software	145	118	263	55.1
Computer peripherals	32	74	106	30.2
Information storage	38	168	206	18.4
Semiconductor devices	688	208	896	76.8
Other	23	37	60	38.3
All electronics and ICT patents	1,004	721	1,725	58.2

Source: USPTO various years.
Note: Unassigned patents are considered to be Singapore based.

to foreign subsidiaries. However, of the largest ICT patent holders in Singapore in 2004 (those owning more than 10 patents each), two-thirds were foreign firms (14 of 21) (table 4.8). Of the seven indigenous patent holders, three are universities or public research institutes and three are in semiconductors (with patents primarily in process technologies), leaving only one firm—Creative Technology—with substantial capabilities in product technology innovation.

Information Content and ICT Services Industry

The information content industry comprises all forms of information content publishing and distribution, from print media publishing to television and video production and broadcasting, music, software development, IT services, multimedia games, Internet and e-business services, and other creative content (Howkins 2001). In contrast to the United States, where the information content industry as a whole is significantly larger than the ICT manufacturing industry in terms of value added (U.S. Department of Commerce 2003), Singapore's information content industry has traditionally been proportionally much smaller than its ICT manufacturing industry—only about one-fourth in 1994 (Wong 1998). Unlike in Hong Kong (China), which has developed a thriving Chinese movie, television, and video industry, the leading subsector in the information content industry in Singapore has traditionally been publishing, printing, and distribution of print media. Although the government has strongly promoted the IT services and software industry since the early 1980s, Wong (1998) estimated that together they accounted for less than 30 percent of the

Table 4.8. Top USPTO ICT and Electronics Patent Holders of Singapore, 1976–2004

Rank	Company	Country	Electronics and ICT patents (1976–2004)
1	Chartered Semiconductor Manufacturing	Singapore	575
2	Seagate Technology	United States	122
3	Hewlett-Packard[a]	United States	88
4	Texas Instruments	United States	64
5	Creative Technology	Singapore	61
6	Micron Technology	United States	53
7	Matsushita Electric Industrial Company	Japan	47
8	Institute of Microelectronics	Singapore	45
9	National University of Singapore	Singapore	42
10	ST Assembly Test Services Pte Ltd.	Singapore	33
11	TriTech Microelectronics	Singapore	32
12	Motorola	United States	31
13	Kent Ridge Digital Labs	Singapore	22
14	Infineon Technologies	Germany	19
15	Advanced Micro Devices	United States	18
16	Amkor Technology	United States	15
16	STMicroelectronics Asia Pacific	Italy and France	15
18	Bridge Semiconductor Corporation	Taiwan (China)	13
19	Agere Systems[b]	United States	11
19	Agilent Technologies	United States	11
19	Thomson Consumer Electronics	France	11
	Total patents		1,328

Source: USPTO various years.
Note: Singapore patents are defined as those that have at least one Singapore-based inventor or are assigned to a Singapore-based company. Patents are classified according to the first named assignee.
a. Includes patents assigned to Hewlett-Packard Development Company.
b. Includes patents assigned to Agere Systems Guardian Corp.

value added by the information content industry in 1994. Although comparable estimates for later years are not available, table 4.9 indicates that growth in the combined value added by IT services, IT wholesale and retail distribution, and telecommunication services in Singapore significantly exceeded the average growth rate of the ICT manufacturing industry during 1986 to 2003. By 2003, this combined value added had grown to 80 percent of the size of ICT manufacturing, up from 30 percent in 1986. Extrapolating from the 2001 estimates of the size of other information content industries (such as print media publishing and television broadcasting) made by Wong, Ho, and Singh (2004), it is likely that the total value added by the overall information content industry might have already exceeded that of the total ICT manufacturing industry by 2003.

Table 4.9. Sectoral Composition of Value Added of Singapore's ICT Industry, 1986–2003

Subsector	Amount (S$ million)					Average annual growth rate (%)		
	1986	1990	1995	2000	2003	1986–90	1990–95	1995–2003
ICT manufacturing	3,781.0	7,716.6	11,987.9	17,228.3	11,678.15	19.5	9.2	–0.3
IT services	86.1	240.8	800.9	1,419.6	1,847	29.3	27.2	11.0
IT wholesale and retail distribution	253.2	623.8	1,075.3	1,731.2	3,196.60	25.3	11.5	14.6
Telecommunication services	804.7	1,433.4	2,739.2	3,159.6	4,286.4	15.5	13.8	5.8
Total	4,925.0	10,014.6	16,603.3	23,538.7	21,008.19	19.4	10.6	3.0
GDP (S$ million)	39,102.5	66,884.5	118,962.7	159,595.9	160,923.6	14.4	12.2	3.8
Value added/GDP (%)	12.6	15.0	14.0	14.7	13.1			
Percentage								
ICT manufacturing	76.8	77.1	72.2	73.2	55.6			
IT services	1.7	2.4	4.8	6.0	8.8			
IT wholesale and retail distribution	5.1	6.2	6.5	7.4	15.2			
Telecommunication services	16.3	14.3	16.5	13.4	20.4			
Total	100.0	100.0	100.0	100.0	100.0			

Sources: Department of Statistics various years a, various years b (reference year 2001), various years c.

Note: Value added for telecommunications for 2003 has been estimated as 90.1 percent of the value added for the post and telecommunication sector in 2003 (S$4,756,317,000), which was telcommunication's share of this sector in 2001.

a. Percentages may not add up to 100 percent because of rounding.

Because the IT wholesale and retail distribution sector includes both hardware and software distribution, it is more useful to examine only the growth of ICT services, even though doing so excludes some of the software development activities that are carried out by firms classified as part of the wholesale and retail sectors. Focusing only on the ICT services sectors (comprising IT services and telecommunication services but excluding IT wholesale and retail distribution), table 4.10 shows that the combined ICT services sector grew quite rapidly from 1986 to 2003. Value added grew from less than S$900 million in 1986 to more than S$6 billion in 2003, while employment increased from 15,500 to 41,800. Thus, unlike ICT manufacturing, which experienced a net employment loss, ICT services have been a major source of employment growth over the past decade.

As table 4.10 indicates, within ICT services, IT services have grown much faster than telecommunication services. In terms of value added, ICT services grew at close to twice the rate of telecommunications, while in terms of employment, ICT services contributed nearly 87 percent of the net employment increase during 1986 to 2003. As a result, the share of telecommunication services has declined steadily over the years, from more than 82 percent in 1991 to about 69 percent in 2003.

Table 4.11 provides a more detailed breakdown by subsector of the value added by ICT services for the period 1991 to 2003. IT development has expanded the fastest, compared with IT consulting and other IT services. It is also interesting to note that the value added by telecommunication services, after a steady decline in the 1990s, appears to have stabilized at about 70 percent in the 2000s.

Although the growth of Singapore's IT services and software development industry is indeed impressive, a significant proportion of it took the form of personnel-intensive contract programming or systems integration services, rather than the creation and commercialization of intellectual properties. In addition, a significant amount of IT wholesale and retail distribution activities involved the distribution of packaged software products from overseas. In this regard, the development of Singapore's IT services and software development industry has not differed significantly from the earlier experience of India, which has grown even more rapidly as an outsourcing outlet for contract programming and IT services to foreign firms. Whereas India quickly generated its own share of global IT services providers such as Wipro, Infosys, and Satyam, Singapore has not done so. In Singapore, the presence of foreign subsidiaries in IT services remains significant—although not as dominant as in the ICT manufacturing industry.

Table 4.10. ICT Services Industry Growth in Singapore, 1986–2003

	Establishments	Employment	Operating receipts	Value added	Value added/labor
IT services (S$ million)					
Year					
1986	134	2,823	224	86	30,506
1990	338	5,524	581	241	43,600
2000	1,753	18,011	4,019	1,420	78,820
2003	3,892	25,532	5,046	1,847	72,341
Average per annum growth (%)					
Period					
1986–90	26.0	18.3	26.9	29.3	9.3
1990–2003	20.7	12.5	18.1	17.0	4.0
Telecommunication services (S$ million)					
Year					
1986	2	12,712	988	805	63,299
1990	4	10,207	1,677	1,433	140,436
2000	256	12,677	5,484	3,160	249,240
2003	597	16,254	8,348	4,286	263,715
Average per annum growth rate (%)					
Period					
1986–90	18.9	−5.3	14.1	15.5	22.0
1990–2003	47.0	3.6	13.1	8.8	5.0
ICT services sector (S$ million)					
Year					
1986	136	15,535	1,213	891	57,340
1990	342	15,731	2,258	1,674	106,432
2000	2,009	30,688	9,504	4,579	149,220
2003	4,489	41,786	13,394	6,133	146,782
2003 (% of total service sector)	3.3	4.4	1.9	8.0	
Average per annum growth rate (%)					
Period					
1986–90	25.9	0.3	16.8	17.1	16.7
1990–2003	21.9	7.8	14.7	10.5	2.5

Sources: Department of Statistics various years a (reference year 2001), various years b (reference year 2001), various years c, various years d.

Note: ICT services comprise IT services and telecommunications. Telecommunication figures prior to 2000 include postal services. Data for telecommunications in 2003 has been estimated using its share for the post and telecommunication sector in 2001 applied to the total for the post and telecommunication sector in 2003.

Table 4.11. Sectoral Composition of Value Added of Singapore's ICT Services Industry, 1991–2003

Subsector	Share of value added (%)				
	1991	1996	2001	2002	2003
IT consulting	5.3	2.4	5.6	7.1	6.1
IT development	5.5	11.4	18.0	15.7	15.5
Hardware maintenance	7.1	12.4	1.3	1.3	1.2
Other IT services			5.5	6.7	7.3
Telecommunication services	82.1	73.8	69.6	69.1	69.9
Total ICT services	100.0	100.0	100.0	100.0	100.0

Sources: Department of Statistics various years a, various years b (reference year 2001), various years c, various years d. Additional information obtained from the Department of Statistics.
Note: Separate data are not available for "hardware maintenance" and "other IT services" for 1991 and 1996. Telecommunication figures prior to 2000 include postal services. Value added for telecommunications for 2002 and 2003 has been estimated as 90.1 percent of the value added for the post and telecommunication sector in the respective years, which was telcommunication's share of this sector in 2001.

As can be seen from table 4.12, the number of new entrant firms in the ICT services sectors far exceeds the number in ICT manufacturing. In particular, during the Internet boom years of 1999 and 2000, the rate of new firm formation in the ICT services cluster rose dramatically. However, many of these new firms subsequently vanished, and most of those that survived remained small, with the result that the industry remained dominated by a relatively small number of large firms. As shown by Wong (2006), of the top 30 IT services and telecommunication services firms operating in Singapore in 2001, 18 were local-majority firms, up from 11 in 1991. However, excluding the four local firms in the telecommunication carrier services sector, which are subject to regulatory controls by the government, the majority of the local ICT services firms are in reality government-linked corporations (GLCs)—that is, firms in which the government has significant equity investment and control. Only 3 of the local IT services firms in the top 30 were indigenous entrepreneurial firms, and although they are listed on Singapore's stock exchange, their size remains modest and their market reach is regional. The picture had not changed much by 2003: while local firms accounted for 12 of the top 20 ICT services firms by sales (up from 7 in 1991), virtually all are either telecommunication services firms or government-linked IT services firms (see tables 4.13 and 4.14).

It should also be noted that, despite the government's aim to promote Singapore as a regional ICT services hub, only slightly more than half of the combined sales from the IT services, software and hardware retail,

Table 4.12. Number of New Firms Registered in Electronics and ICT Industries, 1998–2004

	Year of registration						
	1998	1999	2000	2001	2002	2003	2004
Manufacturing of electronic products and components	90	147	137	104	115	98	93
Post and telecommunications	164	440	997	352	319	417	394
IT and related services	1,104	1,831	2,564	1,699	1,805	1,643	1,466
Total new ICT companies	1,358	2,418	3,698	2,155	2,239	2,158	1,953
Total new companies	29,870	34,604	36,457	33,202	36,675	39,337	41,164
Total new ICT companies/total companies (%)	4.5	7.0	10.1	6.5	6.1	5.5	4.7

Source: Wong and others 2006.

Table 4.13. Top 20 ICT Services Companies in Singapore, 1991–92

Rank	Company	Nationality	Sales (S$ million), 1991–92
1	Singapore Telecommunications	Singapore	2,479
2	AT&T Consumer Products	United States	311
3	Singapore Computer Systems	Singapore	127
4	AT&T Singapore	United States	86
5	CSA Holdings	United States	106
6	Matsushita Graphic Communication Systems	Japan	70
7	Fujitsu	Japan	67
8	Folec Communications	Singapore	38
9	Toshiba Data Dynamics	Japan	38
10	BT Services	United Kingdom	20
11	Transmarco Data Systems	Singapore	23
12	Teledata	Singapore	17
13	Ericsson Network Engineering	Sweden	16
14	Singapore Network Services	Singapore	20
15	ABB Nera	Norway	16
16	Centralab Components	Hong Kong	13
17	Siemens Nixdorf Information Systems	Germany	14
18	Isolectra Far East	Netherlands	12
19	Radac	Singapore	11
20	Nokia Telecommunications	Finland	9
	Total revenue for top 20 companies		3,493

Source: DP Information Network 1994.

and telecommunication services in 2001 and 2002 were exported (IDA 2003b). Thus, many IT services firms, especially the smaller ones, continue to rely on the domestic market.

Network Infrastructure Deployment and Informatization

As documented elsewhere (see, for example, Wong 1996, 2004), Singapore has been among the first to promote ICT diffusion among developing countries. As table 4.15 indicates, the diffusion of IT use in homes and in enterprises rose rapidly from the mid-1980s to the late 1990s. Likewise, the diffusion of Internet access, mobile telephone subscription, and e-commerce rose rapidly from the mid-1990s until 2000 (table 4.16). Such rapid diffusion enabled Singapore to leapfrog ahead of many other countries, including even some member states of the Organisation for Economic Co-operation and Development (OECD). International rankings of countries by ICT adoption indicators put Singapore generally in the top 10 countries in the world on most

Table 4.14. Top 20 ICT Services Companies in Singapore, 2003

Rank	Company	Nationality	Sales, 2003 (S$ million)	Description
1	Singapore Telecommunications	Singapore	11,994.7	Telecommunications
2	Microsoft Operations	United States	4,093.5	Software
3	STT Communications	Singapore	2,530.3	Telecommunications and IT services
4	ECS Holdings	Singapore	1,422.8	IT services
5	StarHub	Singapore	1,118.2	Telecommunications
6	MobileOne	Singapore	717.3	Telecommunications
7	Singapore Technologies Electronics	Singapore	621.1	IT services
8	NCS	Singapore	594.0	IT services
9	Datacraft Asia	United Kingdom	576.3	IT services
10	CSA Holdings	United States	484.2	IT services
11	Singapore Computer Systems	Singapore	418.9	IT services
12	Autodesk Asia	United States	350.6	IT services
13	Keppel Telecommunications & Transportation	Singapore	242.4	Telecommunications and IT services
14	Abacus International	Singapore	244.8	Other services
15	Reuters Asia	United Kingdom	218.4	Other services
16	CET Technologies	Singapore	188.1	IT services
17	Avaya Singapore	United States	184.0	Telecommunications
18	CSE Global	Singapore	169.0	IT services
19	Nera Telecommunications	Norway	167.6	Telecommunications
20	Accenture	Luxemburg	159.4	IT services
	Total revenue for top 20 companies		26,495.6	

Source: DP Information Network 2005.

Table 4.15. Information Communication Use in Singapore Households, 1988–2004

Indicator	1988	1990	1993	1996	1997	1999	2000	2001	2002	2003	2004
PC ownership	11.0	19.1	26.6	35.8	41.0	58.9	61.0	63.9	68.4	74.0	74.0
Home internet access	—	—	—	8.6	14.0	42.1	49.3	56.3	59.4	65.0	65.0
Home broadband access	—	—	—	—	—	—	3.0	17.7	24.2	—	—
IT use in enterprises	50.0				70.0		80.0		83.0	83.0	83.0

Sources: IDA 2003a, various years; Wong 2001a.

Note: For ICT use in enterprises, basic ICT technologies refer to computers, laptops, or workstations. From 2002, personal digital assistants and wireless application protocol–enabled mobile phones are included.

Table 4.16. Selected ICT Diffusion Indicators for Singapore, 1990–2004

Year	Main lines in use per 1,000 inhabitants		Cellular mobile telephone subscribers per 1,000 inhabitants		Internet hosts per 1,000 people		Internet users per 1,000 people		Computers per 1,000 people	
	Rank	Number	Rank	Number	Rank	Number	Rank	Number	Rank	Number
1990	19	371[a]								
1991	20	384[a]								
1992	20	383							12	116
1993	21	402							15	125
1994	21	426	7	57.7					14	151
1995	18	498	8	75.1	12	7.62	14	30.1	12	207
1996	15	529	9	147.5	15	8.35	9	141.2	13	233
1997	24	465	8	229	12	13.27			10	316
1998	23	484	13	280.7	19	13.45			11	344
1999	23	477	18	381.5	17	22.19			12	391
2000	25	472	19	583	13	43.8	6	482.9	13	440
2001	25	472	20	687.9	16	47.92	9	469.0	10	580
2002	25	450	20	761.1			12	511.3	11	596
2003	26	432	19	852.5			19	479.5	15	534
2004			20	894.7			16	574.8	15	573

Sources: IMD various years b; WEF various years.
a. Number of telephones in use per 1,000 inhabitants.

indicators in the late 1990s (IMD various years a). Aggregate measures such as IT spending as a percentage of gross domestic product (GDP) and ICT employment as a share of total employment also indicate that Singapore had achieved a level of investment in IT that is high relative to even advanced OECD countries. As can be seen in table 4.17, in 1999, Singapore spent 3.2 percent of its GDP on ICT, higher than the OECD average and the highest of all Asian countries.

Consistent with studies conducted in the United States and other advanced OECD countries (see, for example, OECD 2004; Pohjola 2001), the aggressive investment in IT has been found to have contributed significantly to the economic growth of Singapore from the late 1970s to the late 1990s (Wong 2001a). In particular, IT capital investment in the 20-year period of 1977 to 1997 was estimated to have contributed 18.7 percent of the real GDP growth of Singapore during that period—and yielded returns that were more than twice those of capital investment outside IT (Wong 2001a).

Notwithstanding the rapid progress made in the past, the diffusion of ICT use in Singapore appeared to have slowed from the late 1990s to the early 2000s (see tables 4.15 and 4.16). Although this slowdown was to some degree inevitable, given that ICT adoption levels in Singapore had already reached a fairly high level by international standards, closer examination suggests that Singapore may have started to experience a relative decline in comparison with some of its international competitors in several ICT adoption indicators.

Table 4.18 shows the relative ranking of Singapore based on the Information Society Index (ISI) maintained by International Data Corporation since 1997 (IDC and *World Times* various years). Singapore's relative ranking has declined steadily from 4th in 1999 to 9th in 2001,

Table 4.17. International Comparison: IT as Percentage of GDP, 1999

Country	IT as % of GDP
Singapore	3.22
United States	4.14
Japan	2.06
Korea, Rep. of	1.61
OECD[a]	3.09
Taiwan (China)	1.34
Hong Kong (China)	1.32

Source: IDC 1999, which defines *IT* as "the revenue paid to vendors (including channel markups) for systems, software, and/or services."
a. Iceland, Luxembourg, and the Slovak Republic are excluded.

13th in 2002, and 17th in 2003, before recovering to 13th again in 2004 (see panel a of table 4.18). In contrast, the Scandinavian countries, particularly Finland and Sweden, have consistently maintained their positions among the top 10 in the world (see panel b of table 4.18). Closer examination of the four subindices (computer, Internet or Web, telecommunication infrastructure, and social) shows Singapore to be weakest in the social subindex and to be losing ground in the Internet or Web subindex (see panel c of table 4.18).

Examination of individual diffusion indicators appears to corroborate the ISI trend. According to the *World Competitiveness Report* (IMD various years a), Singapore's international ranking in the early 2000s declined relative to the late 1990s in the penetration rate of mobile phones, Internet, and broadband. Its ranking by the number of Internet hosts per thousand population and the number of e-commerce transactions per capita similarly dropped.

It is true that a new annual ranking since 2001 by World Economic Forum's annual *Global Information Technology Report* (WEF various years) in the overall Networked Readiness Index (NRI) found Singapore

Table 4.18. Ranking of Singapore in the Information Society Index, 1999–2004

a. Singapore's rank, 1999–2004

Year	Rank
1999	4
2000	11
2001	9
2002	13
2003	17
2004	13

b. Rank of Singapore relative to selected countries, 2001–04

Country	2001	2002	2003	2004
Singapore	9	13	17	13
United States	4	4	7	3
Germany	13	15	14	15
Japan	11	12	15	18
Finland	3	8	4	7
Sweden	1	1	2	2
Hong Kong (China)	15	11	16	11
Korea, Rep. of	19	18	12	8
Taiwan (China)	18	10	23	20

(continued)

Table 4.18. (continued)

c. Rank of Singapore relative to selected countries on ISI component indices

Country	2002				2003				2004			
	Computer	Internet	Information	Social	Computer	Telecom-munications	Web	Social	Computer	Telecom-munications	Web	Social
Singapore	8	2	21	33	11	8	15	28	5	3	10	26
United States	1	10	14	17	2	24	8	8	1	13	12	8
Germany	17	11	9	13	13	17	7	19	12	24	6	16
Japan	5	17	12	2	6	31	2	17	8	27	16	22
Finland	14	9	6	6	16	11	6	1	15	10	7	1
Sweden	6	1	8	4	7	6	1	3	10	7	1	3
Hong Kong (China)	3	16	10	3	9	1	18	30	11	1	20	34
Korea, Rep. of	22	18	16	8	20	2	10	18	20	2	2	22
Taiwan (China)	19	14	1	9	29	3	22	27	25	4	15	28

Source: IDC and *World Times* various years.

to have improved its ranking from eighth in 2001 to 2002, to second in 2002 to 2003 and 2003 to 2004, and first in 2004 to 2005 (Dutta, Lanvin, and Paua 2003; Kirkman and others 2002). However, because several important component indices of the NRI are based on subjective assessments, the ranking methodology is not compatible with the more objective measures of the ISI or the individual diffusion indicators. Moreover, closer examination of the subindices of the NRI reveals that Singapore actually ranked relatively poorly on such components as individual usage (22nd) and individual readiness (18th), although it received high ranking on business usage (2nd) and business readiness (4th) and top ranking for government usage and readiness (1st for both). The high ranking of Singapore's e-government services has been corroborated by a number of other surveys—for example, Accenture's annual e-government surveys (Accenture 2003)—while a high ranking of Singapore in terms of business IT use has also been made by senior managers surveyed by the annual *World Competitiveness Report* (IMD various years a).

These contrasts in ranking suggest a very interesting feature of Singapore's information society development: while ICT usage in the business sector and the public sector has been highly developed, diffusion to the social and community arena and to household and personal activities such as entertainment appears to have been less developed.

Particularly notable is the slower takeoff of broadband use in the home in Singapore relative to other IT-savvy countries, even though Singapore was among the first countries in the world (in 1992) to articulate a vision of a nation fully wired by a broadband national information infrastructure (NCB 1992). As can be seen in table 4.19, Singapore's broadband penetration rate had not kept pace with the rapid growth in not only Korea, Hong Kong (China), and the advanced Scandinavian countries, but also Japan, Taiwan (China), and the United States. More significantly, the cost of broadband access is higher in Singapore than in every one of those economies.

Likewise, Singapore has trailed Hong Kong (China), Korea, and Japan in deploying third-generation mobile infrastructure and applications. Although fixed Wi-Fi deployment achieved rapid growth, access is still far from ubiquitous, owing partly to an inability to roam across Wi-Fi service operators. More significantly, reflecting the lower readiness of individuals in Singapore found by the annual NRI survey, the household and consumer sector in Singapore also appears to lack sophistication with respect to using fixed or mobile creative content and e-commerce applications. This lack of sophistication is reflected in the lower readiness score of Singaporean individuals on the NRI, compared with individuals

Table 4.19. Broadband Market Data as of December 31, 2004

	Total broadband subscribers (millions)	Broadband penetration (subscriptions per 100 inhabitants)		Broadband penetration (% of Internet subscribers)	Cost of broadband (US$ per 100 kilobytes)
		Rank	Number		
Singapore	0.51	16	11.9	23.0	1.59
United States	37.89	15	12.8	59.5	0.49
Japan	1.91	12	14.9	56.4	0.07
Finland	0.80	11	15.3	57.1	0.73
Sweden	1.30	14	14.7	40.6	0.25
Hong Kong (China)	1.51	2	21.3	60.3	0.83
Korea, Rep. of	11.92	1	24.9	99.1	0.08
Taiwan (China)	3.75	8	16.5	28.0	0.18

Source: ITU 2005.

in Japan, Korea, and Scandinavian countries. Although this finding may be related to the underdevelopment of a vibrant creative content publishing industry in Singapore noted earlier, the lack of widespread and competitive deployment of network infrastructure at low cost may also be a factor constraining the growth of creative content. For example, mobile communications operators in Singapore, operating under oligopolistic competition, demand a higher share of revenue generated from content offered by providers of value-added services applications than prevails in such countries as Japan and Korea. That factor may stifle new content offering by small independent content providers.

Distinctive Features of Singapore's ICT Development versus That of the United States, Scandinavia, and Other Asian Newly Industrialized Economies

In summary, Singapore's ICT industrial development appears to exhibit quite different characteristics than that of three other groups of nations that have advanced ICT development: (a) the United States, the world's most advanced technological leader in a wide range of ICT and home to Silicon Valley, the most advanced seedbed for high-tech entrepreneurial capitalism; (b) the Scandinavian countries, which combine a high emphasis on innovation with a high regard for social welfare and egalitarian access to technological progress; and (c) the late-industrializing economies of Korea and Taiwan (China), with their emphasis on acquiring external technologies and developing indigenous capabilities to catch up and compete with the advanced countries.

In contrast to the entrepreneurial dynamism of the U.S. information economy—and to a certain extent the economy of Taiwan (China) well—Singapore's information economy has been characterized by an enterprise ecosystem dominated by subsidiaries of large foreign MNCs. Singapore's information economy is also distinctly different from those of Finland and Korea, where large dominant firms provide key anchors to their ICT industrial clusters (Nokia in Finland and the large ICT *chaebols* like Samsung, LG, and Hyundai in Korea).

Another clear contrast is that, while the U.S. information economy manifests a large number of vibrant creative content industrial clusters (Hollywood movies, computer games, television broadcasting, Internet content publishing, and e-commerce), Singapore's information economy is dominated by ICT manufacturing. Although the software industry is growing, it is primarily focused on business applications, with little in the way of creative content industries. In contrast, apart from having a strong base of ICT manufacturing, Korea has in recent years started to emerge as a major exporter of creative content to youth around Asia in the form of movies, television entertainment programming, and pop music (Yusuf and Nabeshima 2006).

In terms of network infrastructure, the United States deploys a multitude of technology platforms, a consequence of the U.S. public policy of (by and large) emphasizing private market competition in the development of telecommunication infrastructure. In contrast, in Finland and Korea, the state has historically played key roles in proactively investing in emerging technology platforms. It thereby creates the favorable home market conditions for the national firms to leverage their early-entrant advantage to become global players. For example, Nokia capitalized on the early deployment of the GSM (Global System for Mobile) standard in Finland and, more generally, Europe. Similarly, Samsung and LG took early advantage of Korean government's promotion of the CDMA (code division multiple access) platform. Although Singapore moved toward market liberalization, it was a controlled move, and the major players were limited to government-controlled companies, as will be discussed.

Finally, whereas all the advanced information societies emphasize the deployment of ICT to enhance the quality of life of their citizenry, the pattern of deployment appears to differ. Ensuring access by ordinary citizens to government information and protecting the privacy of individuals' information have been major drivers in the United States and in the Scandinavian countries. Singapore has emphasized a more utilitarian, transactional approach in its e-government strategy, one that stresses enabling the public to make efficient transactions with the government, with less focus on facilitating the assertion of their information rights. Similarly, while grassroots initiatives to use ICT for community-based interactions and interest group advancement are quite vibrant in the United States and Scandinavia, such community-based innovations appear to be less frequent in Singapore.

The Role and Influence of the Developmental State

The key to comprehending how the characteristics and developmental path of Singapore's information society differ from those of other advanced information societies is the role and influence of the developmental state. As highlighted in Wong (1998), the rapid pace of ICT manufacturing industry growth and ICT diffusion in Singapore in the 1980s and the first half of the 1990s could not have been possible without a strong interventionist role by the state. However, the influence of the developmental state on ICT growth in Singapore has its downside as well, and some of the negative features in Singapore's information society that were highlighted earlier can be traced to the dominant developmental strategies adopted by the state.

As argued by Wong (2001c, 2004), the developmental state of Singapore takes an approach to promoting economic development that is distinctly different from that of other developmental states, such as Korea and Taiwan (China). In essence, Singapore's economic model in the 1980s and 1990s can be characterized as an MNC-leveraging strategy to generate economic growth. This strategic thrust is complemented by two others. One involves proactively investing public funds in relevant public infrastructure, in human resources, and in enabling technologies to support the development of industries that need such technologies, coupled with relevant incentives to firms in these industries that use them. The other involves establishing government-controlled companies to operate in business sectors deemed strategic to the Singaporean economy, either because of their national strategic role (for example, defense technologies or air transport) or because no private sector firms are willing to take the initial high-capital risk (as in fabrication of semiconductor wafers).

It must be noted that these three thrusts are not implemented in isolation but are integrated with a larger, overall economic development strategy that seeks to position Singapore as a major business node in the global system of trade and capital flows. As pointed out in Wong (2006), Hong Kong (China) and Singapore were among the first developing economies to adopt an open-economy policy emphasizing free trade and movement of capital and welcoming foreign investment in export-oriented manufacturing. Both also adopted the policy of providing a business-friendly environment by emphasizing the rule of law, relatively clean and efficient government services, and stable macroeconomic policies. Beyond these similarities, however, the state played a much more important role in the island economy of Singapore than in the laissez faire approach of Hong Kong (China). Besides playing a virtual monopoly role in providing such traditional social and physical infrastructure services as public education and health care, seaports and airports, telecommunications, and public utilities, the Singaporean state had extensive direct business involvement in many sectors of the economy normally deemed private, through a web of quasi-state enterprises (the GLCs) that are effectively owned or controlled by a number of government investment holding companies. The business involvement of the state through these GLCs covers a range of strategic industries such as airlines, aerospace and defense manufacturing, and telecommunications, as well as other industries such as banking, logistics services, shipbuilding, construction, and even food manufacturing.

Besides such direct business involvement, the state's control over the financial system also goes significantly beyond the normal monetary and fiscal policy instruments, through institutions such as the Central Provident Fund (a compulsory wage-savings scheme) and through licensing control over domestic consumer banks. In addition, the state exerts significant influence over the functioning of the labor market, through highly selective policy instruments such as permanent residency and employment control, a levy on foreign workers, and an extensive public scholarship system that skims off the best students to staff the upper echelons of public service and GLCs. Finally, through its significant ownership of land and its active participation in the provision of public housing and social community facilities, the state's influence weighs heavily on the property markets and extends deep into the social fabric. Through these control levers, the state in Singapore has been able to exercise significant industrial policy intervention over the domestic economy, and because these policies have primarily been market enhancing, Singapore nonetheless has a very open economy that is highly dependent on foreign investments and external trade (Wong 2001c). Indeed, Singapore consistently has been ranked as among the freest economies in the world (Miles, Feulner, and O'Grady 2004), in contrast to other developmental states like Korea and Taiwan (China), which were ranked substantially lower.

The three strategic thrusts identified earlier constitute the principal levers of influence on the development of Singapore's information economy and society.

MNC-Leveraging Strategy for Industry Development
As mentioned earlier, this proactive approach to attracting investment by global MNCs in selected industrial clusters is aimed at accelerating Singapore's competitive entry into these clusters. Although the strategy does not explicitly favor foreign firms at the expense of local firms—indeed, separate programs target domestic firms—it does emphasize attracting the global leaders to help anchor the targeted industrial cluster. Once a global player is rooted in Singapore in a particular activity (such as manufacturing), the strategy is to leverage the presence of that player

through various policies and programs to encourage it to continuously expand its role (to regional procurement or technical support, for example); to upgrade its operations (to handle more complex products or to add R&D and product design); and to develop or work with other players in the local industrial cluster (to develop and qualify local suppliers or to undertake joint R&D with public research institutes and local universities). This MNC-leveraging strategy has been most pronounced in the ICT manufacturing industry, where the success of Singapore in key ICT industrial clusters—hard disk drives (McKendrick, Doner, and Haggard 2000); semiconductor wafer fabrication (Mathews and Cho 2000); and contract manufacturing (Wong 2002a)—would not have been possible without such a proactive industry promotion strategy.

This MNC-leveraging strategy for industry development is implemented through a high-powered agency, the Economic Development Board (EDB). Besides focusing on attracting investment by relevant global MNCs, the EDB also coordinates the subsequent leveraging activities with other agencies, including industry-specific human resource training programs, upgrading programs for local suppliers, and R&D collaboration with public research institutes. Although the EDB also runs programs that target local enterprises, the focus in those programs is on local firms that have the potential to be significant regional players in the key strategic industries; the broader task of helping local small and medium-size enterprises in general to improve their productivity, quality, and innovative capacity is entrusted to a separate agency, the Standards, Productivity, and Innovation Board.

Although this MNC-leveraging strategy of the developmental state is clearly responsible for the rapid growth of the ICT manufacturing industry in Singapore over the past 30 years, it has also resulted in the continuing high dependence of Singapore on foreign firms. Some critics of the policy have argued that it stifled the development of local enterprises, but what the counterfactual outcome might have been had the state pursued a more pro-indigenous firm strategy is by no means clear. Although the share of local firms in the ICT industry might have been higher, the overall size and competitiveness of the industry might have been much reduced as well.

To a lesser degree, the rapid growth of Singapore's IT services and software industry is also likely to have been partly driven by this MNC-leveraging strategy, although the diffusion policy may have contributed even more, as will be discussed. However, as highlighted earlier, Singapore's IT services and software industry suffers from a number of weaknesses, particularly the lack of a critical mass of indigenous entrepreneurial firms that can be globally competitive. This weakness, too, could be a consequence of the MNC-leveraging strategy.

There has been little research into the factors behind the relative overall weakness of Singapore in other creative content industries (such as movies, videos, and music; Internet publishing; computer games; and mobile entertainment). From this analytical framework, however, an important factor would appear to be a lack of strategic recognition of the economic importance of such industries by the government until recently. Because they have not been targeted as strategic industries, they have not received the kind of preferential treatment that has been accorded to the industries promoted by the developmental state. One possible cause for this lack of preferential treatment may be that these industries come under the purview of governmental agencies that are more regulatory than developmental; for example, much of the publishing and the performing arts industry is regulated by the Ministry of Information and the Arts. Some foreign observers have argued that a policy of the Singapore Broadcasting Authority (SBA) that regulates pornographic content and political speeches on the Internet has had an adverse impact on Internet publishing. Another cause may be the diverse nature of these industries, resulting in each being seen as too small a niche to be promoted strategically.

Indeed, not until the early 2000s were these diverse industries recognized by the government as belonging to a strategic industrial cluster—the creative content industry—that needs to be promoted in an integral way (ERC 2002). Only after that strategic recognition did the government establish the Media Development Authority (MDA) in 2003 to replace the regulation-oriented SBA. The MDA has rolled out a strategic plan for promoting the industry (called Media 21), similar to the EDB's MNC-leveraging development strategies for promoting other strategic industries, albeit with a stronger focus on attracting individual foreign talent (in addition to firms) and with more emphasis on nurturing local players (MDA 2003).

Public Sector's Role in Diffusion Promotion

To complement the MNC-leveraging strategy, the developmental state of Singapore also takes a proactive approach to promoting infrastructure and human resource development. Such an approach ensures that the industries that are promoted do not face bottlenecks in terms of factor inputs. More generally, the state in Singapore has evinced an ability to adopt a comprehensive, integrative approach to the promotion of technology diffusion. That approach combines incentives to individual businesses to adopt and use the identified new technologies or innovations, industrywide or economywide human resource and infrastructure development programs, and strategic use of the public sector itself as a lead user or early adopter of new technologies.

This integrated approach to diffusion promotion has been applied successfully in other areas in Singapore, including the promotion of industrial automation, the adoption of ISO 9000 quality practices, and the implementation of electronic road pricing. Yet the state was most successful in promoting IT diffusion in the early phases. Implemented through a centralized coordinating agency, the National Computer Board (NCB), the state's integrated policy contributed significantly to the rapid diffusion of IT adoption, particularly in the 1980s and early 1990s (Wong 1998). By integrating IT human resource development programs, offering assistance to local enterprises to implement computerization, and providing incentives to IT services firms to establish their operations in Singapore, the NCB was able to achieve synergies across different policy instruments. In addition, its ability to integrate the policy of making the public sector an early user of computerization and new IT applications, through its aggressive Civil Service Computerization Program, was critical to the early growth of the IT services industry in Singapore (Wong 1996). Another early success story of the NCB was the development of TradeNet, which contributed significantly to improving productivity in the documentation of external trade transactions.

One area in which the NCB did well was to accelerate the training and development of IT professionals, which increased the supply of IT personnel significantly from 1980 to the mid-1990s (Wong 2002b). Although part of this training and development was through increased enrollment in IT programs in tertiary educational institutions, important also were the various professional training and upgrading programs introduced or subsidized by the NCB, in close consultation with industry. Indeed, workers with nontertiary professional qualifications represented 26 to 38 percent of IT professionals in 1995 to 1999. In addition, in 1995 to 1997, companies devoted a substantial part of their IT payrolls (6 percent) to training, partly motivated by a reimbursable subsidy provided by the NCB (Wong 2002b). Although data from 1999 onward are not comparable with those of earlier years because the coverage was expanded to include a broader range of information communication professionals, the continuing role of the state in promoting human resource development remains important, not only in terms of training but also through the state's efforts to attract foreign talent to work in Singapore.

Strong and early commitment by the Singaporean government to the development of telecommunications infrastructure was also responsible for the emergence of Singapore as a leading regional telecommunication hub. Recognizing the importance of telecommunication infrastructure to its ambition to make Singapore a regional business hub, the government invested heavily in telecommunication infrastructure during the 1970s and 1980s through its postal, telegraph, and telephone (PTT) monopoly, Singapore Telecom. During that period, Singapore Telecom could be regarded as a model PTT monopoly among less developed countries. It achieved above-average standards (relative to global industry) in terms of capital efficiency and labor productivity, and it was among the first such companies in the world to achieve 100 percent conversion of its public switching network to digital technology.

However, with the increasing convergence of IT and telecommunications in the 1990s and with the dramatic rise of the Internet in the mid-1990s, Singapore was arguably less successful in implementing an integrated policy of ICT diffusion because of its relative slowness in managing the transition from dealing with three separate policy domains—telecommunications, IT, and content publishing—to a world of digital convergence. On the telecommunication side, responding to global trends, the Singaporean government began to gradually liberalize the telecommunication market in the early 1990s by privatizing the incumbent PTT monopoly, allowing the entry of new players, and promoting the development of alternative access to the home in the form of cable television (Wong 1996). As the government grappled with the challenges of managing this gradual market liberation through the Telecommunications Authority of Singapore (TAS), the NCB was unable to expand the scope of its diffusion promotion policy to integrate areas that were under the purview of the TAS. In addition, because regulation and control over Internet publishing came under another government agency, the SBA, the ICT diffusion policy became even more fragmented. It was not until the late 1990s that the government decided to merge the NCB and the TAS to become a single agency, the Infocomm Development Authority (IDA). Since then, the IDA has rolled out a new developmental strategy called Connected Singapore (IDA 2003a), which appears to be much more comprehensive and integrated than the piecemeal approaches that characterized the second half of the 1990s.

Notwithstanding the greater policy coherence arising from the integration of the NCB and the TAS, the IDA's policy coverage remains incomplete, because the regulation of creative content publishing still falls outside its purview. As pointed out earlier, although the effects of the SBA policy to regulate pornographic content and political speeches on the Internet are debatable, the lack of a proactive developmental strategy covering creative content may be more serious and represents a clear gap in the government's otherwise proactive developmental approach. This gap was filled only in 2003 with the government's release of a new strategy for promoting creative industries and the subsequent conversion of the SBA from a largely regulatory agency into the MDA. However, significant areas of overlap exist between the policy domains of the IDA and the MDA (for example, the development of "infotainment" software and broadband deployment policies), and the extent to which the two agencies can coordinate their efforts to achieve synergy in these overlapping areas remains unclear.

Government-Linked Corporations and Oligopolistic Competition

The establishment of GLCs dates back to a period when the local capitalist class was weak and the developmental state needed to resort to establishing operating companies to enter industries in which no local businesses were prepared to take risks. Their continuing strong presence in the Singaporean economy is controversial. It is true that, unlike the typical state-owned enterprises in many developing countries, GLCs are run on an arm's-length basis with management that is highly professional, and their business operations are often subject to the discipline of the market, with many of them listed on the local stock exchange and hence subject to the scrutiny of significant outside investors and independent security analysts. Many of these GLCs are indeed profitable (for example, Singapore Airlines has long been one of the most profitable airlines in the world), and some have grown to become significant regional players in key high-tech industries targeted by the developmental state. Two of the four local firms that made it to the top 20 ICT manufacturing firms in Singapore in 2003 are such GLCs, operating in the key cluster of semiconductor wafer fabrication. While proponents argue that without GLCs Singapore would become even more dependent on foreign MNCs, critics are concerned that GLCs may crowd out independent start-ups and stifle local entrepreneurship.

A possible consequence for the development of the ICT industry of the establishment of GLCs is the controlled nature of the telecommunication liberalization process. Although two new major telecommunication carriers had been allowed entry into the telecommunication market of Singapore (in addition to the incumbent, privatized PTT company), both were GLCs with significant ownership and control by the government.

Although it is clear that the increased competition has driven down prices and increased product innovations in the market, there remain lingering concerns that the oligopolistic competition among GLCs has not been as conducive to entrepreneurial start-ups as true free market competition might have been.

The concerns about dominance by GLCs extend to the larger public domestic market for IT services, including public procurement of IT services. Indeed, as part of the legacy of the Civil Service Computerization Program, it was only in the 1990s that systems integration work for various government ministries was opened to independent firms, after the public organizations that previously held monopoly roles for such work were privatized. Despite the liberalization, certain projects for ministries such as defense remain the preserve of some GLCs. This legacy partly explains the strong presence of large GLCs among the top 20 firms in Singapore's ICT services sector and suggests the possibility that independent entrepreneurial start-ups will continue to face playing fields that are not level. Given the small domestic market of Singapore, this obstacle adds to the barriers that independent start-ups must overcome to secure a foothold in the domestic market before venturing overseas.

More generally, some argue that both the MNC-leveraging and the GLC strategies have helped stifle local entrepreneurship in the ICT sector in another way: by providing lucrative career paths, these large enterprises bid talent away from the independent enterprise sector and raise the opportunity costs to technical talent who leave to start their own enterprises. In this sense, the very success of the MNC-leveraging and GLC strategies undermines the development of a more entrepreneurial enterprise ecosystem in Singapore's economy.

The same "paradox of success" argument can perhaps be extended to the success of the public sector in appropriating the top talent to work in public service. This strategy is implemented through a system of public scholarship that skims off the best students from high schools to study in top universities overseas before returning to serve in government services under bond. Rapid promotion opportunities, coupled with high remuneration by international standards and the options for subsequent transfer to senior management positions in GLCs, further help to retain these high flyers in the public sector, thereby reducing the number who shift to entrepreneurial pursuits.

Although not the direct consequence of any of the three strategic thrusts, the generally strong developmental role of the state in Singaporean society may also have an effect on the pattern of ICT use in households and the social community. As noted earlier, although Singapore has some of the most advanced e-government services in the world, they tend to focus on facilitating efficient transactions between the citizenry and government agencies rather than on promoting community interactions among the citizenry. An entrenched habit among the citizenry of turning to the government whenever a problem arises, rather than initiating and fostering community self-help, may also be a contributing factor.

Opportunities and Challenges: Imperatives for New Strategic Thrusts to Information Society Development

The last section highlighted the positive and negative influences of the developmental state on the development of the information economy and society in Singapore. But the global economic environment is constantly changing, and this change will give rise to new opportunities and challenges for the development of Singapore's information society. This section briefly examines some salient changes in the global economic environment that are likely to have a significant influence on Singapore in the medium term and highlights their implications for the formation of new strategic thrusts in Singapore's development effort.

First and foremost, the continuing shift toward a globalized information economy will accelerate two contradictory trends: On the one hand, there will be increasing consolidation of players in various ICT industrial clusters on a global scale; on the other hand, this consolidation process will from time to time be punctuated by gales of Schumpeterian creative destruction, as new disruptive innovations arise in various ICT fields, often pioneered by new entrepreneurial entrants. In addition to creatively destroying incumbents, some of these new entrepreneurial innovations will also seed the emergence of new industries. Thus, both new entrepreneurial firms and global MNCs will continue to be important in the global information economy landscape, and it is prudent for any country to try to ride on both.

Although Singapore has done well in the past through leveraging global MNCs, it is imperative that it try to add a new strategic thrust—that of promoting a more vibrant entrepreneurial ICT enterprise ecosystem— in order to achieve a more balanced strategic development portfolio. Indeed, the state has recognized this need since the late 1990s and started to make significant policy shifts toward a more balanced approach that combines leveraging MNCs and promoting indigenous entrepreneurship (Wong 2006).

Another important trend in the shift toward a global information economy is the growing importance of the creative content industry (Florida 2002). Despite the significant global dominance of U.S. MNCs in a wide range of creative content and media publishing industries, the continuing demand for local and regional content that caters to idiosyncratic specificities of cultural and social interests points to the potential for the rise of indigenous creative content industrial clusters in many emerging economies, particularly in Asia. The recent surge in popularity of Korean pop culture among East Asian youth, the rise of Bollywood in India, and the blossoming of new creative arts in China are manifestations of these new market potentials. Korea also demonstrated the potential of exploiting new ICT to establish new creative content industries through its success in developing interactive online games, just as the Japanese have done in pioneering a host of innovative mobile content services.

Having focused in the past on promoting Singapore as a global business and financial services hub, the Singaporean government has not really made a concerted effort to nurture a significant creative content industrial cluster. It is thus critical to start catching up quickly, in order to carve out a viable niche in the rapidly growing global and regional creative content markets. The recent formation of the MDA to promote creative industries as a strategic industrial cluster represents a move in the right direction, but much remains to be done.

Last, but not least, the growing importance of the two giants—China and India—in the global information economy will have major implications for the future of Singapore as an information economic hub in Asia. On the one hand, these economies offer vast new ICT market opportunities to tap. On the other hand, their growing competitiveness in ICT, coupled with the advantage of a huge supply of low-cost skills and a large domestic market, represents significant competitive threats. As table 4.20 shows, the significant expansion of China's share of the export of electronics goods to the European, Japanese, and U.S. markets is at the expense of the four Asian newly industrialized economies and the four Association of Southeast Asian Nations (ASEAN) countries. Likewise, India is becoming dominant in the global IT service export markets.

The competitive position that India has achieved over the years as a global IT services outsourcing hub has certainly made it very difficult for Singapore to realize its regional ambitions. Not only does India have significant advantages in cost and the supply of skills; it also has developed a critical mass of global IT services firms that possess the advanced project

Table 4.20. China's Rising Share in Electronics Exports to the United States, Japan, and the European Union, 1989–2004

Source of imports	1989–90 (%)	1994–95 (%)	1999–2000 (%)	2003–04 (%)
U.S. imports				
China	1.1	3.3	6.1	13.4
Hong Kong (China) + Korea, Rep. of + Taiwan (China)	9.6	9.8	10.2	9.5
Singapore	3.5	4.4	2.9	1.8
ASEAN-4	2.7	5.3	7.2	6.5
Others	83.0	76.3	73.6	68.8
Japanese imports				
China	1.2	5.2	11.6	25.9
Hong Kong (China) + Korea, Rep. of + Taiwan (China)	7.1	9.0	9.6	10.0
Singapore	2.4	5.6	4.0	2.7
ASEAN-4	9.1	16.4	24.5	21.7
Others	80.2	63.4	50.4	39.8
European Union imports				
China	0.3	1.1	2.2	5.4
Hong Kong (China) + Korea, Rep. of + Taiwan (China)	2.7	3.6	4.7	4.7
Singapore	0.9	1.6	1.4	1.2
ASEAN-4	1.5	3.2	3.8	3.7
Others	95.5	92.1	89.3	86.2

Source: Compiled from United Nations Statistical Division various years (import records, Standard International Trade Classifications 75 and 76).

management and organizational capabilities needed to manage globally dispersed teams around the clock. Indeed, building on the reputation established with Western firms, these global Indian IT services firms are now leveraging the global information infrastructure to rapidly expand their operations into a wide range of emerging opportunities for business process outsourcing (for example, accounting, financial analysis, medical diagnosis, and engineering design), thereby hastening the outsourcing of professional work from higher-cost locations.

To compete effectively with China and India and to tap their market opportunities, Singapore needs to develop new capabilities in its ICT clusters. Central to the development of such new capabilities is the need to invest more intensively in indigenous innovation capabilities and the creation of IP-based ICT businesses in niche business application domains where Singapore has some specialization advantages (such as information systems for health care and public transportation, security, and logistics and supply chain management). Singapore can also leverage its multicultural heritage as well as its status as a trusted independent business hub to facilitate business links between India and China.

Emerging Responses to the Challenge of Production Network Globalization and Digital Convergence

There are indications that the twin challenges of production network globalization and digital convergence are being recognized by the Singaporean government agencies responsible for development of the information economy and that a more coherent and concerted strategic approach has begun to take shape over the past couple of years. This approach takes the form of a new 10-year ICT master plan called iN2015 (Intelligent Nation by 2015) that the IDA launched in June 2006 (IDA 2006a) (see box 4.1), as well as new foreign direct investment promotion initiatives offered by the EDB and new public R&D funding offered by the new National Research Foundation (NRF) that specifically target the ICT industry.

More Active Promotion of New Emerging Digital Content Clusters

In addition to continuing promotion of ICT manufacturing, the EDB has made a significant shift over the past two to three years toward promoting the development of a number of emerging digital content clusters in Singapore, particularly PC games and digital animation, mobile communication, and e-commerce software and services.

Table 4.21 highlights some of the key new investments in the ICT clusters by major global firms over the past three years. It shows the emergence of a critical mass of new activities in the new digital media industries with the entry of notable global players such as Lucasfilm, Electronic Arts, Koei, and Genki (PC games, animation, and design); Rohde & Schwarz, Motorola, and Mobileway (mobile communications); and IBM, Cisco, and NEC (e-commerce software and services). In particular, the PC games and animation industry received a boost when DigiPen, a leading degree-granting training institute for computer games and animation, agreed to establish a branch campus in Singapore—its first outside the United States. Singapore also hosted the World Cyber Games for the first time in 2005, and shortly afterward the government announced a S$1

Box 4.1

Vision, Goals, and Strategy of iN2015

Vision

The vision of iN2015, Singapore's plan for an Intelligent Nation by 2015, is a global city, powered by information communications.

Innovation

The iN2015 plan will fuel creativity and innovation among businesses and individuals by providing an ICT platform that supports enterprise and talent.

Integration

The iN2015 plan will connect businesses, individuals, and communities, giving them the ability to harness resources and capabilities—speedily and efficiently—across diverse businesses and geographies.

Internationalization

The iN2015 program will be the conduit for providing easy and immediate access to the world's resources as well as for exporting Singapore's ideas, products, services, companies, and talent into the global markets.

Goals

The plan sets ambitious goals for Singapore:

- To be number one in the world in harnessing ICT to add value to the economy and society
- To realize a twofold increase in the value added by the ICT industry to S$26 billion
- To realize a threefold increase in ICT export revenue to S$60 billion
- To create 80,000 additional jobs
- To achieve 90 percent home broadband usage
- To achieve 100 percent computer ownership in homes with schoolchildren

Strategy

A bold strategy characterizes iN2015:

- To spearhead the transformation of key economic sectors, government, and society through more sophisticated and innovative use of ICT
- To establish an ultra-high-speed, pervasive, intelligent, and trusted ICT infrastructure
- To develop a globally competitive ICT industry
- To develop an ICT-savvy workforce and globally competitive ICT professionals

Source: IDA 2006a.

Table 4.21. Major Recent Foreign Investments in Singapore ICT Manufacturing and ICT Services Industries, 2002–05

Company	Nationality	Nature of investment	Year	Size of investment
Electronics manufacturing				
Linear Technology	United States	Testing facility for high-performance analog and mixed-signal integrated circuit chip	2005	S$100 million
Hewlett-Packard	United States	Integrity server R&D center	2005	S$20 million
Schott AG	Germany	Wafer-level packaging manufacturing plant	2005	S$80 million
Xilinx	China	Regional headquarters and testing operation	2005	US$40 million
Showa Denko	Japan	Hard disk media plant	2005	S$850 million
Seagate	United States	New media plant	2004	S$200 million
STMicroelectronics	France and Italy	Wafer fabrication plant	2004	S$2 billion over 2 years
MediaTek	Taiwan (China)	R&D center	2004	S$50 million
Nidec	Japan	Manufacturing center of fluid dynamic bearing spindle motors	2004	S$85 million
ASM International	Netherlands	Plant to manufacture vertical furnaces	2004	S$50 million
Hewlett-Packard	United States	Manufacturing center for Superdome server, facility for hardware development, and manufacturing center for HP ProCurve Networking products	2004	Plans to invest S$1.6 billion
Fuji Xerox	Japan	Singapore Epicenter to advise Southeast Asian customers on production issues and solutions	2004	S$8 million
Infineon Technologies	Germany	Asia Pacific headquarters, including R&D and logic integrated circuit testing hub	2003	Plans to increase its R&D headcount to more than 350
Matsushita Electric Industrial	Japan	Assembly and test facility for charged coupled device image sensors	2003	S$150 million

Company	Country	Description	Year	Investment
Panasonic AVC Networks	Japan	Digital video disc recorder production and development facility	2003	S$160 million
Siemens Dematic	Germany	Design, development, and manufacturing facility for high-speed placement machines	2003	—
AFPD	Japan	Liquid crystal display manufacturing plant	2002	S$1.8 billion
3M	United States	Optoelectronics Center of Excellence and manufacturing, design, and product and process development facilities	2002	S$60 million
IT services and software				
Dell	United States	Design center for display and imaging products	2005	35,000 square foot facility
Sybase	United States	Wireless solution center	2005	About 16 employees
Sun Microsystems	United States	iForce Solution Center, developings IT solutions and proofs of concept	2005	S$8.1 million
Oracle	United States	Advanced Technology and Solutions Center	2004	S$11 million
T-Systems	Germany	Asia Pacific headquarters to host production centers for services and solutions	2004	110 employees
IBM	United States	Regional data center	2004	S$21 million
Cisco	United States	Networked Solutions Integration Test Engineering laboratory	2003	S$68 million
Philips	Netherlands	Connected Planet Center: emporium of ideas and prototypes that are developed, produced, and tested before full-scale production and commercialization	2003	US$150 million
NEC	Japan	3 R&D centers for biometrics, hospital information systems, and global e-procurement; also includes plasma support center and disaster recovery center	2003	Will increase Singapore investments to almost S$50 million

(continued)

135

Table 4.21. **Major Recent Foreign Investments in Singapore ICT Manufacturing and ICT Services Industries, 2002–05** (*continued*)

Company	Nationality	Nature of investment	Year	Size of investment
IBM	United States	Business resiliency center offering business continuity and recovery services	2003	
Polaris	India	Center for disaster recovery and business continuity	2002	150-seat capacity
IBM	United States	Singapore Trading Center: builds, maintains, and operates e-commerce procurement services	2002	More than 100 personnel
Microsoft	United States	.NETMySingapore: develops XML-based web services	2002	
Sun	United States	Java Smart Services: research, pilots and trials, incubation and human resources development in Web services	2002	S$8 million
Hewlett-Packard	United States	Test-bedding center	2002	4,000 square feet
Mobileway	United States	Regional headquarters and R&D center (R&D in mobile payment and content management solutions)	2002	
Open Mobile		Regional headquarters and R&D center (mobile payment and content management solutions)	2002	
Telecommunications				
Rohde & Schwarz	Germany	Technical competence center to develop software for testing third-generation handsets, and oversee its Asia Pacific operations, including R&D and headquarters functions	2004	S$18 million
Bridge Mobile (joint venture comprising 7 leading regional mobile service providers)	Singapore	Global headquarters and R&D center	2004	Close to S$70 million over 3 years

Company	Country	Activity	Year	Staff/Investment
Mobile 365	United States	Global network services hub and Asia headquarters	2004	45 staff members and will recruit an additional 70
Motorola	United States	R&D center for third-generation handsets	2004	60 staff
Ericsson	Sweden	Network Operations Center	2005	
Digital media				
Electronic Arts	United States	Studio	2005	22 quality assurance testers and 17 development personnel
10TACLE Studios	Germany	Studio	2005	24 staff members
Lucasfilm	United States	Animation studio	2005	Up to 300 animators
Koei	Japan	Studio to develop online PC games	2004	S$3 million
Genki	Japan	Studio producing games	2004	12 staff members, to increase to 50
Southern Star	Australia	Animation studio	2003	40 staff members
GlobeCast	France	Digital broadcast hub	2003	17 staff members
Top Notch Productions	United Kingdom	Content creation venture with VHQ	2002	S$30 million
HI CORP	Japan	R&D activities in 3D-rendering technology, development of 3D-mobile content	2002	6 engineers; will expand to 25

Source: EDB various years a.
Note: — = not available.

billion fund to promote the development of the PC games and animation industry over the next 10 years. This announcement was followed in 2006 by the announcement that interactive media constituted a new priority technology area for major new public funding support for R&D (S$1 billion over the next five years) under the newly established NRF. IT security (including antiterrorism security technology and services and business continuity and disaster-recovery services) is also emerging as an industry that the Singaporean government is actively promoting.

A More Proactive Approach to Promoting Broadband Network Infrastructure and Applications

Recognizing that Singapore has fallen behind Hong Kong (China), Korea, and other economies in terms of broadband deployment, the IDA's iN2015 master plan has identified the need to accelerate the pace of deployment of both wired and wireless broadband network infrastructure in Singapore. A key strategic thrust of iN2015 is to establish an "ultra-high speed, pervasive, intelligent, and trusted infocomm infrastructure." (IDA 2006b: 8). This infrastructure will comprise a national fiber network (NFN) that offers high-speed (more than 1 gigabytes per second) access to all homes, schools, and businesses, as well as a wireless broadband network (WBN) that provides wireless hotspots in all major public spaces. In addition to such physical investment, the plan also calls for the development of a national trust framework to address issues of security, privacy, and identity.

Although the plan does not provide specifics about how this new infrastructure is to be financed, significant public funding in the form of investment incentives is expected, as well as new policies to promote greater competition in access. For example, the anticipated increase in competition in so-called triple-play digital convergent services—combining telephony, video and television programs, and Internet access—have so far not occurred because the key incumbents in traditional fixed-line telecommunication services (SingTel) and cable television (StarHub) hold dominant positions in their domains and have been rather cautious in leveraging digital convergence to enter each other's territories. True competition in converged digital services is unlikely to emerge until a second broadband pipe (fiber-to-the-home) is widely deployed under iN2015, to provide an alternative to the current cable television pipe. Given that, the NFN and WBN proposals of iN2015 appear to signal a more interventionist role by the state in helping Singapore catch up with or even overtake other advanced ICT hubs.

Development of Differentiation Advantages in Specialized Business ICT Applications That Leverage Lead-User Interaction Dynamics

For Singapore-based ICT services firms to compete with firms in locations that have a lower-cost professional workforce (for example, India), they need to develop differentiation advantages. One way to do so is to focus on developing specialized ICT applications for niche business sectors in which Singapore has a critical base of sophisticated and demanding lead users. For example, Singapore has world-class air- and sea-based logistics and transport operators, as well as relatively advanced health care and legal services. Singapore has also established a reputation for trust and security. Thus, the Singaporean government should develop policies and programs to facilitate and enhance network interaction between the ICT services cluster and selected industries as lead users so that ICT firms in Singapore have a better chance to develop specialized products and services that will differentiate them from other ICT firms. For example, with the high concentration of logistics firms in Singapore, the early deployment of advanced sensor networks, especially RFID (radio frequency identification) networks, may help Singapore's ICT firms develop competitive capabilities in logistics-related RFID applications. Likewise, Singapore's well-run public hospitals could be test beds for advanced ICT applications such as biometric identification and wireless biosensor systems. The iN2015 has recommended intensified investments in deploying new ICT applications in the major sectors where Singapore has competitive strengths—manufacturing and logistics, tourism, hospitality, retail, and financial services.

Intensification of Policies to Promote Technology Entrepreneurship

As highlighted in Wong (2006), the Singaporean government has since the late 1990s made a significant policy shift toward achieving a more balanced high-tech enterprise ecosystem by promoting greater indigenous entrepreneurship in technology in addition to attracting high-tech foreign direct investment. These new pro-enterprise policies may have contributed to the improving propensity for forming new firms recorded by Singapore over the past two years, as measured by the annual Global Entrepreneurship Monitor study (Wong, Lee, and Ho 2005). It is imperative that the government sustain such a policy shift over the long haul, with continuing refinement of policies as necessary. Indeed, several policy refinements and incremental program extensions have been introduced over the past two years, including a business angel fund scheme to complement the existing business angel coinvestment program,

Start-up Enterprise Development Scheme; a program to encourage student enterprises, Fund for Student Entrepreneurship; and various venture capital funds targeted at new media industries and defense and security technologies. These initiatives are all positive steps in the right direction, although there is room for more and bolder programs.

Development of ICT Professionals

A key factor in the past success of Singapore in achieving rapid ICT deployment and industry development has been its strong emphasis on the development of human resources (see Wong 2006). However, in the past three to four years, particularly after the dot-com crash, ICT as a field of tertiary education has become less attractive to the top young talent in Singapore; this shift is evidenced by the declining quality of high school graduates who opt to major in computing and management information systems in local universities. In addition to the growing attractiveness of such new fields as biotechnology, the perceived increasing competition from Indian and Chinese ICT talent may have contributed to this declining interest in ICT among the top high school students in Singapore. This worrying trend has been recognized in the iN2015, which calls for a significant increase in efforts to promote interest in new ICT among the nation's top young talent. In addition, the plan calls for new curricula and programs that address the new educational requirements of emerging disciplines, such as interactive digital media and game design, to be developed among local tertiary educational institutions, including collaborative programs with leading universities in the world.

Further Strengthening of IP Support Services

A key factor that has led ICT MNCs to locate their R&D activities in Singapore in recent years is the relatively strong IP protection regime put in place by the government. This factor clearly influenced some of the new computer games and animation studio investors such as Electronic Arts and Lucasfilm. Moving forward, however, Singapore needs to go beyond IP protection by further strengthening the depth and scope of professional expertise. Singapore must be able to provide the wide range of specialist IP services needed to entrench it as a hub for technological innovation and creative content development. This effort includes increasing not only the pool of engineers competent to file patents but also the number of experienced IP licensing and marketing professionals, business consultants specializing in IP strategies, and specialist IP lawyers to handle IP litigation and media and design copyright issues.

Conclusion

Singapore has made great progress in building a strong ICT manufacturing cluster as well as an ICT services hub. However, with increasing regional competition, particularly from China and India, Singapore's ICT manufacturing growth has slowed in recent years, while its IT services have not been able to capture much of the global outsourcing business. After exerting a relatively strong developmental role in the 1980s and first half of 1990s, the government appears to have retreated to a less active approach, with the expectation that market forces would become the primary driver for ICT network infrastructure deployment and applications diffusion. However, recent experience has shown that the pace of network deployment and new ICT services innovation in Singapore has fallen behind that of other East Asian economies, partly because of the relatively small domestic market and the oligopolistic nature of competition among the players permitted to compete in the domestic telecommunication industry.

With digital convergence driving the growth of new digital content industries such as PC games and animation, mobile content, security services, and e-commerce on a global scale, the challenge is for Singapore to make itself a viable hub for these new industries not only by attracting a critical mass of key global players to locate activities in Singapore, but also by promoting the growth of a critical mass of indigenous firms with innovative capabilities to compete in these new industries. A rapid deployment of broadband network infrastructure is needed to enable the growth of these new digital convergence industries. The recent strategic initiatives by the Singaporean government such as the iN2015 master plan, the EDB technology entrepreneurship support programs and ICT industry promotion programs, and the NRF R&D funding for interactive media are certainly moves in the right direction. Whether Singapore succeeds in meeting the twin challenges of digital convergence and production globalization depends ultimately on how well the new strategies are executed.

References

Accenture. 2003. "e-Government Leadership: Engaging the Customer." Hamilton, Bermuda. http://nstore.accenture.com/acn_com/PDF/Engaging_the_Customer.pdf.

Department of Statistics. Various years a. *Economic Survey Series: IT and Related Services*. Singapore: Department of Statistics.

———. Various years b. *Economic Survey Series: Post and Telecommunications*. Singapore: Department of Statistics.

———. Various years c. *Economic Survey Series: Real Estate and Business*. Singapore: Department of Statistics.

———. Various years d. *Economic Survey Series: Transportation and Communications*. Singapore: Department of Statistics.

DP Information Network. 1994. *Singapore 1000 1994*. Singapore: DP Information Network.

———. 2005. *Singapore 1000 2005*. Singapore: DP Information Network.

Dutta, S., B. Lanvin, and F. Paua. 2003. *Global Information Technology Report, 2002–2003: Readiness for the Networked World*. New York: Oxford University Press.

EDB (Economic Development Board). Various years a. *EDB Yearbook*. Singapore: EDB.

———. Various years b. *Report on the Census for Industrial Production*. Singapore: EDB.

———. Various years c. *Report on the Census of Manufacturing Activities*. Singapore: EDB.

Elsevier. Various years. *Yearbook of World Electronics Data*. Oxford, U.K.: Elsevier Advanced Technology.

ERC (Economic Review Committee). 2002. *Creative Industries Development Strategies: A Report by the ERC Services Industries Subcommittee Workgroup on Creative Industries*. Singapore: Ministry of Trade and Industry.

Florida, Richard. 2002. *The Rise of the Creative Class and How It's Transforming Work, Leisure, and Everyday Life*. New York: Basic Books.

Howkins, J. 2001. *The Creative Economy*. London: Penguin Press.

IDA (Infocomm Development Authority). 2003a. *Connected Singapore: A New Blueprint for Infocomm Development*. Singapore: IDA.

———. 2003b. *IDA Annual Report 2002–2003*. Singapore: IDA.

———. 2006a. *iN2015: A Living Plan for Every Individual and Business in Singapore*. Singapore: IDA.

———. 2006b. *Innovation. Integration. Internationalisation: Report by the iN2015 Steering Committee*. Singapore: IDA.

———. Various years. "IDA Annual Survey on Infocomm Usage," various years. IDA, Singapore. http://www.ida.gov.sg.

IDC (International Data Corporation). 1999. *The 1999 IDC Worldwide Black Book*. Framingham, MA: IDC.

IDC (International Data Corporation) and *World Times*. Various years. "Information Society Index." Framingham, MA: IDC. http://www.idc.com/groups/isi/main.html.

IMD (International Institute for Management Development). Various years a. *World Competitiveness Report*. Lausanne, Switzerland: IMD.

———. Various years b. *World Competitiveness Yearbook*. Lausanne, Switzerland: IMD.

ITU (International Telecommunication Union). 2005. *ITU Internet Report 2005: The Internet of Things*. Geneva: ITU.

Kirkman, Geoffrey S., Peter K. Cornelius, Jeffrey D. Sachs, and Klaus Schwab. 2002. *Global Information Technology Report, 2001–2002: Readiness for the Networked World*. New York: Oxford University Press.

Mathews, John A., and Dong-Sung Cho. 2000. *Tiger Technology: The Creation of a Semiconductor Industry in East Asia*. New York: Cambridge University Press.

McKendrick, David G., Richard F. Doner, and Stephan Haggard. 2000. *From Silicon Valley to Singapore: Location and Competitive Advantage in the Hard Disk Drive Industry*. Stanford, CA: Stanford University Press.

MDA (Media Development Authority). 2003. "Media 21: Transforming Singapore into a Global Media City." MDA, Singapore. http://www.mda.gov.sg/wms.ftp/media21.pdf.

Miles, Marc, Edwin J. Feulner, and Mary Anastasia O'Grady, eds. 2004. *2004 Index of Economic Freedom*. Washington, DC: Heritage Foundation.

NCB (National Computer Board). 1992. *IT2000: Vision for an Intelligent Island*. Singapore: NCB.

OECD (Organisation for Economic Co-operation and Development). 2002. *Measuring the Information Economy*. Paris: OECD.

———. 2004. *OECD Information Technology Outlook 2004*. Paris: OECD.

Pohjola, Matti, ed. 2001. *Information Technology, Productivity, and Economic Growth: International Evidence and Implications for Economic Development*. Oxford, U.K.: Oxford University Press.

United Nations Statistics Division. Various years. UN Commodity Trade Statistics Database (UN Comtrade Database). United Nations, Geneva.

U.S. Department of Commerce. 2003. *Digital Economy 2003*. Washington, DC: U.S. Department of Commerce.

USPTO (U.S. Patent and Trademark Office). Various years. Database of the USPTO. USPTO, Washington, DC. http://www.uspto.gov/patft/index.html.

WEF (World Economic Forum). Various years. *The Global Information Technology Report*. Geneva: WEF.

Wong, Poh-Kam. 1996. "Implementing the National Information Infrastructure Vision: Singapore's Experience and Future Challenges." *Information Infrastructure and Policy* 5 (2): 95–117.

———. 1998. "Leveraging the Global Information Revolution for Economic Development: Singapore's Evolving Information Industry Strategy." *Information Systems Research* 9 (4): 323–41.

———. 2001a. "The Contribution of IT to the Rapid Economic Development of Singapore." In *Information Technology, Productivity, and Economic Growth: International Evidence and Implications for Economic Development*, ed. Matti Pohjola, 221–41. Oxford, U.K.: Oxford University Press.

———. 2001b. "Leveraging Multinational Corporations, Fostering Technopreneurship: The Changing Role of S&T Policy in Singapore." *International Journal of Technology Management* 22 (5–6): 539–67.

———. 2001c. "The Role of the State in the Industrial Development of Singapore." In *Rethinking the East Asian Development Paradigm*, ed. Poh-Kam Wong and Chee-Yuen Ng, 503–79. Singapore: Singapore University Press.

———. 2002a. "Globalization of American, European, and Japanese Production Networks and the Growth of Singapore's Electronics Industry." *International Journal of Technology Management* 24 (7–8): 843–69.

———. 2002b. "Manpower Development in the Digital Economy: The Case of Singapore." In *Human Resource Development in the Information Age: The Case of Singapore and Malaysia*, ed. Minoru Makishima, 79–122. Tokyo: Institute of Developing Economies and Japan External Trade Organization.

———. 2003. "Global and National Factors Influencing E–Commerce Development in Singapore." *Information Society* 19 (1): 19–32.

———. 2004. "The Information Society and the Developmental State: The Singaporean Model." In *The Global Information Society: Development Paths from Silicon Valley to Singapore* [in Finnish], ed. Pekka Himanen, 11–31. Helsinki: Tekes.

———. 2006. "The Re-making of Singapore's High Tech Enterprise Ecosystem." In *Making IT: The Rise of Asia in High Tech*, ed. Henry Rowen, Marguerite Gong Hancock, and William F. Miller, 123–74. Stanford, Calif.: Stanford University Press.

Wong, Poh-Kam, Yuen-Ping Ho, and Annette Singh. 2004. "Singapore as an Innovative City in East Asia: An Explorative Study of the Perspective of Innovative Industries." Paper presented at the World Bank Workshop on Innovative Cities in East Asia, Bangkok, February 22–23.

Wong, Poh-Kam, Lena Lee, and Yuen-Ping Ho. 2005. *Global Entrepreneurship Monitor 2004: Singapore Report*. Singapore: National University of Singapore Entrepreneurship Centre.

Wong, Poh-Kam, Lena Lee, Yuen-Ping Ho, and Finna Wong. 2006. *Global Entrepreneurship Monitor 2005: Singapore Report*. Singapore: National University of Singapore Entrepreneurship Centre.

WTO (World Trade Organization). 2005. *International Trade Statistics 2005*. Lausanne, Switzerland: WTO. http://www.wto.org/english/res_e/statis_e/its2005_e/its05_toc_e.htm.

Yusuf, Shahid, and Kaoru Nabeshima. 2006. *Postindustrial East Asian Cities*. Palo Alto: Stanford University Press.

CHAPTER 5

Bangalore Cluster

Evolution, Growth, and Challenges

Rakesh Basant

The competitiveness of firms in some industrial clusters, even in the wake of globalization and liberalization in the 1990s, has led researchers to explore the causes of dynamic efficiencies at the cluster level. Earlier explanations focused on cost- and resource-based advantages arising from the co-location of firms. Cluster studies in the 1980s argued that horizontal collaboration between small and medium-size enterprises could yield collective efficiencies in the form of reduced transaction costs, accelerated innovation through more rapid problem solving, and greater market access. In addition, positive externalities are generated by agglomeration through the availability of skilled labor and inputs, certain types of infrastructure, and innovation-generating informal exchanges. These processes of networking and clustering contribute to the competitiveness and growth of the participating firms. Furthermore, political and social institutions, along with various policies, can play a crucial role in supporting the emergence and development of partnering activities

The author is thankful to Rajesh Upadhyayula and Radhika Bhuyan for their help in preparing the paper. Thanks are also extended to the participants at the Second Asian Development Conference on the Information and Communication Technology Industrial Clusters in East Asia at Kitakyusha, Japan, during December 12–14, 2005, who provided useful comments.

among firms and stimulating the transformation of such networks into broader systems of innovation and production. In fact, in most of the European success stories of networking in industrial clusters, regional and local governments played a crucial role (see Schmitz and Musyck 1994). Recent studies have focused on dynamic efficiencies that emanate from learning at the cluster level. They emphasize the importance of knowledge flows to firms, social and relational capital, and capabilities of firms as critical factors necessary for the continued success and growth of industrial clusters. It is argued that geographically bounded clusters should be viewed as systems of knowledge accumulation rather than just production systems (Bell and Albu 1999). The focus on knowledge accumulation shifts the policy to focus on processes that convert the cluster-based production systems into innovation systems (Mytelka and Farinelli 2000; Mytelka and Pellegrin 2001).[1]

An application of the innovation systems concept to a cluster would require an analysis of capabilities internal to the cluster (or firms in a cluster) and their links with external knowledge sources, including organizations such as universities, research and development (R&D) institutions, certification agencies, external firms, and customers. On the basis of a detailed review of the available literature, it has been argued that an understanding of the dynamism of a cluster would require a systematic analysis of links between knowledge flows, cluster characteristics (including capabilities and links), external links, and external policy and the economic environment (Basant 2002). Knowledge flows can take various forms but are generally embedded in products, processes, and practices, which get transferred to cluster firms through a variety of mechanisms. Industrial clusters use a variety of sources for knowledge acquisition. Box 5.1 summarizes these sources. Although the literature has highlighted the importance of interorganizational links, the links between firm-level resources and the knowledge flows facilitated through such links have attracted much less attention (Basant 2002; Bell and Albu 1999). Consequently, knowledge diffusion in clusters is often seen as passive and automatic. Related to the question of firm-level learning in the context of geographically bounded clusters is the issue of the linking of various sources of knowledge. Recent research has highlighted the increasing role of links external to the cluster in facilitating knowledge flows.

---

1 In simple terms, "combinations of internally organized capabilities with external knowledge resources, and the links between them" are referred to as innovation or knowledge systems (Bell and Albu 1999: 1718).

Box 5.1

Sources of Knowledge in Industrial Clusters

Intrafirm sources include the following:

- "Learning by doing," the passive experience of productions
- Improved process and practices derived from trial-and-error experimentation
- Adaptation and improvement of existing technologies (such as reverse engineering)
- Aligning of products, processes, and practices within the firm.

Intracluster sources include the following:

- Knowledge spillovers and diffusion between producers
- Knowledge spillovers, diffusion between users and producers of machinery, and material or production-related services
- Intracluster mobility of skilled labor
- Training and skill development through cluster-based and cluster-mediated initiatives
- Links between enterprises and cluster-based technology institutions, such as technology development, adaptation, testing, and certification
- Collaboration among cluster-based enterprises for adaptation and technology development, including machinery and product design
- Links between enterprises and customers located in the cluster, including multinational corporations and large firms

Sources outside the cluster include the following:

- Customers and traders
- Machinery and other input suppliers
- Collaborative testing or technology development with technology institutions and enterprises outside the cluster
- Externally sourced training
- Visits to outside clusters and firms

Source: Basant 2002.
Note: Bell and Albu (1999) inspired the creation of this list.

Various dimensions of a cluster contribute to knowledge flows. These cluster-specific factors include size of the cluster, extent of diversification, division of labor (and the associated buyer-supplier relations), nature of products (high-tech versus traditional), levels of competition, nature of markets, location (developing or industrial economy), links with other clusters and with noncluster firms (such as global networks and multinational corporations), and so on. Other important factors relate to public policy and the macroeconomic environment. Figure 5.1 summarizes the variety of factors and processes that impinge on knowledge flows in a geographically bounded cluster. Table 5.1 provides a summary of variables that have been identified as contributors to knowledge flows in a cluster.

The information and communication technology (ICT) cluster in Bangalore, India, has attracted much research and media attention. It is often referred to as the Silicon Valley of India. It currently boasts of having more than 1,500 information technology (IT) firms and many more in other sectors such as electronics.[2] Furthermore, most of the large IT firms in India such as Infosys and Wipro are headquartered in Bangalore. Wholly owned subsidiaries of multinational corporations (MNCs) such as Motorola, Texas Instruments (TI), and Hewlett-Packard (HP) have their bases in Bangalore. The IT firms provide a range of services, including customer software application development, maintenance, facility management, and training. A number of firms are also moving up the value chain to provide wholly integrated packages (Balasubramanyam and Balasubramanyam 2000; Caniels and Romijn 2003). Although the IT sector has brought the city into the limelight, it has a fairly diverse portfolio of activities, with firms manufacturing machine tools, telecommunication equipment, electronics products, and some automotive components. In recent years, the city has emerged as a premier biotechnology center in the country. Evidence also shows that diversity is on the rise even within sectors in Bangalore.[3] Recently, the Indian Institute of Management in Ahmedabad conducted a survey of electronics and IT firms in the Bangalore, Pune, and National Capital Region clusters and in some noncluster areas (IIMA 2005–06). What advantages do firms perceive of being in Bangalore, in other clusters, and in noncluster locations? Table 5.2 provides some insight. The respondent firms were

---

2 Even in the late 1980s, Bangalore included 375 large and medium-size industries and had 3,000 companies employing 100,000 people in the electronics industry alone. The city contained up to 10,000 small firms and eight large industrial parks (Madon 1997).

3 For example, Bangalore is emerging as a diverse biotechnology cluster. Production embraces enzymes (Biocon); biotherapeutics (Biocon and GangaGen); bioinformatics (Strand Genomics; Bigtech; Kshema, now part of MphasiS Technologies; CDC Linux; and Molecular Connections); plant genetics and genomics (Avesthagen, Monsanto, Metahelix, and Advanta); contract R&D (Syngene, Aurigene, Genotypic Technology, Avesthagen, and Bangalore Genei); and bioprocessing and bioinstrumentation (Sartorius, Wipro GE, Photonics & Biomolecules, Bangalore Genie, and Millipore).

Figure 5.1. Cluster Characteristics, Links, Policies, and Knowledge

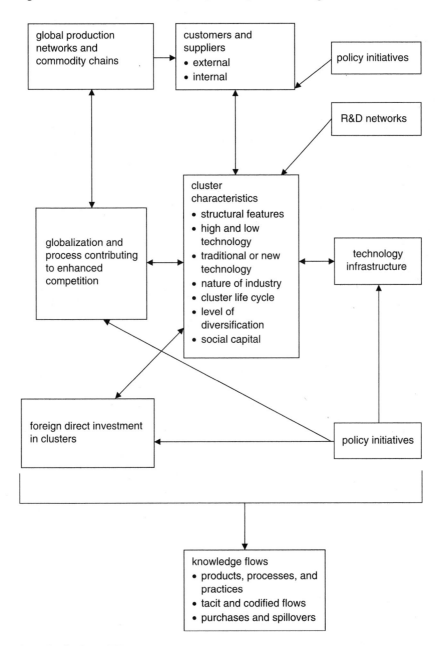

Source: Based on Basant 2002.

Table 5.1. Summary of the Determinants of Knowledge Flows in Geographically Bound Clusters

Factor	Likely effect on knowledge flows (empirical evidence)
Factors internal to the cluster	
Spatial proximity	Positive, with passive externalities and potential for active cooperation, as well as flow of tacit knowledge
Horizontal interfirm links between firms producing similar products	Positive, but generally weak collaboration
Vertical interfirm links (user-producer)	Positive, with relatively strong collaboration
Demanding customers	Positive
High technology (tacit knowledge and complexity of technology)	Generally positive, depending on production organization
Traditional industries	Mixed results
Social capital	Positive, with difficult measurement
Cluster structure	
Role of large firms	Probably positive, but limited evidence
Type of clusters	Limited evidence
Cluster life cycle	Higher during early phases
Existence of facilitating institutional framework	Tacit knowledge critical
Universities and R&D institutions	Critical for high-tech and some traditional industries
Associations (standards, testing, and so forth)	Important for all types
Nature of industry	Limited evidence, with knowledge flows seemingly more important for science-based industries
Diversified or industry-specific cluster	Limited evidence, with possibly differing nature of knowledge flows
External links of the customers and suppliers	
External customers	Positive, if customer is demanding and has less market power
Links with equipment suppliers or R&D institutes	Generally positive
Links with global production network or commodity chain	Location in the network or chain important
Foreign direct investment	May be positive, depending on technology gap and objectives of foreign direct investment
Policy initiatives and environment	
Enhancement of competition (trade liberalization)	Encouragement of efforts to access knowledge Possibly allows optimal levels of competition
Foreign direct investment policies	Local manufacturing

Source: Basant 2002.

Table 5.2. Summary of Responses from Cluster and Noncluster Firms in IT and Electronics Industries about the Perceived Advantages of Locating in a City Cluster

Advantages of location	Bangalore cluster	Pune and National Capital Region clusters	Nonclusters	Significant difference	
				Bangalore and other clusters	Bangalore and nonclusters
Proximity to customers	3.46	3.04	3.29	Yes	No
Access to information from competitors	3.08	3.00	2.68	No	Yes
Access to information about competitors	3.17	3.12	2.63	No	Yes
Availability of skilled labor from competitors	3.16	3.17	2.78	No	Yes
Access to skilled labor	3.99	3.74	3.29	Yes	Yes
Presence of hardware and software suppliers	3.95	3.60	3.22	Yes	Yes
Better access to support services	3.89	3.60	3.08	Yes	Yes
Better access to training facilities	3.94	3.48	2.91	Yes	Yes
Better access to R&D institutions	3.61	3.25	2.56	Yes	Yes
Better access to information on fairs and exhibitions	3.74	3.55	2.53	No	Yes
Availability of maintenance and repair services	3.85	3.70	3.38	No	Yes
Availability of better infrastructure	3.30	3.79	3.68	Yes	Yes

Source: IIMA 2005–06.
Note: The sample was 166 for Bangalore, 141 for the Pune and National Capital Region, and 105 for nonclusters. The perceived advantage was measured on a five-point scale, with the advantage being higher if the score was closer to five. The significance of the difference in the mean responses for clusters and nonclusters has been tested at 5 percent.

asked about the perceived advantages of locating in the city where they operate. As compared with noncluster firms, the cluster firms seem to be benefiting from proximity to customers and competitors and from better access to suppliers and providers of various services. Among the clusters studied, Bangalore seems to be better off than the other two.

The Bangalore ICT cluster is also a more advantageous location for access to labor and to R&D and training facilities. All these advantages contribute to the growth of the cluster.

A large variety of factors have contributed to the evolution and growth of the cluster in the city. In the context of the broad analytical framework enunciated in figure 5.1 and the processes and factors identified as critical for the growth of the clusters (see box 5.1 and table 5.1), this chapter pools evidence on the evolution and growth of the Bangalore ICT cluster. The remainder of the chapter is divided into six sections. The next section highlights the role played by the public policy initiatives at the federal and the state levels. The section that follows is a brief discussion of how the Indian diaspora contributed to the growth of the cluster through a variety of links. The importance of links is emphasized further in the next sections: the third section looks specifically at the role of MNCs and large firms in the city, the fourth section brings out the role of academia-industry links in the city, and the fifth section analyzes the role of links at a generic level. The final section summarizes the main findings and identifies some policy imperatives.

Public Policy: Initial Capability Building and Creation of an Enabling Environment

Public policy has been one of the most important contributors to the emergence of Bangalore as a preeminent industrial cluster in the country. A wide variety of policies at both the federal and the provincial levels have played a role. Table 5.3 summarizes the evolution of the policy regime. This section discusses some key policy initiatives and their implications. It must be emphasized at the outset that macro policy changes made after the 1970s benefited the Bangalore cluster in a significant manner because the city had the capabilities to exploit the emerging opportunities. This point will be discussed later.

The Initial Investments
The city's emergence as an IT center stems from decisions made by the federal government shortly after independence to locate strategically sensitive industries well away from borders and coastlands. Bangalore became a city of choice for the headquarters of the Indian air force and other public sector institutions. This strategy promoted, in turn, the establishment of a number of universities, institutions, and colleges

Table 5.3. Summary of Policy Changes Contributing to the Emergence and Growth of the Bangalore Industrial Cluster

Period	Policies
1947–60: Public sector policies and creation of large firms	• A state monopoly existed in several defense and infrastructure industries, with most of them located in Bangalore. • Large public enterprises, such as Hindustan Machine Tools, Bharat Electronics Limited, and Indian Telephone Industries, were set up. • Licenses were given for large private firms, such as Motor Industries Company (better known as MICO), an automotive components manufacturer and a subsidiary of Robert Bosch GmbH, and Widia, the machine tool manufacturer.
Early 1970s: Export focus training and procurement policies	• The Software Export Scheme included imports of hardware for exporting firms with duty concessions. • Emphasis was placed on computer and software education and training, with institutions that focused on training being allowed to import hardware at much lower import duties. • The Department of Electronics of India began to encourage public sector projects that dealt with software development, with public procurement of software giving priority to Indian companies.
Mid-1970s: New restrictions	• Restrictions were placed on foreign ownership in accordance with the Foreign Exchange Regulation Act.
1976–77: Export-import liberalization	• Hardware import duties were reduced from more than 100 percent to 40 percent. • Software export applications had faster clearance. • Software exporters could take advantage of export incentives, including locating in export processing zones. • Nonresident Indians were allowed to import hardware for the purposes of software export with a 100 percent export obligation.
Early 1980s: Export-import liberalization for foreign investment	• The Department of Electronics was more supportive of the domestic software industry, encouraging software exports and export-oriented foreign investment. • Import duties on hardware were raised. • Firms were allowed to use the hardware for the development of domestic software as well as for exports. • Software exporters could also import loaned computers.
1984: New computer and software policy	• Import procedures for hardware and software were simplified. • Import duties for hardware and software were reduced from 135 percent to 60 percent for hardware and from 100 percent to 60 percent for software. • Software was recognized as an industry, and licensing procedures were simplified. • Access to foreign exchange for software firms was improved.

(continued)

Table 5.3. Summary of Policy Changes Contributing to the Emergence and Growth of the Bangalore Industrial Cluster *(continued)*

Period	Policies
	• The income tax exemption on net export earnings was reduced from 100 percent to 50 percent.
1985: Software Technology Park	• The Department of Electronics of Karnataka formed an electronics park—Karnataka State Electronics Development Corporation—that housed the Software Technology Park.
1986: Computer software export, software development, and training policy	• Imports of hardware and software were further deregulated; anyone could import software at a 60 percent duty. • Software production units that were completely export oriented were permitted to import hardware duty-free. • Indian firms were allowed to sell foreign software by becoming distributors. • Export obligations for hardware importers increased by 50 percent, and the time in which to meet the obligations was reduced to 4 years.
1989: Tax on travel	• A 15 percent tax was imposed on foreign exchange expenditure on travel.
1989: Telecommunication infrastructure	• Videsh Sanchar Nigam Limited (VSNL) commissioned a direct 64-kilobits-per-second satellite link to the United States—a new gateway switching system that operated through Intelsat and was directly linked to AT&T's earth station at Coram, New York.
1988–91: Software Technology Parks of India Scheme	• The Software Technology Parks of India Scheme involved the creation of software technology parks for the production of software for export • The government provided office space and computer equipment, access to high-speed satellite links, and an uninterrupted supply of electricity. • The Department of Electronics installed appropriate telecommunication equipment to provide easy access to the clients of software firms and to expedite delivery of software exports. • Firms that were completely export oriented received tax-free status for 5 years within the first 8 years of operation. • Single-window clearance was given for projects, and for projects valued at less than Rs 30 million, only the park's clearance was required. • Total foreign equity was permitted, and no restrictions were placed on location.[a]

(continued)

Table 5.3. Summary of Policy Changes Contributing to the Emergence and Growth of the Bangalore Industrial Cluster (continued)

Period	Policies
	• Videoconferencing services were provided between Bangalore and the rest of the world.
1991: Foreign exchange policies and trade liberalization	• The rupee was devalued and partially converted.
	• The tax on foreign exchange for travel was abolished.
	• Telecommunication charges for satellite links were reduced.
	• Duty-free and obligation-free imports of telecommunication equipment were permitted in the parks.
1992: Telecommunications	• The exclusive satellite international gateway for export industry was set up.
1992: Tax policies	• Software exports were brought under the Income Tax Act, which exempted exporters from income tax[b]
	• The income tax exemption that was offered to enterprises established in export processing zones and to completely export-oriented units was extended to software exports from companies taking part in schemes that were established in or after 1993.
1994–95: Further trade liberalization	• Import duties on software were reduced to 20 percent (10 percent in 1995) for applications software and 65 percent (10 percent in 1995) for systems software.
	• Hardware import duties were liberalized, and loans for importing hardware were given certain export obligations, which could be met by earnings from onsite services.
1997: State IT policy	• An IT policy was announced by the government of Karnataka, which was the first state in India to have such a policy.
1999–2001: Foreign direct investment policy	• The Department of Electronics allowed 100 percent foreign direct investment in the IT industry.
	• The government favored foreign investment in infrastructure and high technology over foreign investment in consumer products.
2001–05: Deregulation	• Deregulation continued, albeit at a slow pace.

Source: Author's compilation based on several sources.

a. The parks are connected by an integrated network, SoftNet, whereby subscribers can lease a point-to-point digital 64-kilobits-per-second channel and have access to the Internet with their own transmission control protocol/Internet protocol number, which would give them e-mail, remote log in, file-transfer services, and access to the World Wide Web.

b. Confirmation of this status occurred on an annual basis until 1995, when confirmation became open ended. The tax exemption continues, but because software exports were brought under the same chapter of the tax code as merchandise exports, some of the benefits were eroded on account of the different characteristics between merchandise and software exports. Although the same tax code persists for software exports today, the profits of software industry have been adversely affected by the recently introduced tax on certain services.

providing engineering and scientific training (Holstrom 1994).[4] During the 1950s and 1960s, the government invested heavily in large public sector units such as Hindustan Machine Tools, Bharat Electronics Limited, Bharat Heavy Electricals Limited, Hindustan Aeronautics Limited, and Indian Telephone Industries. Several other defense and infrastructure industries also sprang up in Bangalore. In fact, the city became an important defense research center. Apart from strategic reasons, the choice of Bangalore for these investments was also related to the existence of an educated workforce (how the engineering colleges and the Indian Institute of Science contributed to this will be shown later) and the availability of cheap electrical power (Heitzman 2004: 45).

A few large private sector undertakings were also given licenses. For example, Motor Industries Company (MICO), the automotive components manufacturer and subsidiary of Robert Bosch GmbH of Germany, and Widia, the machine tool manufacturer, were established during that period. One can partly attribute the presence of IT industry in Bangalore to the initial establishment of electronics firms in the city. Because software in the initial phases was more hardware centric, it was more appropriate for IT firms to locate in the vicinity of producers of hardware units (Balasubramanyam and Balasubramanyam 2000; Madon 1997).

The initiation of the industrialization process in Bangalore city was *not* a postindependence phenomenon. In fact, Hindustan Aeronautics Limited was created by the British in 1940 to support the war effort. Subsequently, two more state-owned firms were set up by the British: the Radio and Electric Manufacturing Company was set up in 1942 to make radio receivers and components, and Mysore Electrical Industries was started in 1945 to produce switchgear and motor control gear. The latter was set up in collaboration with a U.K. company (Heitzman 2004: 45). The emergence of modern industry in Bangalore, therefore, predated independence and, with postindependence investments, created a large modern industrial workforce in the city. In fact, Hindustan Aeronautics Limited had as many as 21,000 workers by 1960 (Heitzman 2004: 45). The existence of such a workforce was conducive for the emergence of the IT and electronics sectors, and therefore, Bangalore was better able to exploit the potential than other regions.

---

4 Key educational institutions, such as the Institute of Science, already existed in the city at the time of independence. The role of educational institutions is explored in a later section.

Early Recognition of the Importance of Software Exports and Public Procurement

The potential of software exports was recognized as early as 1972, when the Software Export Scheme was launched. The scheme provided a variety of concessions to software exporters, including hardware imports at low tariffs. Simultaneously, computer and software education and training were emphasized and institutions that focused on training were allowed to import hardware at much lower import duties. Around the same time, Karantaka's Department of Electronics (DoE) began to encourage public sector projects that stimulated software development. In addition, public procurement of software gave priority to Indian companies. This focus on the software industry began to create some domestic demand for software.

The Foreign Exchange Regulation Act and Exit of Foreign Firms

The other major policy change in the mid-1970s was the Foreign Exchange Regulation Act, which sought to reduce foreign ownership of firms in India. Computer firms were no exception. A fallout of the government's decision to reduce foreign ownership was that software development occurred in-house. Some companies, such as International Computers Limited (a U.K. company), accepted this policy change, reducing their share of the company's equity to 40 percent, whereas others, such as IBM, chose to leave India in 1978. The departure of IBM had significant implications for India's computer industry in general and especially for the industry in Bangalore. Some companies created 8-bit microprocessors and sold them in the local market. One of them was Wipro, based in Bangalore.[5] The exit of IBM released an estimated 1,200 software personnel into the Indian market. According to Heeks (1996: 70), this influx had an interesting effect on the software export business. Many of these people had no option but to leave India if they wanted to pursue IT careers. Others set up their own small companies, because very few companies were dedicated to the development of software and to software services. Many of these companies were established in Bangalore. Initially, the focus of many of the IT companies that sprang up during this period was on providing services for domestic clients. But the domestic market proved too difficult to penetrate because of the very low level of computerization and the high level of in-house development, so the focus shifted to the export market.

---

5 Other companies were DCM Data Systems and HCL Technologies in Delhi.

Trade Protection and Liberalization

For a brief period in the second half of the 1970s, hardware imports were liberalized with a reduction in duties,[6] especially for software exporters, and a variety of incentives to export was put in place. But by the early 1980s, stricter controls were put on hardware imports; import duties on hardware were increased, but firms were allowed to use the hardware for the development of domestic software as well as for exports. In addition, software exporters could import loaned computers.[7] Moreover, DoE's approach to the domestic software industry became more supportive than the previous restrictive and regulatory approach. It also encouraged software exports and export-oriented foreign investment.

The policy to protect the hardware industry had an important effect on the software industry. It forced Indian computer firms to shift their focus away from mainframes, which were the mainstay of the MNCs, toward producing and using microcomputers or personal computers (PCs). Hence, a new generation of software engineers gained a great deal of experience in programming for PCs, especially in operating systems such as MS-DOS (the Microsoft disk operating system) and particularly Unix, which was an operating system for non–IBM compatible computers based on Intel and Motorola chips. This operating system was preferred and pushed by CMC Limited and the DoE (Heeks 1996). Policy changes in 1986 enabled the import of the Unix source code, and Unix emerged as the de facto standard in the super microcomputer and the minicomputer markets. According to an IDC India study (see *Dataquest* 2002), 1,400 Unix systems were shipped from India in 1987 and 1988, compared with just 480 the year before. Meanwhile, the PC had come to India, and within a couple of years, a price war triggered by Sterling Computers led to vendors slashing prices. By 1988, more than 70,000 microcomputers were in the market. The market for PCs and PC compatibles boomed, which stimulated the demand for local software packages. By December 1988, more than 500 software companies were

---

6 This reduction had some interesting positive spillovers. In 1981, NIIT was started in Delhi by HCL Technologies as a training company to exploit the tax waiver on hardware imports and thus enter the hardware industry. Such training initiatives multiplied many times in subsequent years.

7 After a brief hiatus, deregulation of hardware and software imports continued in the second half of the 1980s; apart from reducing tariff rates on these imports, the policy allowed Indian firms to become distributors for foreign software. The reduction of import duties on software and hardware continued in the 1990s, combined with more flexible ways of fulfilling export obligations (see table 5.3).

making packaged software—a major share of which were cheap accounting packages.[8]

One of the effects of the policies was that some Indian companies—HCL Technologies, Wipro Information Technologies Limited, and DCM DP—became the first in the world to build PCs that were based on Unix.[9] This research and the knowledge that was created provided Indian software engineers with a competitive edge after 1984, when the computer policy was liberalized and when the mainframe technology gave way to the PC technology in the global software industry in the latter half of the 1980s (Heeks 1996: 214–16). In response to the success of companies such as HCL Technologies, Tata Consultancy Services (TCS), and Wipro, a new computer policy was introduced in 1984 that reduced many constraints on the industry (see table 5.3). The IT sector was recognized as an industry, and several measures were introduced to facilitate imports, improve foreign exchange availability, and reduce the tax burden on exporting firms. The new software policy further liberalized the regime that advocated imports. It was this regime that allowed the entry of a TI subsidiary in Bangalore in 1985 and 1986. The subsidiary was a 100 percent export-oriented, foreign-owned, and foreign-operated subsidiary (the parent company's first outside the United States) with a direct satellite link to the United States. The government and the Indian telecommunication provider, Videsh Sanchar Nigam Limited (VSNL), then a public company, softened many rules to allow this connectivity.[10]

Establishment of Electronics Parks and Infrastructure

As far back as 1976, the government of Karnataka attempted to encourage the electronics industry through the establishment of Karnataka State Electronics Development Corporation. The corporation entered into production with its own initiatives and with joint initiatives with domestic and foreign industrial houses. It promoted private enterprises through marketing support, created testing and development centers, and operated

---

8 This discussion is based on reports in several issues of *Dataquest*, mainly *Dataquest* (2002).

9 Wipro, located in Bangalore, is often cited as the first IT success story in the city (Heitzman 2004: 180).

10 The DoE and the Indian government processed the license fairly quickly, and DoE apparently broke 26 separate rules to accommodate Texas Instruments' Bangalore subsidiary and were willing to break more (Heeks 1996: chapter 7). Texas Instruments played a very important role in the growth of the cluster. This role will be discussed in a subsequent section.

personnel training centers. In 1977, the Department of Electronics of Karnataka state formed an electronics park that also housed the first software technology park (STP) in the country. The new park facilitated the exploitation of emerging IT opportunities in Bangalore. Between 1988 and 1991, the federal government launched the Software Technology Parks of India Scheme (Heitzman 2004: 188–89). The scheme provided many facilities (see table 5.3) and helped the fledgling STP that the Karnataka government had launched earlier as more resources became available from the central government for the STP in Bangalore. Around the same time, VSNL commissioned a direct 64-kilobits per second satellite link to the United States. It was a new gateway switching system, which operated through Intelsat and was directly linked to AT&T's earth station at Coram, New York, on the U.S. East Coast. This system offered software exporters a completely new way of functioning and enhanced the facilities available through the STP. These facilities saw further enhancement in 1992 when an exclusive satellite international gateway for export industry was set up. The STP in Karnataka took care of a variety of infrastructural constraints, especially those related to telecommunications.[11]

One can argue that the software park in Karnataka was created at just the right time. Market forces were already at work inducing the cluster.

---

11 The Bangalore STP became an Internet service provider even before VSNL, and it had a large number of corporate customers for its SoftNet service. In 1991 to 1992, soon after the SoftNet service was set up, the STP bypassed the Indian Department of Telecommunications and the local loop to provide a microwave link to IBM. And in 1993, the STP was the only place in India with an asynchronous transmission mode connection, providing an incubation center for nearly 60 start-ups. Subsequently, the Bangalore STP's communication facility at Electronics City on Bangalore's outskirts became a connectivity exchange, with seven satellite gateways and three metropolitan fiber networks residing at the same place, apart from the country's biggest microwave radio network for data covering more than 150 buildings in Bangalore. The STP has also expanded this infrastructure to Mysore and Manipal, the nearby cities. The park has three more unique features: (a) by 2001, it had provided a global gateway for 125 VSATs (very-small-aperture terminals) across the country, including the remote areas of the northeast; (b) it manages a Nortel hub that is one of only a dozen in the world; and (c) it has an internal process that coordinates all communication for the other STPs with consoles monitored around the clock for network management (Seshan 2001). In 2003, India's VSNL entered into an agreement with AT&T, the U.S.-based voice and data communications company, to offer managed data networking services to local enterprises. According to the agreement, AT&T set up network nodes that are enabled with multiprotocol label switching-at Mumbai and Bangalore (*World IT Report* 2003b). In the same year, Sify Limited made Bangalore city Wi-Fi enabled with broadband connectivity from more than 120 hotspots. Sify chose Bangalore for the launch of Wi-Fi services because of the population's use of laptops and their familiarity with working online and because international visitors needed such services while moving around the city (*World IT Report* 2003a).

This policy of setting up software parks further facilitated the process with better infrastructure and other support. The quality of other infrastructural facilities in the city was an additional plus, although these facilities have deteriorated in recent years.[12] A recent survey of IT and electronics firms in Bangalore, in two other clusters (Pune and National Capital Region), and in other noncluster areas showed that a much larger proportion of Bangalore firms (55 percent) find physical infrastructure a major constraint than do firms in other areas; the proportion of firms reporting such a problem was 33 percent in other cluster areas and only 31 percent in noncluster areas (IIMA 2005–06). The growth of industry in recent years without a commensurate investment in supporting facilities is responsible for the inadequacy of the infrastructure. Similarly, availability of power and transportation facilities is increasingly becoming a constraint (see table 5.4).

Taxes, Offshoring, Devaluation, Foreign Direct Investment, and Other Factors

To represent the interest of the Indian software industry, the National Association of Software and Service Companies was formed in 1988. In the very next year, a policy decision was made that reduced the potential profits that Indian firms could derive through "body-shopping" activities by imposing a 15 percent tax on foreign exchange expenditure (especially on travel) (Heeks 1996: 47). There may have been some effort on the part of the Indian firms around this period to reduce the onsite component of outsourced work. The tax was abolished in 1991, but the process of reducing the onsite component had begun, which facilitated the growth of centers such as Bangalore that were ideal for offshore activity, given the capabilities and the infrastructure availability. The transition from onshore to offshore activities continued because of another policy decision—one that was made by the U.S. government. In 1993, the U.S. Immigration and Naturalization Service proposed changes to the regulation that would have made B-1 visas difficult to obtain.[13] As a result, clients had less incentive to hire software

---

12 It is quite interesting to note that Bangalore was the first city in India to be electrified. The state-run utility company was started in 1900 in cooperation with the U.S.-based General Electric Company (Heitzman 2004: 33).

13 Most onshore workers visit the United States under a B-1 visa. Under a B-1 visa, a foreign national who has a permanent residence in another country and who does not intend to abandon his or her home country may enter the United States for a brief specified period in order to conduct limited business activities. Individuals eligible for this visa include entrepreneurs investigating investment opportunities in the United States, employees of a foreign corporation entering the United States to provide consultation services, and employees of a foreign employer entering the United States to solicit services, negotiate contracts, or finalize contracts.

Table 5.4. Firms Facing Infrastructure Constraints

Infrastructure constraints	Bangalore (%)	Pune and National Capital Region clusters (%)	Nonclusters (%)	Significant difference	
				Bangalore and other clusters	Bangalore and nonclusters
Availability of power	49.10	65.97	45.10	Yes	No
Telecommunication services	28.74	26.39	22.55	No	No
Transportation facilities	50.30	45.14	36.27	No	Yes
Industrial safety and security	12.57	11.11	18.63	No	No
Centers for better technical education	6.59	5.56	29.41	No	Yes
Basic education facilities	9.58	4.17	16.83	Yes	No
Consulting and support services	5.39	6.94	22.55	No	Yes
Credit line availability	11.98	6.94	18.63	No	No
Technology development centers	10.18	7.64	41.18	No	Yes
Presence of industry associations	5.39	7.64	22.55	No	Yes
Livability of the city	22.75	20.83	5.88	No	Yes
Entertainment services	12.12	7.64	7.84	No	No

Source: IIMA 2005–06.
Note: The sample was 167 for Bangalore, 144 for the Pune and National Capital Region clusters, and 102 for nonclusters. The significant difference between the proportions of firms facing constraints has been tested at 5 percent.

engineers from India. At the same time, cost pressures were on the rise, and a larger share of the offshore component made good business sense. One observed a rapid increase in the offshore segment of the Indian software and services exports.[14] Whatever may have been the underlying motivations, the transition from the onshore to the offshore model benefited

---

14 The onsite share declined from 90 percent in 1990 to 1991 to about 39 percent in 2002 to 2003.

locations that had a large pool of workers who had the requisite skills, and Bangalore was one of them. The cost advantage of the offshore model increased with the devaluation of the rupee in 1991, the reduction in telecommunication charges for satellite links, and the duty-free and obligation-free imports of telecommunication equipment in the STPs. A variety of tax and other benefits introduced in the 1990s made IT business more profitable (see table 5.3). As a complementary policy, 100 percent foreign direct investment was allowed in 1999 in the IT industry. Partly as a result of this policy, many MNCs set up development centers in India as their own offshore arms, most of them conducting high-end work. In the same year, the Indian Institute of Information Technology in Bangalore and the Karnataka Information Technology Venture Capital Fund were also established. The effect of these developments is discussed later.

It has been argued that social and political stability within the state, absence of labor conflicts, and extensive support of the government during the initial setup phases of a firm (for example, simplifying the procedures for establishment of a software unit) have also contributed to the growth of the Bangalore cluster (Balasubramanyam and Balasubramanyam 2000; Madon 1997). All these factors are broadly policy and governance linked. Overall, several policy measures over the years have contributed to the growth of the Bangalore cluster. Although many of these policy initiatives in the 1980s and 1990s were undertaken by the federal government, they benefited the Bangalore cluster, because it already had the basic capabilities—skill pool, enterprises, links, and so on—to take full advantage of the policies.

The Diaspora: Building Networks and Reducing the Cultural Differences

Entire graduating classes from the elite Indian Institutes of Technology emigrated during the 1970s and 1980s. These émigrés often achieved impressive professional and economic successes abroad. In 1998, Indian engineers were running more than 775 technology companies in California's Silicon Valley, which together accounted for US$3.6 billion in sales and 16,600 jobs. Talented immigrants who have studied and worked abroad increasingly return to their home countries to pursue promising opportunities there. As engineers and other professionals return home—either temporarily or permanently—they transfer not only technology and capital, but also managerial and institutional expertise to formerly peripheral regions. They also link local producers more directly to the market opportunities and networks of more advanced economies (Kapur 2002; Kapur and McHale 2005; Saxenian 2006).

As mentioned, during the 1980s, Bangalore's main software industry exports were not products, but people—highly skilled software engineers and programmers who took jobs in the United States for low wages. Managers of Indian origin in IT working in U.S. firms have played an important role in helping their firms consider outsourcing to India. Entrepreneurs who have started companies such as Mastech, Syntel, CBSi, and Information Management Resources in the United States have relied on Indian programmers to provide software development services to domestic clients (Arora and others 2001).[15] Furthermore, during the 1960s and 1970s, a number of skilled Indian professionals migrated to the United States (many from Bangalore) and returned to India in the early 1980s. These entrepreneurs set up centers in Bangalore, taking advantage of a large, English-speaking local population (Arora and others 2001).

According to one estimate, 71 of the 75 MNCs in Bangalore's STP were headed by Indians who had lived and worked overseas, especially in the United States (Ghemawat 2000). Companies such as Yahoo!, HP, and General Electric opened operations in India largely because of the confidence engendered by the presence of many Indians working in their U.S. operations (Kapur 2002). In fact, most MNC India development centers are headed by Indians who have worked in the parent company in the United States for several years and who have seized an opportunity to return home without jeopardizing their careers.[16] The overseas Indian presence has helped to diffuse knowledge through a variety of mechanisms. Given the technological frontier in the United States, Indian technology professionals who work in the United States have a substantial opportunity to upgrade their skills. To the extent that some return while others circulate between the two countries, technological diffusion occurs through imitation—mimicry being an effective way to reduce search

---

15 Firms such as Mastech, Information Management Resources, Syntel, Cognizant Technology Solutions (a subsidiary of Dun & Bradstreet), and CBSi use their India operations in much the same way as do Indian software export firms. For example, they tap a large pool of relatively cheap but skilled labor for providing software services to U.S.-based clients. These firms are similar in many respects to the Indian software firms. Virtually all are headed by entrepreneurs of Indian origin, and all began, as did many of the leading Indian firms, by supplying software professionals, such as programmers and analysts, to clients in the United States. As Indian software exporters establish overseas subsidiaries, the distinction between the two will diminish.

16 This observation is based on personal communications with IT professionals in Bangalore.

costs (Kapur 2002). Moreover, as Indian software professionals become knowledgeable about the U.S. economy and culture, their ability to develop software for the U.S. market—the largest and the leading market—is enhanced. If they return to India, both the Indian and the U.S. economies benefit (Arora and others 2001). Consequently, outsourcing becomes even more cost-effective.

MNCs and Large Private Firms: Links, Capabilities, and Spillovers

According to a study conducted by the Administrative Staff College of India, 77 global firms have established R&D centers as direct subsidiaries in India; and several others have formed R&D alliances with or have contracted research to local firms. Bangalore, with nearly 40 of the 77 centers, is clearly far ahead of the rest of the country as the most preferred location. Existing companies are expanding, and on an average, six new MNCs were opening centers in Bangalore per month during 2002 (*Business Line* 2003).

Spending on R&D increased from 2.5 percent in 1997 and 1998 to more than 4 percent during 2000 and 2001, and it has continued to rise as firms try to climb the value chain (Kapur 2002). Several studies have highlighted the role of MNCs in developing capabilities through several mechanisms (Patibandla and Peterson 2002). The spillovers associated with the activity of MNCs in a cluster can be varied. The annex (see page 178) summarizes the activity profile of some important MNCs operating in Bangalore. It is evident that the activity profile of most of these firms has become more complex through the years with more R&D and patenting activity. The details also show that these firms contribute to the local cluster through training and collaborations with entities in the cluster. These entities include firms as well as educational institutions. Virtually all observers who have commented on the evolution of the Bangalore cluster believe that the entry of TI in the mid-1980s was critical for the growth of the cluster because it demonstrated the potential of offshore activities in a significant manner. Because TI persisted with its vision of building a unit in India and managed to negotiate all the bureaucratic obstacles to achieve Internet connectivity, it inspired other firms to do the same.

One major source of capability creation in the cluster has been links between small IT firms and MNCs. Some of these links are evident in the summaries provided in the annex (see page 178). Small IT companies in India have started to offer their workforce on a project basis to the large companies in an arrangement reminiscent of the old body-shopping practice. Although small companies such as SystemLogic, Datacons, Intertec Communications, and Nagaraj Technologies are lending a part of their workforce, the demand for contract professionals is mainly from the Indian arms of MNCs, such as HP, TI, Robert Bosch, and Philips Software, and companies such as Wipro and MindTree Consulting.[17]

Just as the activity profile of MNCs has enhanced the capability of the Bangalore cluster, the large domestic firms and a few R&D-intensive small firms have also contributed to the process. Recent evidence shows that these firms are evolving software development methods and project management skills that enable them to undertake larger and more complex projects and to execute high-value-added parts of such projects. Studies show that firms in Bangalore invest in training, professional development programs, infrastructure, techniques and methods, and process and people management initiatives. Although more recent estimates are not available, in 2001, training constituted about 5 percent of revenues of such firms. Furthermore, firms such as Infosys spent about 5 percent of their revenue on R&D. In Bangalore, TI's subsidiary designs sophisticated chips and owns about 200 patents. Several MNC firms are also making R&D investments. In addition, the attrition of labor at 30 percent is common across firms in Bangalore. This circulation of the workforce helps firms exchange information—not only specific types of software, but also generic principles and organizational methods. Despite these factors, until recently there were few formal alliances between large Indian software companies (such as TCS, Infosys, and Wipro) and the MNCs (such as Nortel and HP). However, collaboration is increasing. For example, the Software Productivity Improvement Network, a group of 10 large firms, shares information or benchmarks on software practices in each of the firms. All these elements have combined to contribute to the capability development of IT firms in Bangalore in recent years (Arora and others 2001). Overall, although the MNCs have been active in patenting a majority of Indian software services, R&D efforts are aimed at generating other forms of intellectual property, such as reusable software components. At a very simple level, intellectual property in the IT services context can be defined as an ownership of code and the ability to sell the same piece or block of code to multiple customers (Mahalingam 2003).

---

17 For example, a few years ago, Datacons had a team of professionals managing the infrastructure services at Motorola India and employees were deputed to Wipro for specific projects. The company had deputed nearly 30 of its 225-person workforce to various companies (Kulkarni 2002). Similarly, SystemLogic caters to companies such as LG Soft India, Robert Bosch, MindTree Consulting, and Wipro. At any point, 50 of SystemLogic's 80 professionals were on deputation to different companies.

Overall, the success of TI increased the interest of other U.S. technology companies in setting up their own operations. The details in the annex (see page 178) show that only a few MNCs, such as Motorola and HP, entered Bangalore in the 1980s; many more set up operations in the early and mid-1990s. The rate of entry of MNCs increased significantly after the late 1990s. Although the role of TI—and to some extent Motorola and HP—has been to put Bangalore on the horizons of the MNCs, subsequent MNC entry has facilitated the learning process and has probably also stimulated the labor market. Over time, the nature of activities undertaken by MNCs in Bangalore has become more diverse and complex. The externalities associated with all these activities have contributed to the growth of the Bangalore cluster. The links of firms with academia, other firms, and other entities may have enhanced the benefits of these externalities.

Academia-Industry Links: Providing Labor and Knowledge

Education—especially English education—has a long history in Bangalore. The creation of a British military base (cantonment) in the city in 1807 unleashed a variety of processes that may have contributed to the emergence of the city as an educational center. The cantonment attracted a wide range of service providers from all over southern India, making the population very diverse. The cantonment commissioners subsequently supported the establishment of the first English medium school in 1842 (Heitzman 2004: 29–30). Another English medium school for poor Anglo-Indians was set up in 1854. Following India's independence, the preference for such schools even among the poor has persisted, and Bangalore today has more English medium schools than does Kannada (Pani 2005). Before independence, Mokshagundam Visvesvaraya contributed tremendously to the creation of the technical educational system in Bangalore. He set up an engineering college in 1917 and, about the same time, steered the creation of Mysore University, with which many colleges in Bangalore became affiliated. The Indian Institute of Science was created in 1911. Visvesvaraya firmly believed in the role of the technically educated workforce in the industrialization process, and his efforts made Bangalore a hub of technical education even before independence.

As a result of all these efforts, Bangalore had high literacy rates even in the 1950s (43 percent in 1951), and these rates increased rapidly to 65 percent in 1981 and to 86 percent in 2001 (Heitzman 2004: 223). Following India's independence in 1947, a large number of educational institutions were established in Bangalore, including 4 universities, 14 colleges providing scientific and engineering education, and 47 polytechnic schools. Wages were initially low because of the excess supply of skilled workers in Bangalore. By the late 1990s, India was producing about 65,000 engineers and 95,000 diploma-holders annually in engineering and technology (World Bank 2000) through a large network of public and private colleges. The system was producing nearly 100,000 IT professionals annually, many through private institutes (the figure was close to 500,000 in 2006). Karnataka has 132 engineering colleges with 25,000 places, in addition to 200 diploma institutes. Furthermore, 78 colleges in engineering and science are to be permitted, with a possible addition of another 10,000 students (Kapur 2002).

The advantages of locating in a cluster, especially Bangalore, were briefly discussed in the introductory section. In the context of the role of academic institutions, it can be seen from table 5.2 that firms in the Bangalore cluster rate access to skilled labor as the most important advantage (with a rating of 3.99 on a five-point scale) of locating in these cities. This response strongly recognizes the role of academic institutions as key suppliers of labor in the market, especially in the knowledge sectors of IT and electronics. Bangalore-based firms found the advantage of having access to specialized services such as training and R&D services and facilities to be high—and greater than the other cluster and noncluster firms (see table 5.2).

An earlier study showed that almost all the domestic and foreign firms located in the STPs have had some form of professional contact with research laboratories or institutes in Bangalore in the past five years; about one-third of the firms surveyed agreed that these institutes provided new ideas that helped them to improve their existing products or designs and to introduce new products (Srinivas 1997). A more recent study has also found that the academia-industry links in Bangalore are very diverse; the local academic institutions are the providers of labor as well as knowledge. Initially, these institutions focused on providing labor to the growing cluster, but now they are making efforts to transition into knowledge-based links. However, the number of spinoffs from academic institutions is still quite small (Basant and Chandra 2007). In fact, the available data suggest that such activity has still not taken root in the Indian milieu—not even in a place such as Bangalore, which has grown very rapidly in recent years, represents modern entrepreneurial culture, and hosts many academic institutions with significant research programs.[18]

---

18 For some details of spinoff activity, see Basant and Chandra (2007).

Although the role of academic institutions as a key source of talent is widely recognized, other links are formed as firms in a city cluster move up the capability ladder or begin to service complex order requirements of advanced customers. The difference in perceived benefits of links with academic institutions between Bangalore and other cluster firms could also reflect how the city cluster has evolved to date and may indicate the demand (and likely supply) for the particular nature of the institutions and the accompanying capabilities (see table 5.2). There is a significant difference in the mean value of responses on these links between firms located in a city cluster versus those that are not part of one (see table 5.2), implying that these locational benefits are appropriated when there are others with whom such links can be formed.

Inter- and Intracluster Links: Knowledge Flows and Capability Building

Other factors that contributed to the growth of Bangalore include social and political stability within the state; absence of labor conflicts; establishment of technology parks; investment in the physical infrastructure, especially in the earlier stages; high-quality residential complexes; and extensive support of the government during the initial phases (that is, simplifying the procedures for establishment of a software unit) (Balasubramanyam and Balasubramanyam 2000; Madon 1997).

Many firms also depended on a local network of firms (private and public) to carry out tests of various levels for different products. For example, a particular software company may send a test version of its product to potential client firms. Most companies located within an STP agreed that such interaction with local firms on a regular basis has helped them to adapt their products and services more quickly for global markets (Madon and Sahay 2001: 273).

The role of these links is reflected in the perception of firms regarding advantages of locating in clusters, especially Bangalore. Table 5.2 also shows that, compared with firms in other clusters (and firms in noncluster regions), firms in the Bangalore cluster derive more benefits because of their proximity to customers and suppliers. However, these advantages are not significantly higher for Bangalore firms than for their counterparts in other clusters, presumably because a large segment of customers for the IT firms in all clusters are located in other countries. Still, cluster firms derive more advantages from proximity to customers than do noncluster firms. An unexpected result is that the Bangalore firms do not find the availability of infrastructure to be a major benefit as compared with firms elsewhere—possibly because infrastructural facilities in the city are over-stretched now and are seen more as a constraint. Overall, table 5.2 reveals that cluster firms derive a large variety of advantages, many of which have been mentioned. Moreover, within clusters, Bangalore continues to be a preferred location because of the scope for local links, the availability of R&D institutions, the availability of skilled labor, and so on.

Why are links important? One of the many advantages could be the building of capabilities through the adoption of various best processes and practices. This change could be through demonstration effects attributable to the right location or through explicit knowledge flows built around a variety of links. A recent survey undertaken by the Indian Institute of Management in Ahmedabad collected data on good processes and prac-tices adopted by IT and electronics firms (IIMA 2005–06). The list of these processes and practices was developed with the help of detailed interviews of experienced industry professionals. Combining all types of processes and practices, tables 5.5, 5.6, and 5.7 provide summary informa-tion on their adoption in cluster and noncluster firms.[19] It is evident from

Table 5.5. IT Firms Adopting Various Processes

Process	Bangalore (%)	Pune and National Capital Region clusters (%)	Nonclusters (%)	Significant difference	
				Bangalore and other clusters	Bangalore and nonclusters
High-end application development process	88.60	88.13	76.67	No	Yes
Low-end application development process	90.99	92.97	91.67	No	No
Package implementation process	56.51	50.42	53.00	No	No
Quality process	34.30	31.77	10.83	No	Yes

Source: IIMA 2005–06.
Note: The sample was 86 for Bangalore, 96 for the Pune and National Capital Region clusters, and 60 for nonclus-ters. The significant differences in proportions have been tested at 5 percent.

19 For details of the processes and practices covered in the survey, see Basant, Chandra, and Upadhyayula (2006) and Upadhyayula (2006).

Table 5.6. IT Firms Adopting Various Practices

Practices	Bangalore (%)	Pune and National Capital Region clusters (%)	Nonclusters (%)	Significant difference	
				Bangalore and other clusters	Bangalore and nonclusters
Coding practices	76.74	82.50	66.33	Yes	Yes
Knowledge management practices	70.93	72.71	57.00	No	Yes
Security (data and physical) practices	71.40	75.83	57.67	No	Yes
Human resources practices	70.64	78.13	57.50	Yes	Yes

Source: IIMA 2005–06.
Note: The sample was 86 for Bangalore, 96 for the Pune and National Capital Region, and 60 for nonclusters. The significant differences in proportions have been tested at 5 percent.

Table 5.7. Electronic Firms Adopting Various Processes and Practices

Capabilities	Bangalore (%)	Pune and National Capital Region clusters (%)	Nonclusters (%)	Significant difference	
				Bangalore and other clusters	Bangalore and nonclusters
Process capability	28.40	37.08	25.56	Yes	No
Design capability	53.50	43.75	51.11	No	No
Practice capability:					
Planning	47.69	57.29	40.41	Yes	Yes
Quality	53.54	55.68	46.72	No	Yes
Training	62.35	71.88	69.19	Yes	No

Source: IIMA 2005–06.
Note: The sample was 81 for Bangalore, 48 for the Pune and National Capital Region clusters, and 43 for nonclusters. The significant differences in proportions have been tested at 5 percent.

table 5.5 that IT firms in clusters are significantly better than noncluster IT firms at adopting some processes. Although, Bangalore-based IT firms are not significantly different from other cluster firms at adopting any of these processes shown in table 5.5, this pattern changes when the adoption of practices by IT firms are considered (see table 5.6). By this criterion, on average, Bangalore-based IT firms are worse than firms in other clusters at adopting coding and human resource management practices. But overall, cluster firms are significantly better than noncluster firms at adopting all types of practices. Thus, while noncluster firms are still behind, the other cluster firms have caught up with Bangalore firms in the adoption of good practices.

In the case of electronics, on average, Bangalore firms lagged firms in other clusters in all areas except design but were ahead of noncluster firms in all but training (table 5.7). Evidently, electronics firms in other clusters not only have caught up with Bangalore firms in terms of adoption of good processes and practices but have also moved ahead. This development could affect the competitiveness of Bangalore firms in the future. With official policy promoting the equitable distribution of electronics firms, the National Capital Region and Pune clusters caught up much earlier than Bangalore with respect to electronics (Joseph 2004).

Is the adoption of good processes and practices affected by firms' links with outside entities within and outside the city? The survey conducted by the Indian Institute of Management in Ahmedabad survey (IIMA 2005–06) also compiled data on the variety of links firms have with other entities.

Tables 5.8 and 5.9 provide a summary picture of links of electronics and IT firms, respectively, in Bangalore and elsewhere. Links of firms in Bangalore in both sectors are generally higher than those of firms in other clusters and in nonclusters. Bangalore-based firms are in an advantageous situation with respect to international and national customer networks and other international networks. The variation in the number of links across firms is quite high (see tables 5.8 and 5.9), and the same is true for the adoption of processes and practices (data not reported here). Tables 5.10 and 5.11 show that, on average, employee productivity in cluster firms is much higher than in noncluster firms. On average, firms based in Bangalore tend to be more productive than other cluster and noncluster firms in the electronics sector; in the case of IT, they are significantly better than noncluster firms but not compared with other cluster firms. Once again, the variability across firms in productivity (not reported here) is quite high among both electronics and IT firms in clusters. Preliminary econometric estimates based on firm-level equations show that these links facilitate capability building through adoption of good processes and practices. These capabilities, in turn, have a positive effect on profitability of firms.[20] Overall, therefore, there is some evidence that links—especially international links—build capabilities, which, in turn, have a positive effect on the profitability of firms. Because firms in Bangalore have been able to build these links through the years, they are better placed in terms of opportunities and growth prospects.

---

20 For details of these results, see Basant, Chandra, and Upadhyayula (2006) and Upadhyayula (2006).

Table 5.8. Number of Networks for Electronics Firms: Weighted Means and Standard Deviations

Networks	Bangalore		Pune and National Capital Region clusters		Nonclusters		Significant difference	
	Mean	Standard deviation	Mean	Standard deviation	Mean	Standard deviation	Bangalore and other clusters	Bangalore and nonclusters
Internal (within the city) customer networks	25.77	224.96	154.36	1,024.34	12.15	73.57	No	No
National customer networks	250.85	2,235.97	6.96	31.99	20.59	105.08	No	No
International customer networks	14.24	112.14	2.11	14.42	0.01	0.02	No	No
Other internal networks	12.77	111.19	0.15	0.19	0.20	0.23	No	No
Other national networks	0.40	1.38	0.08	0.17	0.34	0.91	No	Yes
Other international networks	0.37	1.78	0.01	0.04	0.13	0.76	No	Yes

Source: IIMA 2005–06.

Note: The sample was 81 for Bangalore, 48 for the Pune and National Capital Region clusters, and 46 for nonclusters. The significant differences in proportions have been tested at 5 percent.

Table 5.9. Number of Networks for IT firms: Weighted Means and Standard Deviations

Networks	Bangalore		Pune and National Capital Region clusters		Nonclusters		Significant difference	
	Mean	Standard deviation	Mean	Standard deviation	Mean	Standard deviation	Bangalore and other clusters	Bangalore and nonclusters
Internal (within the city) customer networks	38.22	155.83	15.49	44.52	95.10	309.42	Yes	No
National customer networks	121.17	766.74	17.34	48.99	203.15	1,094.04	No	No
International customer networks	125.24	686.82	103.56	567.44	7.40	18.25	Yes	No
Other internal networks	18.72	28.54	14.91	30.01	12.97	15.29	No	No
Other national networks	14.23	23.18	30.39	160.22	29.62	130.67	No	No
Other international networks	11.36	19.40	11.94	39.04	0.52	1.68	Yes	Yes

Source: IIMA 2005–06.
Note: The sample was 86 for Bangalore, 97 for the Pune and National Capital Region clusters, and 60 for nonclusters. The significant differences in proportions have been tested at 5 percent, except for international customer networks, for which the significant differences have been tested at 10 percent.

Table 5.10. Performance of Electronics Firms

Performance	Bangalore	Pune and National Capital Region clusters	Nonclusters	Significant difference	
				Bangalore and other clusters	Bangalore and nonclusters
Sales (Rs 100,000)	9,454.71	6,006.42	813.81	No	Yes
Number of employees	73.84	85.73	37.14	No	Yes
Employee productivity (Rs 100,000)	93.35	42.98	20.93	No	Yes

Source: IIMA 2005–06.
Note: The sample was 58 for Bangalore, 40 for the Pune and National Capital Region clusters, and 44 for nonclusters. The significant differences in proportions have been tested at 5 percent, except for number of employees, for which the significant differences have been tested at 10 percent.

Table 5.11. Performance of IT Firms

Performance	Bangalore	Pune and National Capital Region clusters	Nonclusters	Significant difference	
				Bangalore and other clusters	Bangalore and nonclusters
Sales (Rs 100,000)	3,533.37	15,141.88	522.53	No	Yes
Number of employees	126.38	159.98	49.35	No	Yes
Employee productivity (Rs 100,000)	53.86	54.23	9.80	No	Yes

Source: IIMA 2005–06.
Note: The sample is 69 for Bangalore, 71 for the Pune and National Capital Region clusters, and 50 for nonclusters. The significant differences in proportions have been tested at 5 percent.

Some Concluding Observations

Broadly then, Bangalore benefited a great deal from initial conditions and policy initiatives immediately after India gained independence. Investments in education during the pre- and postindependence period paid off when the city became a focus of a state-sponsored industrialization process. Early emergence of a large and diversified public sector in the city created a large pool of trained workers who understood technology well. The existence of this labor pool, in turn, prepared the cluster to exploit business opportunities that emerged during the period of the Y2K problem and subsequently as the ICT industry grew rapidly through outsourcing. Presence of diaspora links and the early entry of MNCs created a base for a variety of international links that facilitated transfer of knowledge and adoption of good processes and practices. Existence of decent educational and R&D institutions and their subsequent growth expanded the local labor market and provided good R&D and other related facilities. The state government provided good governance that facilitated the exploitation of emerging opportunities. However, survey data seem to suggest that other clusters are now catching up and that Bangalore is facing a variety of constraints that may hamper its growth.

Is diversity of the cluster important for technology flows and cluster growth? Although it is difficult to explore this link systematically, the available evidence suggests that diversity may have contributed to the growth and sustainability of the Bangalore cluster. The recent emergence of biotechnology firms is gradually leading to some synergies across sectors (IT, electronics, and biotechnology) that may result in changes in the activity profile of new firms in the cluster. Similar changes have occurred in Silicon Valley (see chapter 2). This issue is important from the point of view of policy makers as they design new clusters. Policy instruments should facilitate the exploitation of these synergies. Creating interdisciplinary courses and research activity in the cluster may be helpful in this regard.

The earlier literature has clearly shown that exposure to demanding markets generally enhances capability building (see Basant 2002 for a review). Bangalore is no exception, with significant exposure to demanding international markets. How can strategy maximize such learning? As many earlier studies have suggested, policies enhancing export orientation should help, but the previous analysis does not give any additional insight on this issue. The chapter also lends support to the hypothesis that the presence of MNCs in the cluster can create positive spillovers through demonstration effects and competition effects. Bangalore as a cluster seems to have benefited a great deal from the activities of MNCs.

Annex: The Role of Major MNCs Operating in Bangalore Cluster

A large number of MNCs operate in the Bangalore cluster and have contributed to the growth of the cluster in many ways. Their contributions include training and knowledge spillovers through direct and indirect links with other entities in the cluster. The annex summarizes the activity profile of a few major MNCs so as to indicate their likely effect on the cluster.

Texas Instruments

Area of work and activity—In 1985, TI India was incorporated in Bangalore. It started with just 20 people but now has more than 1,000 engineers and about 200 business associates. The center began with the production of CAD (computer-aided design) software in Bangalore. It has two divisions: (a) very-large-scale integration design and (b) embedded software. The former team designs chips for DSP (digital signal processing), ASIC (application-specific integrated circuit), broadband, and wireless systems. Two-thirds of engineers are involved in this area. The embedded software team designs software applications for DSP, broadband, and wireless systems.

The center has developed chips for mobile and third-generation communications and collaborates with other TI design centers. A huge talent gap exists in very-large-scale integration design. To bridge that talent gap, TI India began master's degree programs in very-large-scale integration design and signal processing at 15 universities. Its plan is to set up DSP labs in several hundred universities across India. It has already sponsored DSP labs in 29 leading institutions, including the Indian Institute of Science at Bangalore, the five Indian Institutes of Technology, and leading regional engineering colleges.[21]

Size—Employees include more than 1,000 engineers.

Market—As an export-oriented company, TI designs chips for wireless handsets, wireless local area networks, digital still cameras, Internet audio players, and Internet protocol telephony markets. Every design that is shipped out of TI worldwide has components designed by an Indian team.

Research and development—During the past 15 years, about US$25 million had been invested in the Bangalore location, which was TI's biggest facility in the Asia Pacific.

Patents and products—The Indian center of TI holds 225 patents. It developed the world's first single chip on mobile phones and the world's fastest fixed-point DSP for emerging video and imaging applications. It also designed a single combined chip for high-speed modems. By 2003, TI had released many "Made in India" products (about 20), including the

---

21 For additional information, see http://neasia.nikkeibp.com/nea/200308/intvw_259901.html.

Ankur digital signal processor; Sangam, a bridge router for DSL (digital subscriber line); and Zeno, which runs multimedia applications.

Training—The facility has a partnership with four off-campus development centers, and more that 400 partner engineers are working closely with TI.

Local collaboration—TI sees third-party software developers as a key part of its growth plans. It is working in partnership with several Indian software firms, such as Wipro, Sasken, and Tata Elxsi, to design and develop embedded software.

Effect—Many highly skilled Indian professionals in the United States have been persuaded by TI to return to their home country.

Intel

Area of work and activity—The first Intel R&D center was started in Bangalore in 1998 with 20 engineers. Today, it has about 1,400 engineers. It is mainly involved in e-business applications. Intel expects to invest more than US$40 million in a second R&D center, where it will employ more than 1,000 people. The new center will focus on microprocessor chip designing, large-scale integration, and embedded software applications for mobiles. The development center is already working on Xeon processors and will be involved in developing the next generation of Intel's mobile Centrino platform. The 32-bit processor was designed entirely in Bangalore and has 1 billion transistors. In comparison, Intel's Pentium 4—previously the company's most advanced 32-bit chip for desktop computers—had 55 million transistors).

Size—Intel employs about 1,400 engineers.

Patents and products—More than 14 patents have been granted to the two centers. The first center has developed a network switch product.

Training—Intel has started a computer literacy program in line with its corporate social responsibility. It has already provided 240,000 teachers with computer literacy training.

Local collaboration—Intel and Nokia are collaborating with the Indian Institute of Science and are accelerating work in many domain areas. Intel has set up an R&D lab in the Indian Institute of Information Technology in Bangalore. The Technology Centre at Bangalore also oversees the company's multimedia labs in various Indian Institutes of Technology. Intel started a capital fund, which invested in 15 companies within 18 months. Among the companies Intel invested in were Rediff.com, Network Solutions, Eastern Software, Ritechoice, Bharati, Indus Software, and Silicon Automation Systems. It has sold its 5 percent stake in Rediff.com to Warburg Pincus for US$3.5 million. It is also selling its 15 percent stake in Bharti Telespatiale (an Internet service provider) and its 10 percent interest in Bharti Telesoft. Intel's acquisition of Bangalore-based Thinkit Technologies would supplement design capability sourcing from India. Pramati Technologies in Hyderabad also received investments from Intel in the Java technologies area. Intel India announced plans to acquire the 120-person consulting group of systems integrator Network Solutions, located in Bangalore.

Effect—As Intel India was expanding its R&D operations, and Intel USA embarked on downsizing, it relocated personnel from the United States to its Indian operations Of the 1,400 engineers who work in Intel India, nearly 10 percent are repatriated Indians who have spent significant time working abroad. Most moved voluntarily, many taking significant cuts in pay and bringing their compensation closer to Indian salaries. Evidently, the opportunity to return home and the lower cost of living made the tradeoff acceptable.

General Electric
Area of work and activity—The General Electric (GE) R&D Centre in Bangalore was inaugurated in 2000. In 2001, phase 2 of the center was built so that it could accommodate an additional 700 scientists, researchers, and engineers, bringing the total number of technical staff members to 1,800. Employees work in 11 multidisciplinary labs supporting various GE businesses. They are part of a global GE research team, which also has centers in Schenectady, New York; Munich, Germany; and Shanghai, China—all of which are able to collaborate by computer networks.

Size—Employees include 1,800 scientists, researchers, and engineers. More than 20 percent of them have global experience, and 31 percent have Ph.D.s.

Market—GE plans to invest US$800 million in IT and expected software exports from India to rise to US$3 billion by 2004, with software outsourcing expected to account for one-third of the export targets.

Patents and products—Research engineers in GE Bangalore filed for 95 patents in the four years since the research facility was set up in 2000.

Local collaboration—Initially, GE contracted with four companies, including Infosys and Wipro. John Welch forged a joint venture with Wipro for medical systems, and GE became one of the largest outsourcers to the Indian software industry. Today, GE accounts for more than 2 percent of the software outsourced to India. Wipro benchmarked GE's Six Sigma process and became a well-known symbol of the Indian high-tech industry. Since then, Indian software firms—essentially services firms—have not only benchmarked the best practices, but have also begun competing with major global companies.

IBM

Area of work and activity—IBM left India in the late 1970s, when severe restrictions on MNCs were put in place. It reentered India in 1992 through a joint venture with Tata Consultancy Services. In 1997, it started IBM Global Services India. In Bangalore, its Software Testing Center has level-5 Capability Maturity Model accreditation from the Software Engineering Institute. Currently, the center is working on IBM's Blue Gene Project and on verifying IBM's Giga Processor for the next generation of IBM systems. In 2000, IBM launched a new facility in its Solution Partnership Centre in Bangalore to support Web-based application development in the country. It is just one of 10 such facilities worldwide. IBM's new initiative is aimed at partnering with independent software vendors to provide Web-based solutions to end users. Subsequently, it was involved in the development of the WebSphere application server and commerce suite. In 2003, IBM Global Services India set up a call center in Bangalore, which could accommodate close to 1,000 callers. A new center will provide technology support to global customers of IBM worldwide.[22]

Size—Employees include 3,100 engineers, with 400 professionals working at the Software Testing Center.

Patents and products—There have been 85 patents filed.

Training—To promote cooperation between its employees and key engineering institutes in India, IBM established the Centre for Advanced

---

22 The Indian operation of IBM Global Services has won a 10-year project from AT&T. More than 5,000 people could be working on this project.

Studies at its Bangalore facility. The Bangalore center, one of eight such centers opened worldwide, will offer students with master of technology, master of science, and doctoral degrees from premier engineering institutes in India access to IBM's research areas, technical staff, and other resources, with the goal of solving research problems of the utmost importance to software developers. Moreover, NIIT and IBM India Limited have entered into an alliance to expand the pool of technical labor skilled in IBM software technologies. Also, IBM India held a national entrance test for its advanced certificate course in software engineering. This structured, short-term software development course is offered at 44 IBM Authorized Centers for Education in India. The entrance test was held in 29 cities in India.

Local collaboration—In 2002, IBM and Wipro signed a nonexclusive alliance. In the agreement, Wipro Infotech will market, integrate, and offer solutions and services for IBM's wide range of servers and storage products in India, the Asia and Pacific region, and Japan. In exchange, IBM will get entry into Wipro Infotech's large domestic market.

Oracle
Area of work and activity—Oracle entered India in 1987 through a distribution tie-up with TCS. It formed its Indian subsidiary in 1993 in Bangalore with just three people. Initially, engineers worked for the company on a project-by-project basis. Later, Oracle hired regular employees. Currently, IDC Bangalore works on Oracle's database, development tools, application servers, and e-business applications, including work on components of the Oracle9i Database Server and the Oracle9i Application Server. It is also working on grid computing tools. Bangalore houses Oracle's largest development center outside the United States. The center has introduced consulting services and also provides tech support to the company's global customers for a range of Oracle products, including databases, tools, and applications. It has deployed a pilot project for the National Stock Exchange of India and e-Governance Center. Oracle is in the process of establishing a second center in Bangalore. Oracle has also decided to bring the Asia and Pacific region under the purview of its venture capital fund.

Size—More than 3,200 staff members are working in India, with a large share in Bangalore.

Market—About 60 percent of Oracle's sales come from outside the United States, and India is the company's fifth-largest market in Asia, with more than 6,000 customers.

Patents and products—Oracle has filed 10 patents.

Training—Oracle employees have enrolled for master of science degree programs at the Illinois Institute of Technology. Up to 75 percent of the cost of this course is subsidized by the company. Oracle India hosts Oracle Developer Days, a series of one-day workshops in Bangalore and New Delhi. Participants include software developers from various organizations across industries, such as manufacturing and financial services; from government departments; and from IT companies, as well as independent software vendors and systems integrators. These workshops are specifically designed to teach developers the latest in emerging technologies while showing them how to take advantage of their existing skills and technology investments.

Local collaboration—Oracle started an e-Governance center in partnership with HP. Several other companies, including National Informatics Centre are part of this initiative. This center will promote packaged software through a partnership model.

Analog Devices
Area of work and activity—Analog's liaison office was started in 1990 in Bangalore, and the software subsidiary was launched in Bangalore in 1996. The software subsidiary is now known as the India Product Development Center (IPDC). The focus of IPDC is on digital signal processing, both DSP integrated circuit design and DSP software development. Products by Massachusetts-based Analog Devices Inc. have been sold in India since the mid-1970s. Channel partners include BBS Electronics and the Capricorn Group. Currently, IPDC develops software tools for real-world signal processing applications. Tools developed here are used to program DSP for different applications. In 2002, Analog opened an analog and mixed signal design center in Bangalore.

Size—Employees include about 70 engineers (35 to 40 are in chip design and about 30 are at the analog and mixed signal design center).

Market—The chip used in manufacturing electronic metering systems is supplied by Analog in India. Analog had about 80 percent of market share for these chips in India, especially from mid- to late 2000.

Patents and products—A landmark achievement by the IPDC was the indigenous designing of a 32-bit digital signal processor, ADSP–21065L, code-named "Shark," which Analog claims is the world's highest performance 32-bit general purpose DSP today.

Training—In 2001, Analog entered into an agreement with the Indian Institute of Technology in Madras to fund a DSP learning center for training 500 engineers a year. The center, funded by Analog with an investment of about Rs 40 million (about US$1 million), caters to the growing need for DSP skills.

Local collaboration—Analog has tie-ups with several Indian companies, for which it will design and develop solutions to be incorporated in products that will be sold worldwide. A decade ago, Analog Devices Inc. launched a series of initiatives with local companies that included development of DSPs for electronic meters and work on a low-cost wireless local loop using its chips. It is planning to make the IPDC home to its application engineering support group to provide technical training, support, and advice to customers in South and East Asia.

Philips Innovation Campus

Area of work and activity—Established in 1996, the Philips Innovation Campus develops software for Philips products. Drawing on an investment of US$2.5 million, the campus focuses on television, telephony, and video-communication products. Almost all Philips products that use software have some contribution from this campus. It is the largest software center for Philips outside the Netherlands. The campus's primary expertise is in embedded software and information system engineering, architecture design, programming, and testing. It specializes in logic and circuit design for integrated chips. The campus has five product divisions: Philips Mainstream Consumer Electronics, Philips Semiconductors, Philips Medical Systems, Philips Research, and Philips Center for Industrial Technology. These product divisions work on technologies ranging from speech recognition and video telecommunication to embedded memories, systems-on-silicon design flow, digital rights management, and wireless (802.11×) systems. Software for digital entertainment and advanced medical diagnostics and design for some enabling microelectronic circuits are areas of research focus.

Size—There are about 2,000 employees.

Market—Philips India contributes nearly 20 percent of the software for Philips operations globally.

Training—The campus, which has the ownership of a complete software stack for DVDs (digital video discs), has a tie-up with the Indian Institute of Technology in Delhi for a master of technology degree in very-large-scale integration technology. It collaborates with the Indian Institute of Science in Bangalore for research activities. Since 1996, Philips participates in a master's degree program at the Indian Institute of Technology in Delhi in the area of very-large-scale integration design, tools, and technology. Philips Research also has an embedded-systems architecture laboratory at the Indian Institute of Science in Bangalore.

Hewlett-Packard

Area of work and activity—The HP operation in India, known as HP ISO (India Software Operations), began commercial operations in 1989 in Bangalore, but a major expansion occurred after 2000. In Bangalore, HP set up two labs—one at its software development facility and another at the Indian Institute of Science campus. A third one was set up at the Electrical Engineering Department of the Indian Institute of Technology in Chennai. The operations in Bangalore play a strategic role in developing and enhancing many HP products by partnering with HP divisions and businesses. In addition, HP ISO acts as a backup for HP India in supporting its customers with consultancy and technology services. In 2003, HP decided to invest US$20 million in its Bangalore software unit, even as the services division of that unit was merged with a subsidiary, Digital GlobalSoft (begun in 1988 in Bangalore). Digital GlobalSoft works on application management, enterprise package implementation, and infrastructure services. It recently acquired two products from Compaq: Digital Infolife (a suite of storage management products) and tools for electronic data interchange. The company's Advanced Technology Center is involved in enterprise mobility solutions and has significant .NET capability. Intellectual property includes work in speech technology, a third-generation protocol stack, a unified messaging platform called mFortis, and several initiatives in voice-over Internet protocol. The R&D facility also works on key R&D program areas, such as operating systems, embedded systems, network management, Cooltown (HP's Web-centric vision of the future), and mobile services, among others.

In 2000, HP established a worldwide e-speak support center at its HP ISO facility in Bangalore. The new establishment brought the total investment value in HP ISO to US$30 million. In 2001, HP invested US$1 million in creating a Partner Technology Access Centre in India, which helps users port and test their applications on Itanium (Intel) processors. It is working with industry partners such as Oracle, SAP, and Microsoft to make more applications available for the new family.

Currently, HP India supplies components to assemblers for the unbranded PC market in the country. It provides the basic PC configuration and certain optional components to these assemblers through distributors such as Redington. It assembles the ProLiant ML 150 servers at its facility in Bangalore, which has an installed capacity of 3,000 servers per month. In 2004, HP became the first company to set up a wholly owned contact center for after-sales support of its consumer products sold in the United States.

Size—About 1,000 engineers work on product development at Bangalore, spread across eight different centers. An equal number of engineers are split between partners such as TCS, Wipro, and Digital GlobalSoft. These engineers focus on maintenance, implementation, and support services. Digital GlobalSoft itself has about 1,500 engineers.

Market—Limited information is available on this issue. Key projects for HP ISO have included a mobile e-services solution for customers in Europe and the Republic of Korea and a project to help Amazon.com move to Linux.

Patents and products—Six to eight patents were under review in 2004.

Training—The company has set up a joint lab with the Indian Institute of Technology in Madras. The lab focuses on technologies for developing markets. Its objective is to provide an environment for HP employees to work with faculty members, research staff members, and students to create communication technologies.

Sun Microsystems

Area of work and activity—Sun Microsystems entered India through a sales-and-support agreement with Wipro in 1987. It set up its own office in Bangalore in 1995 and opened an engineering center in 1998. Initially employing 20 people, the center works mainly on Sun's software, which includes Solaris and Sun ONE. Sun considers India to be a high-growth area and expects to invest nearly US$50 million, mainly in ramping up its infrastructure in India and setting up more offices. Sun gives top priority to R&D and requires that the Indian operations develop a complete stack of servers. About 25 percent of the company's workforce on Sun ONE—its Web services platform—is based in India.

Size—There are about 850 employees.

Patents and products—Ten patents have been filed. Large chunks of Sun ONE—version 6 of its application server, meta directory products, and mail and calendar service—were developed in India. Part of Sun MC—the management console for Solaris—was designed in Bangalore.

Effect—Many of the employees worked previously in the San Francisco Bay Area of California. First-rate talent is returning to India and helping to bridge cultures, bootstrap new work, and build skill sets in organizations at the Sun India Engineering Center in Bangalore. The center has given Indian developers and engineers the kind of work and living conditions that they would normally experience in the United States.

Cisco

Area of work and activity—Cisco entered the Indian market in 1995. Cisco Systems (India) Private Limited in Bangalore is the largest R&D center established by Cisco outside of the United States. Cisco is increasingly looking at Bangalore as its core product and Internet protocol development center. Cisco sells and supports its networking products and services through systems integrators, such as Datacraft RPG, Compaq India, HCL Infosystems, Microland, CMC Ltd., Wipro Infotech, and Tata Infotech, and through distributors, such as D-Link and Godrej Pacific Technology. Since 2002, the company started looking into venture capital funding of Indian start-ups, particularly those that operate in the Internet software segment.

Size—Employees include about 1,500 engineers. In addition to having its own engineers, Cisco India operates through a network of ecosystem partners across India. The engineering partners in the ecosystem consist of three leading Indian IT companies—Infosys Technologies, Wipro, and HCL Technologies. In 2002, more than 1,600 engineers worked for Cisco through these partners (Carless 2002).

Market—India contributes about 10 percent of Cisco's revenues. Punjab National Bank was one of Cisco's largest clients. Cisco helped the bank network 3,870 branches as part of its Rs 1.5 billion plan.

Patents and products—Cisco India has designed an entire gigabit switch fabric application-specific integrated circuit that is used in a giga-Ethernet switching product.

Training—Cisco provides various levels of certification for IT professionals, with several different tracks to meet individual needs.

Local collaboration—In 2001, Cisco invested US$200 million in India. The investment is promoting five development centers, which Cisco has set up with Indian IT companies. Cisco has a formal relationship with Wipro and with HCL Infosystems, an offshoot of HCL Technologies. Infosys, and two other companies, and the joint research centers contribute to a growing pool of knowledge in all three Indian companies. Subsequently, IBM India Limited and Cisco India offered comprehensive and integrated solutions for contact centers in India.

Other MNCs in Bangalore
A few other MNCs are quite active in Bangalore, but detailed information about them is not readily available.

Motorola—A wholly owned subsidiary of Motorola started operating in Bangalore in 1987. It has been assessed at Software Engineering Institute's level-5 accreditation, the only software company in the world to achieve this status until 1998. Motorola India Global Software subsequently integrated its two centers in Bangalore under a single roof. Since the subsidiary was set up, India has been a major hub for Motorola's R&D efforts. The company set up the internal software development division, or global software group, as Motorola India Electronics Limited in 1991 and has centers in Bangalore and Hyderabad. In addition, Motorola also established its chip development operations in the country in 1998 and has chip design labs at Noida and Gurgaon as part of its semiconductor product sector division. Motorola India Electronics Limited focuses on software process engineering and building of large software systems. Products developed in India include libraries for Motorola's DSPs, parallel compilers, software for cellular phone systems and pagers, and subscriber data maintenance. The development center in Bangalore focuses on software development for all Motorola handsets and on cutting-edge research on wireless technologies. The software used in the Motorola Accompli personal digital assistant–GSM (Global System for Mobile) phone that was launched globally in mid-2001 was developed entirely in

India. About 30 percent of all software for Motorola's latest phones is written in India.

Motorola is donating its cutting-edge networking processor technology to design labs in 14 top engineering institutes across the country under the IMPACT-SSS program of the Ministry of Information Technology and Indian Institute of Science in Bangalore. The grant of tools and software of the Asia and Pacific region's PowerPC family is valued at Rs 5 million (US$111,000).

Nortel—Nortel has carried out significant offshore software development through agreements with TCS, Infosys, Wipro, and SAS (now Sasken). It regards them as strategic partners for the long-term success of its R&D activity in India. Nortel Networks and BPL Innovision Business Group have announced a partnership to develop software and sell Internet and GSM cellular services in India. As an element of the partnership, Nortel is setting up an offshore software development center at Bangalore's Electronics City for offering technology solutions to Nortel's global customers. It will provide consulting and technology support for BPL Innovision's domain experts and access to the huge domestic market. The alliance will also allow Nortel to offer its infrastructure expertise to BPL Innovision's Internet and cellular service companies. Nortel, which has already invested about US$30 million in its development partners in India, will continue to invest at least US$2 million per year. The bulk of the investment thus far has gone into installation of about eight captive offices and into associated tools for mainstream product development. Nortel has also invested heavily in the Indian Institute of Science in Bangalore, in a network management center at the Indian Institute of Technology in Kharagpur, and in a telecommunication policy research center at the Indian Institute of Management in Ahmedabad.

Nokia—Nokia has two global software development teams in India. The Intelligent Edge products group, which is based in Bangalore, is involved in developing Nokia's ASR line of routers and released the ASR 2020, an Internet protocol aggregation router. The other team is based in Hyderabad. Nokia sponsors Ph.D. students at the Indian Institute of Technology in Delhi and finances a fellowship in high-speed networking, thereby driving research in that area. Intel and Nokia have tied up with the Indian Institute of Science to accelerate work in many domain areas.

References

Arora, Ashish, V. S. Arunachalam, Jai Asundi, and Ronald Fernandes. 2001. "The Indian Software Services Industry." *Research Policy* 30 (8): 1267–87.

Balasubramanyam, V. N., and Ahalya Balasubramanyam. 2000. "The Software Cluster in Bangalore." In *Regions, Globalization, and Knowledge-Based Economy*, ed. John H. Dunning, 349–63. Oxford, U.K.: Oxford University Press.

Basant, Rakesh. 2002. "Knowledge Flows and Industrial Clusters: An Analytical Review of Literature." Working Paper 2002-02-01, Indian Institute of Management, Ahmedabad, India.

Basant, Rakesh, and Pankaj Chandra. 2007. "Role of Educational and R&D Institutions in City Clusters: An Exploratory Study of Bangalore and Pune Regions in India." *World Development* 35 (6): 1037–55.

Basant, Rakesh, Pankaj Chandra, and Rajesh Upadhyayula. 2006. *Building Technological Capabilities through Strategic Development of Industrial Clusters.* Ahmedabad: Indian Institute of Management.

Bell, Martin, and Michael Albu. 1999. "Knowledge Systems and Technological Dynamism in Industrial Clusters in Developing Countries." *World Development* 27 (9): 1715–34.

Business Line. 2003. "India Emerges Global R&D Base for MNCs." March 24. http://www.blonnet.com/2003/03/24/stories/2003032401830300.htm.

Caniels, Marjolein C. J., and Romijn, Henry A. 2003. "Dynamic Clusters in Developing Countries: Collective Efficiency and Beyond." *Oxford Development Studies* 31 (3): 275–92.

Carless, Jenny. 2002. "Q&A: Samu Devarajan, Director, Engineering, Talks about How Cisco's R&D Efforts in India Contribute to the Company's Global Innovation Strategy." *News@Cisco*, December 30. http://newsroom.cisco.com/dlls/ts_123002.html.

Dataquest. 2002. "The Hot Verticals: The Great Indian Software Revolution." December 22. http://dqindia.ciol.com/content/20years/102122306.asp.

Ghemawat, Pankaj. 2000. "The Indian Software Industry at the Millennium." Harvard Business Case 9-700-036, Harvard Business School, Boston.

Heeks, Richard. 1996. *India's Software Industry: State Policy, Liberalisation, and Industrial Development.* New Delhi: Sage.

Heitzman, James. 2004. *Network City: Planning the Information Society in Bangalore.* New York: Oxford University Press.

Holstrom, Mark. 1994. "Bangalore as an Industrial District: Flexible Specialisation in a Labor-Surplus Economy?" Pondy Paper in Social Sciences 14, French Institute of Pondicherry, Pondicherry, India.

IIMA (Indian Institute of Management Ahmedabad). 2005–06. *Survey of IT and Electronics Firms*. Ahmedabad, India: IIMA.

Joseph, K. J. 2004. "The Electronics Industry." In *The Structure of Indian Industry*, eds. Subir Gokarn, Anindya Sen, and Rajendra R. Vaidya, 238–80. New Delhi: Oxford University Press.

Kapur, Devesh. 2002. "The Causes and Consequences of India's IT Boom." *India Review* 1 (2): 91–110.

Kapur, Devesh, and John McHale. 2005. *Give Us Your Best and Brightest*: The *Global Hunt for Talent and Its Impact on the Developing World*. Washington, DC: Center for Global Development.

Kulkarni, Vishwanath. 2002. "Now, It's Contract Hiring of Skills." *Business Line*, March 29.

Madon, Shirin. 1997. "Information-Based Global Economy and Socio-economic Development: The Case of Bangalore." *Information Society* 13 (3): 227–43.

Madon, Shirin, and Sundeep Sahay. 2001. "Cities in the Developing World: Linking Local and Global Networks." *Information Technology and People* 14 (3): 273–86.

Mahalingam, T. V. 2003. "Intellectual Property: Indian IT Wakes Up to Patents." *Dataquest*, August 4. http://dqindia.ciol.com/content/dqtop202K3/analysis/103080411.asp.

Mytelka, Lynn, and Fulvia Farinelli. 2000. "Local Clusters, Innovation Systems, and Sustained Competitiveness." Discussion Paper 2005, United Nations University Institute for New Technologies, Maastricht, Netherlands.

Mytelka, Lynn, and Julie Pellegrin. 2001. "Can SMEs Survive? Static vs. Dynamic Externalities in the French Biotechnology Industry." United Nations University Institute for New Technologies, Maastricht, Netherlands.

Pani, Narendar. 2005. "Bangalore Turns against Itself." *Times of India*, November 28, 12.

Patibandla, Murali, and Bent Peterson. 2002. "Role of Transnational Corporations in the Evolution of Hi-tech industry: The Case of India's Software Industry." *World Development* 30 (9): 1561–77.

Saxenian, AnnaLee. 2006. "The Bangalore Boom: From Brain Drain to Brain Circulation?" In *Bridging the Digital Divide: Lessons from India*, ed. Kenneth Kenniston and Deepak Kumar, 169–81. New Delhi: Sage.

Schmitz, Hubert, and Bernard Musyck. 1994. "Industrial Districts in Europe: Policy Lessons for Developing Countries?" *World Development* 22 (6): 889–910.

Seshan, Sekhar. 2001. "Beyond Bangalore." *Business India*, July 9.

Srinivas, S. 1997. "The Information Technology Industry in Bangalore: A Case of Urban Competitiveness in India?" Paper presented at the Fifth Asian Urbanization Conference, London, August 26–30.

Upadhyayula, Rajesh. 2006. "Determinants of Knowledge Flows and Firm Performance in Industrial Clusters." Ph.D. dissertation, India Institute of Management, Ahmedabad.

World Bank. 2000. "India-Scientific and Technical Manpower Development in India." Report 20416-IN. Education Sector Unit, South Asia Region.

World IT Report. 2003a. "India's VSNL, AT&T Tie-up." July 9. http://www.world itreport.com/India/&mod=search&searchWords=VSNL&st_id_search= 94184&time=1&sub=1.

World IT Report. 2003b. "Bangalore: India's First WiFi Enabled City." October 15. http://www.worlditreport.com/India/&mod=search&searchWords=Bangalore &st_id_search=94583&time=4&sub=1.

CHAPTER 6

ICT Clusters and Industrial Restructuring in the Republic of Korea
The Case of Seoul

Sam Ock Park

What we call the *digital economy* involves transforming the local economy through the application of information and communication technology (ICT). This economy is being shaped not only by the development and diffusion of computer hardware and software, but also by rapidly increasing low-cost electronic connectivity in the global society. It is being shaped, in addition, by changing patterns of production and consumption mediated by new institutions, new laws, and a new division of labor (Bryson, Daniels, and Warf 2004). ICT and related services now permeate every part of the contemporary economy and society, and they are affecting the use of economic spaces. Clustering of knowledge-intensive activities, on the one hand, and dispersion of production activities, on the other hand, are now two sides of one coin in the knowledge-based economy.

The agglomeration of ICT industries and related services in Seoul has become very evident, especially since the financial crisis in the Republic of Korea in 1997 and the industry restructuring that followed in its wake. Gangnam, located south of the Han River in Seoul, is the center of a cluster of ICT-related industries. The clustering of these industries has led to the emergence of a learning region within the capital city. A high-tech venture environment or high-tech venture habitat has been evolving through the continuous interaction among spinoffs, high-tech venture firms, and advanced services within this region. Formal and informal meetings are the sources of creation and transfer of knowledge. And the synergy arising from strategic alliances and interfirm networks within the capital city has contributed to the clustering. In addition to the Gangnam cluster, the Seoul Digital Industrial Complex is a focus of ICT-related services and industries.

The purpose of this chapter, which draws on recent data and surveys, is to analyze the dynamics of concentration and structuring of ICT industries in the Gangnam area and in the Seoul Digital Industrial Complex.

Dynamics of Economic Spaces in the Knowledge-Based Economy

Economic spaces evolve through interactions. Traditionally, interactions in the space economy focused on commodity flows and migration, Ullman's (1957) triad—transferability, complementarity, and intervening opportunity—being the classic conceptualization of spatial interaction. *Transferability* related to the cost of movement formed the basis for classic location theory, *complementarity* represented relationships arising from the spatial inequalities of supply and demand of commodities, and *intervening opportunities* arose from spatial competition and substitutability among destinations.

In the world of services, however, knowledge is becoming interwoven at all levels of the production process. Production processes now "involve the articulation of various forms of tacit and explicit knowledge, raw material, land, building, and people" (Bryson, Daniels, and Warf 2004: 52). In the premanufacturing stage—as well as during manufacturing, selling, distribution, and consumption—various services, including knowledge-intensive producer services, add value and determine competitiveness. In a complex production process, diverse forms of tacit and codified knowledge are interwoven, converged, and also created. As a consequence of the complex service functions in the production process of the knowledge-based economy, the bases of spatial interaction differ from those arising from traditional commodity flows.

Recently, Park (2004b) suggested four notions regarding interaction of the advanced services in the Internet era: transferability; knowledge genesis for service products; network and collaboration; and hierarchy of control. Transferability is still important in the service worlds. However, the spatial range of advanced services has been extended dramatically, because the effect of distance has decreased significantly for tangible goods and intangible services. Knowledge genesis for service products is critical for interregional and international interaction of advanced services in the knowledge-based economy. Knowledge creation and innovation for services have become more important for regional competitiveness and development (Clark and Lloyd 2000; Glaeser, Kolko, and Saiz 2001). Clustering of talent, innovation, and advanced services is closely related to the process of knowledge creation and transfer.

Networking and collaboration among customers, suppliers, universities, public institutions, research centers, and other functions within a firm are important mechanisms for generating new knowledge and innovation for economic activities. They are why advanced services are concentrated in a few metropolitan areas. The development of ICT has made codified knowledge more ubiquitous, but tacit knowledge is still place based and locally embedded (Park 2003, 2004a). Because of the influence of networking and collaboration, clustering of advanced services is occurring unevenly in the global space economy.

The hierarchy of control is much more important than distance in the flow of advanced services. It derives from the interplay of transferability, knowledge genesis, and networking and collaboration. A major focus center for services is usually the creation of knowledge. Global financial activities are concentrated in the primary financial centers of London, New York, and Tokyo. The location of headquarters and regional centers of multinational firms also represents the hierarchy of control in the global space economy. Advanced services are distributed hierarchically across global, national, and regional centers.

The four elements of interaction in the knowledge-based economy are integrated as a whole in the global space economy. Economic spaces evolve dynamically because centripetal and centrifugal forces coexist in the process of economic restructuring. In this section, four patterns, which were identified by Park (2004b), are introduced as major dynamic spatial characteristics of the knowledge-based economy in relation to the elements of interaction.

Intensified Spatial Division of Labor
It is well known that the spatial division of labor has changed during the course of industrialization. There are two basic types of spatial division

of labor: sectoral and functional (Massey 1984). A sectoral division of labor develops when regions specialize in particular industries and related skills. Historically, the underlying spatial division of labor is a sectoral one, as experienced in Europe and the United States in the 19th century. The development of an industrial district, in which a certain kind of industry localized, is a good example of a sectoral spatial division of labor. A functional division of labor occurs when firms choose to locate different tasks and occupations within an individual industry in different places. With industrial development, different functions within individual industries, such as management, marketing, research and development (R&D) activity, and manufacturing, require different locations. Limited product life cycles can be one reason for the functional division of labor, because standardized production can be dispersed to low-cost locations (Park and Wheeler 1983; Vernon 1966). Firms can also strategically separate well-paid managerial or R&D positions from low-paid production occupations so as to limit the bargaining power of low-paid production workers (Clark 1981). As production becomes more flexible, the spatial division of labor may not coalesce and can remain problematic in some industries (Hayter 1997).

In the Internet era, a spatial division of labor has intensified in the advanced services—for example, between R&D activity and production. During the past decade, however, in addition to this functional division, basic and applied research has tended to concentrate in a core area, while production R&D has tended to disperse to peripheral areas (Park 1993). Within the R&D activities, more complex and basic research activities that require high-quality employees have tended to concentrate in a few major metropolitan areas. This tendency toward spatial separation within the same type of work has intensified the existing functional spatial division of labor, thus indicating that regional disparity is not being reduced in the Internet era.

Clustering Advanced Services and Internet Industry
Clustering of economic activities is one of the most prominent phenomena in the knowledge-based economy. Clustering of the software industry, venture capital, advanced financial services, producer services, and so forth can be clearly identified in the global space economy. Even in the industrializing and newly industrialized economies, the clustering of advanced services can be observed in places such as Bangalore, Beijing, Seoul, Hong Kong (China), and Singapore (Park 2005; Yeh 2005).

Despite the ability of the Internet to transcend space, dot-com companies also cluster in a few major metropolitan areas (Zook 2005). In Korea, more than three-fourths of business-to-consumer (B2C) e-market-places, business-to-business (B2B) e-commerce sites, and Internet domains are clustered in the capital region (Park 2004a). Supplies of skilled labor, the organization of labor, government-support programs, and regional innovation capacity are some of the factors responsible for geographic clustering (Zook 2005).

The process of knowledge generation is another factor. Nonaka and Takeuchi (1995) suggested that an innovation should be understood as a cycle of interaction between tacit knowledge and codified knowledge. Proximity does not matter in transferring codified knowledge in the Internet era because the codified knowledge can be transferred through the Internet globally at low cost. However, the transfer of tacit knowledge usually takes place on a local level, where firms share the same values, background, and understanding of technical and commercial problems (Maskell and Malmberg 1999). Geographic and cultural proximity provide access to local relational networks for the transfer of tacit knowledge (Park 2003). Accordingly, proximity and institutions are also important underlying factors for clustering of knowledge-intensive economic activities.

Globalized Networks of Services

Traditionally, most services were supplied locally and domestically. Central place theory (Christaller 1966; Lösch 1954) explains why services are locally supplied. As the liberalization of the service industry progressed, producer services, such as finance, legal, R&D, advertising, technical, and engineering services, became widely traded and are now increasingly dispersed among cities in the Asia and Pacific region (Daniels, Ho, and Hutton 2005). Global commodity chains and their related services further underscore the importance of global networks of services in the knowledge-based economy (Gereffi and Korzeniewicz 1994).

The global networks of services are more prominent in the B2C e-commerce segments, a leading example of which is Amazon.com. In recent years, many global firms increased their rate of global sourcing through B2B e-commerce (Park 2004a; Timmers 2000). It should be noted that there is a clear hierarchical ordering of the urban centers supplying the services. The distribution of the Internet industry confirms that, on the one hand, the globalization of service networks intensified in the Internet era while, on the other hand, localization of the Internet-related service firms intensified. Accordingly, globalization and localization are intertwined processes in the evolution of the ICT-based services industries.

Virtual Innovation Clusters

In the Internet era, virtual space or cyberspace represents another dimension of communication and social space. In the virtual space, flows of information and knowledge occur along the networks of the Internet. Some places help coordinate a smooth interaction in the network by serving as communication hubs, while other places can be nodes of the networks. The nodes and hubs are hierarchically organized according to their relative importance within the networks, and they give rise to diverse types of innovation clusters depending on the logic of the spatial division of labor and the value chain of economic activities (Castells 2000; Park 2003).

In cyberspace, innovative clusters can be organized through networks of skilled workers. In this case, hubs and nodes are not a necessary condition for the formation of a virtual innovation cluster. In the hubs and nodes of a spatial economy, actual face-to-face contacts take place easily, accompanying the transfer of tacit knowledge and knowledge conversion processes among the highly skilled workforce, such as engineers and information or managerial elites. In the peripheral areas, daily networking of qualified workers through face-to-face contacts is not easy. However, through a combination of online and offline meetings, a clustering of information and knowledge can be possible in a given location. Research groups can be organized through the Internet, and periodic face-to-face meetings of the advanced researchers can be set up for the transfer of tacit knowledge into peripheral areas. In this way, even though no actual clustering of the innovation workforce occurs, an innovation cluster can be formed by combining both online and offline networks.

ICT Clusters in Seoul

Spatial Concentration of the .kr Domain and B2B e-Commerce in Korea

The Internet infrastructure in Korea has developed rapidly during the past few years. By the end of 2004, Korea had 31.58 million Internet users, and the Internet usage rate had risen to 70.2 percent (KRNIC 2005). Just five years earlier, in 1999, the numbers were 9.43 million and 22.4 percent, respectively. In general, younger generations show a much higher usage rate than older generations do, and the usage rate of the male population is somewhat higher than that of the female population. The rate of Internet usage is not significantly different among provincial regions, suggesting that the distribution of Internet users is similar to the male and female population distribution (Park 2004a).

However, there is a considerable difference in the usage rate between urban and rural areas. The average usage rates of large metropolitan areas, small and medium cities, and rural areas were 72.7 percent, 71.5 percent, and 50.9 percent, respectively, at the end of 2004. Overall, the data on the Internet usage rate suggest no significant differences in the access to the Internet infrastructure by regions (as between the capital region and other regions). But the rate does vary between rural and urban areas. This difference may have less to do with access to the Internet infrastructure than with the difference in the age distribution. In rural areas, the proportion of population over age 65 is much higher than in the urban areas. In 2000, the proportion of people in the older age groups in rural areas was 17.9 percent, while in the cities it was only 4.3 percent (KRNIC 2003).

Even though the regional disparity in the usage rate is not significant, .kr domains are concentrated in the capital region, which includes Gyeonggi province, Seoul, and Incheon. According to the survey by the Korea Network Information Center (KRNIC 2005), Seoul had 55.0 percent of the total number of .kr domains in August 2005, and the capital region had 75.9 percent of the total in Korea (see table 6.1). Although the share of .kr domains in Seoul decreased somewhat during 2003 to 2005, that of the capital region slightly increased. The higher concentration of .kr domains in the capital region might be related to some other factors that attract information and communication technology (ICT) firms in Seoul. The distribution of B2C e-marketplaces is also highly concentrated in the capital region; about 73 percent of the total number of B2C e-marketplaces are in Seoul (Choi 2003).

Firms operating B2B e-marketplaces are more concentrated in Seoul and its surrounding areas than are firms operating .kr domains. The capital region had a 79.5 percent share of the total firms operating B2B e-commerce sites in Korea in 2003 (table 6.1). The southeastern region, the second-largest industrial zone in Korea, had only 14.2 percent of the national total of such firms. If one considers only the public B2B e-marketplaces, which many sellers and buyers can access for transactions, the degree of concentration in the capital region is overwhelming. About 95 percent of the firms operating public B2B e-marketplaces are located in the capital region (Choi 2003). The predominance of Seoul, with a share of 84 percent of the total public B2B e-marketplaces, might be related

Table 6.1. Regional Share of .kr Domains and B2B e-Commerce Sites

Region	Population, 2000 (%)	.kr domains, 2003 (%)	.kr domains, 2005 (%)	B2B e-commerce sites, 2003 (%)
Capital region	46.3	74.9	75.9	79.5
Seoul	21.5	56.2	55.0	63.0
Incheon	5.4	3.4	3.4	3.0
Gyeonggi	19.5	15.3	17.5	13.5
Middle region	10.1	4.7	4.9	2.6
Daejeon	3.0	2.3	2.4	1.2
Chungbuk	3.2	1.2	1.1	0.9
Chungnam	3.9	1.2	1.4	0.5
Southwest region	11.3	4.6	4.0	3.7
Gwangju	2.9	2.3	1.8	1.6
Jeonbuk	4.1	1.3	1.3	1.9
Jeonnam	4.3	1.0	0.9	0.2
Southeast region	27.9	14.2	13.2	14.2
Busan	8.0	4.8	4.4	1.4
Daegu	5.4	4.1	3.7	2.3
Ulsan	2.2	0.9	0.8	2.6
Gyeongbuk	5.8	2.0	1.9	3.5
Gyeongnam	6.5	2.4	2.4	4.4
Gangwon	3.2	1.2	1.3	0.0
Jeju	1.1	0.5	0.5	0.0
Total	100.0	100.0	100.0	100.0

Source: KRNIC 2005; KNSO, 2003. The B2B e-commerce data are based on an internal source of the government.
Note: Because of rounding, sums may not total 100.

to the clustering of ICT firms, ICT-related spinoffs, and innovative entre-preneurs and knowledge workers in Seoul, especially in the Gangnam area (Park 2004a). ICT-related firms and advanced producer services are strongly concentrated in the Gangnam district within Seoul (Park and Choi 2005).

The overwhelming concentration of .kr domains, B2B e-commerce sites, and B2C e-commerce sites in Seoul points to a strong tendency for ICT firms to cluster in Seoul even though the Internet infrastructure (transferability) has been well provided throughout the country.

Clustering of ICT Firms in Seoul

The number of ICT-related firms in Korea has increased considerably in recent years. There were 25,637 firms in 1999, and 33,927 in 2003. Almost half of the firms (44.8 percent) in 2003 were concentrated in Seoul (table 6.2). The degree of concentration in Seoul differs by the

Table 6.2. Distribution of ICT Firms in Seoul, 1999 and 2003

District	Manufacturing (%)		Telecommunications (%)		Service (%)		Wholesale and renting (%)		ICT total (%)	
	1999	2003	1999	2003	1999	2003	1999	2003	1999	2003
Jongro	2.6	2.6	3.4	4.1	1.6	2.1	3.4	2.9	2.6	2.6
Jung	3.1	2.4	5.7	8.0	2.9	4.6	4.4	2.2	3.8	3.6
Yongsan	1.8	1.6	4.2	4.3	3.6	3.2	45.7	49.1	19.4	17.6
Seongdong	7.7	5.8	1.6	2.1	1.3	1.6	0.7	0.6	2.5	2.0
Gwangjin	2.9	2.0	2.9	2.9	3.4	3.3	3.0	1.4	3.1	2.5
Dongdaemun	2.2	1.8	1.9	2.0	1.6	1.4	0.9	0.5	1.5	1.2
Jungrang	2.5	1.5	0.5	0.6	0.3	0.8	0.3	0.3	0.8	0.7
Seongbuk	0.9	1.2	0.8	1.7	0.8	1.3	0.4	0.4	0.7	1.0
Gangbuk	1.0	0.9	0.6	1.5	0.3	0.6	0.1	0.3	0.4	0.6
Dobong	0.8	0.6	0.8	1.7	0.2	0.6	0.2	0.2	0.4	0.5
Nowon	1.6	1.3	1.0	1.4	0.5	0.7	0.2	0.2	0.7	0.7
Eunpyeong	1.4	0.7	0.7	0.5	0.3	0.7	0.3	0.3	0.6	0.6
Seodaemun	0.6	0.6	3.5	2.3	1.0	1.5	0.4	0.4	0.9	1.0
Mapo	3.0	2.3	3.7	3.7	4.3	5.2	2.9	3.3	3.4	4.0
Yangchon	4.2	4.5	1.4	3.2	0.8	2.4	0.5	0.9	1.5	2.3
Gangseo	4.9	4.7	2.4	1.1	1.1	1.9	1.0	1.3	2.0	2.1
Guro	13.4	17.5	2.1	2.8	1.8	6.2	3.5	4.5	5.1	7.5
Geumcheon	15.1	15.0	1.5	2.1	0.7	2.1	0.8	1.2	4.1	4.1
Yongdungpo	7.0	8.2	10.6	5.8	14.1	9.2	8.0	6.0	9.9	7.8
Dongjak	1.9	1.1	1.9	2.3	2.0	1.6	0.6	0.5	1.4	1.2
Gwanak	3.1	2.3	2.6	3.7	1.3	2.8	0.7	0.5	1.6	2.0
Seocho	7.2	7.3	17.9	11.8	20.8	14.8	9.5	10.1	13.2	11.8

(continued)

Table 6.2. Distribution of ICT Firms in Seoul, 1999 and 2003 (continued)

District	Manufacturing (%)		Telecommunications (%)		Service (%)		Wholesale and renting (%)		ICT total (%)	
	1999	2003	1999	2003	1999	2003	1999	2003	1999	2003
Gangnam	5.5	8.2	20.7	24.3	30.4	25.3	9.4	10.2	16.0	17.4
Songpa	3.4	4.2	5.3	4.4	3.9	5.1	2.3	2.5	3.3	4.1
Gangdong	2.0	1.6	2.4	1.7	1.0	1.2	0.6	0.5	1.2	1.1
Seoul (number of firms in parentheses)	100.0 (2,523)	100.0 (2,685)	100.0 (887)	100.0 (653)	100.0 (3,482)	100.0 (7,014)	100.0 (4,283)	100.0 (4,850)	100.0 (11,175)	100.0 (15,202)
Seoul (as a % of Korea)	24.25	22.59	31.47	30.66	69.97	56.06	59.71	65.56	44.31	44.81
Korea (number of firms)	10,404	11,888	2,819	2,130	5,241	12,511	7,173	7,398	25,637	33,927

Source: KNSO 2000, 2004.

type of firm. If the ICT-related firms are divided into four sectors— manufacturing, telecommunication, service, and wholesale and renting— several important location-related tendencies can be identified.

First, there is a trend toward spatial division of labor among the sectors of the ICT-related firms. Those in the service and the wholesale and renting sectors are far more concentrated in Seoul than are those in manufacturing, as seen in table 6.2. During the past decade, the number of ICT-related service firms in Seoul has increased about 700 percent, while the number of ICT-related manufacturing firms in Seoul has increased only 27 percent, reflecting the development of the service industry in Seoul. Considering the differences in terms of knowledge intensity and technology between Seoul and the provinces, as well as new core and other areas within Seoul, intensified spatial division of labor has progressed in the Internet era.

Second, there is a clear trend toward the concentration of providers in specific areas within Seoul. Five of 25 districts in Seoul—Yongsan (19.4 percent), Gangnam (16.0 percent), Seocho (13.2 percent), Yongdungpo (9.9 percent), and Guro (5.1 percent)—have more than a 5 percent share of the total ICT-related firms in Seoul (see table 6.2 and figure 6.1). Among the five districts, Yongdungpo and Guro are traditional industrial areas, while Gangnam and Seocho districts have developed since the 1970s. Yongsan is the only region located north of the Han River.

Third, each area specializes in certain types of ICT-related firms (figure 6.1). If one examines the distribution of the IT firms by the type of firm, each district has distinct characteristics. Yongsan district special-izes in ICT-related wholesale and renting firms. It has an electronic com-mercial zone where ICT-related wholesale firms dealing with various ICT-related products, services, and rental activities are concentrated. Gangnam and Seocho districts are newly developed core areas of Seoul since the 1980s and specialize in ICT-related services such as computer software and engineering. Advanced producer services are clustered in Gangnam and Seocho districts (Park and Nahm 1998). Yongdungpo district, which is relatively specialized in ICT-related services and man-ufacturing, was regarded as one of three clusters of advanced services in Seoul, but its role is currently diminishing. Yongdungpo was traditionally an industrial area, but the district was restructured with the entry of the National Assembly and major financial firms in Yeoeido. The most interesting district is Guro, which is the most specialized in ICT-related manufacturing activities in Seoul. A noticeable trend is the rapid growth in ICT-related services (table 6.2).

Figure 6.1. Distribution of ICT-Related Firms in Seoul, 1999–2003

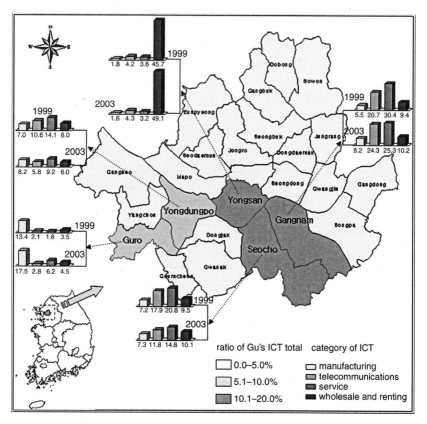

Fourth, there is a spatial dispersion trend within Seoul. Three of the five ICT core districts lost their share of firms between 1999 and 2003, reflecting a trend toward spatial redistribution. Yongdungpo and Yongsan lost a considerable part of their share of ICT-related industries while Gangnam and Guro gained a part. Among the 20 districts of low concentration, 10 districts increased their shares while 6 districts decreased their shares between 1999 and 2003. It is notable that Guro district increased its share about 50 percent from 1999 to 2003 (table 6.2). The spatial restructuring trend within Seoul can be also seen from the distribution of venture firms, most of which have close connections with ICT-related firms. In 2001, venture firms of Seoul were concentrated in the districts of Gangnam (34.4 percent); Seocho (17.7 percent), and Yongdungpo (7.6 percent). These three districts have continuously lost shares of firms during the past five years. However, Guro and nearby Geumcheon districts increased their shares significantly from 2.7 percent to 9.1 percent and from 2.1 percent to 8.3 percent, respectively, during this period (http://www.venturenet.or.kr). Gangnam district is still the most important area in both clusters of ICT-related firms and clusters of venture firms. Guro district has been the most dynamic area in Seoul. It has seen a rapid increase of ICT-related firms and venture firms after renaming its core production area the Seoul Digital Industrial Complex (previously the Guro Industrial Complex).

Restructuring of ICT Clusters in Seoul

During the past decade, ICT clusters in Seoul have taken two distinct forms: first, the natural formation of ICT clusters that comprise networks of knowledge-based advanced services and, second, the concentration of ICT-related firms following the restructuring of the existing industrial system. The development of a new core in the Gangnam area and the restructuring of the Guro Industrial Complex represent the two distinct cases. The development of innovation networks is the major characteristic in the Gangnam area, whereas the recent concentration of ICT venture firms in the newly constructed office-apartment complexes is the major characteristic in Seoul Digital Industrial Complex in Guro district.

Spatial Networks of Innovation in Gangnam, Seoul

Gangnam, a geographic name for the Gangnam and Seocho districts, has become Seoul's new core for economic activities. Gangnam features numerous modern high-rise office buildings. Since the late 1980s, advanced services such as software, engineering, advertising, and design have concentrated in the Gangnam area (Park and Nahm 1998). This process intensified after the financial crises in 1997, with the agglomeration of start-ups in high-tech and software sectors. Many large ICT firms and start-ups are located along Teheran Road, which crosses the Gangnam area from east to west (Shin and others 2001). It has been called "Teheran Valley" because of the overwhelming concentration of ICT firms, advanced service firms, and other high-tech firms. Foreign direct investment in producer services is also concentrated in the area. The concentration of new start-ups, high-tech firms, and R&D institutions of private firms has made this area an innovation center in Korea. Even though the degree of concentration in Gangnam has weakened since 2001, it remains the major cluster of ICT firms.

Supporting infrastructure such as ICT infrastructure and office buildings is excellent. Collective learning processes with formal and informal meetings can be regarded as a distinct culture of Gangnam. The area also hosts international conferences and exhibitions in local convention centers or hotels. There are no leading research universities within Gangnam, but top-ranking research universities and various private R&D centers are located nearby in Seoul.

Gangnam can be regarded as the major learning region in Korea, and it also benefits from collective learning through intensive local networks. According to a survey conducted in 2001 (Gang Nam Gu 2002), about 31 percent of the local firms regard the Internet as the most important source for the acquisition of codified knowledge related to product and process technology (figure 6.2). Related books and journals, exhibitions and trade fairs, and conferences are also regarded as important sources for the acquisition of knowledge by a considerable percentage of surveyed firms.

The sources of tacit knowledge are a completely different story. About one-third of the responding firms regarded R&D activity within firms as the most important source for acquisition of tacit knowledge regarding product and process technology (figure 6.3). However, personal relations and interfirm relations are also important sources of knowledge. For product technology, more than one-fourth of firms regard the personal

Figure 6.2. Sources of Codified Knowledge of Product and Process Technology

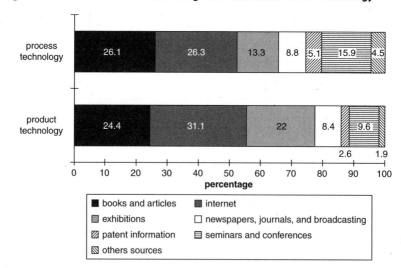

Source: Gang Nam Gu 2002.

Figure 6.3. Sources of Tacit Knowledge of Product and Process Technology

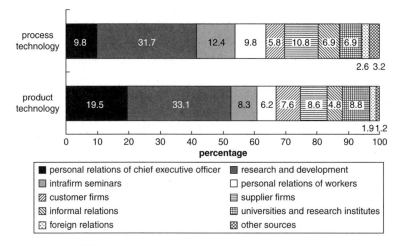

Source: Gang Nam Gu 2002.

relations of the chief executive officer and employees as the most important sources for the tacit knowledge. More than 16 percent of the firms regard suppliers or customers as important sources as well.

The survey results presented in figure 6.3 show that formal and informal relations with personnel and institutions are more important sources for acquisition of tacit knowledge for product and process technology than formal R&D activities. This result is consistent with the survey conducted by the Organisation for Economic Co-operation and Development (OECD) showing that R&D costs comprised only 33.5 percent of the innovation expenditures of the OECD countries (OECD 1999). Informal and formal meetings are important for the acquisition of the tacit knowledge. Entrepreneurs in the Gangnam area have on average two formal meetings and three informal meetings per month. There are many informal meeting groups, such as the E-Business Club, the Software Industry Club, the Network Communication Club, the Venture Leaders Club, and the I-Partnership. These groups bring together many entrepreneurs, engineers, university professors, and venture capitalists to share their information and knowledge.

Spatial networks of innovation in Gangnam are highly localized. Venture firms in Gangnam have strong innovation and cooperative networks with firms, entrepreneurs, private research centers, venture capitalists, professional consultants, and other business services. They also have strong cooperative networks with universities and entrepreneurs located in Seoul outside the Gangnam area. They have relatively weak networks with innovation clusters outside the Gangnam area and with foreign firms. Compared with firms in other industrial or innovation clusters in Korea, firms in the Gangnam area have relatively strong localized networks, revealing that networking and collaboration is an important part of clustering.

It should be noted, however, that firms in Gangnam do network with foreign firms. About 11 percent of firms responding to the survey (Gang Nam Gu 2002) regard foreign firms as contributing to their innovation activities. Another survey result from Park (2002) shows that about 12 percent of firms in Guro Industrial Park, which is located in Seoul, have innovation networks with foreign firms, and only 8 percent of firms in Gumi Industrial Park, which is located in the southeastern part of Korea, have such innovation networks.

Some Korean ethnic networks are in Silicon Valley as well. The Korean American Association of Entrepreneurs has about 2,000 members. The Korean American Professional Society, Korean American Chamber of Commerce of Silicon Valley, and Silicon Valley Korean IT Forum also have many members. The Korean government supports new start-ups, such as I-Park, in the ICT sector by members of the Korean diaspora in Silicon Valley. Korean engineers and entrepreneurs in Silicon Valley also have connections with the Gangnam area, providing flows of information, marketing services, and employees. Korean high-tech firms such as Samsung, LG, and Hyundai have invested in R&D activities in Silicon Valley, helping to connect the knowledge economies of Seoul and Silicon Valley. Gangnam also maintains international networks with innovation clusters in China and India. Overall, firms in the Gangnam area have strong localized networks of innovation leading to knowledge generation and diffusion. The Gangnam area is also a part of innovation networks at regional, national, and international levels. However, the collective learning process within the Gangnam area is more important for innovation than for national and international networks, which suggests that a localized innovation cluster is evolving.

Restructuring of the Guro Industrial Complex into the Seoul Digital Industrial Complex

The former Guro Industrial Complex, located in the southwestern part of Seoul, developed in the late 1960s and early 1970s as a result of the Korean government's export-oriented industrial policy. It was the first national export industrial district and took a leading role in Korea's industrialization in the 1970s. At first, the Guro Industrial Complex specialized in textiles and apparel—the leading export industry in the 1960s and 1970s. In the late 1980s and early 1990s, however, the Guro Industrial District was restructured following labor disputes. These disputes and the rapid rise in wages resulted in the closure of foreign firms and small domestic firms and in the relocation of large plants to other areas. The remaining firms in the Guro Industrial District were vulnerable in the late 1980s and early 1990s. Accordingly, many labor-intensive factories of the textile and apparel industries were restructured so as to maintain or regain competitive advantage.

Four major strategies of restructuring were pursued in the capital region: flexible labor strategy with employment of foreign guest workers and more part-time workers; increased use of subcontracting activities to save costs; research to promote product innovation and improvement of productivity; and foreign direct investment in low-cost areas such as China and Southeast Asia. During the late 1980s and early 1990s, the number of firms and employees in Guro Industrial Complex decreased considerably.

Since the late 1990s, the Guro Industrial Complex has experienced a second industrial change and now specializes in ICT-related industries. During the financial crisis at the end of 1997, labor-intensive factories in the Guro Industrial Complex lost their competitive edge. They attempted to regain their competitiveness by reorganizing so as to improve productivity and, in some cases, by completely shifting their business focus to ICT-related products. Accordingly, in 2000, the National Industrial Complex Management Organization sought to redevelop the Guro Industrial Complex into an ICT cluster and renamed the complex the Seoul Digital Industrial Complex (SDIC). This action has reinvigorated the area and attracted many ICT-related firms. In recent years, many venture firms have also moved into the newly constructed high-rise industrial building (an office-apartment plant).

The number of software firms increased from 16 in 2001 to 281 in 2005. Firms related to the electronic and information equipment industry increased from 303 in 2001 to 995 in 2005. In addition to the Gangnam area, SDIC is now regarded as an emerging ICT cluster.

According to a survey conducted in summer, 2005, the cooperative networks of the ICT firms in SDIC have several notable features. For R&D purposes, 34 percent of the networks are within SDIC and 52 percent are in Seoul outside SDIC. For other purposes, however, most cooperative networks are established with firms or institutions outside

SDIC. For marketing purposes, 83 percent of the cooperative networks are established with institutions in Seoul outside SDIC. For production purposes, Gyeonggi province is the most important region, with almost one-half of the cooperative networks. The pattern of the cooperative networks suggests the presence of strong local and regional networks, as well as the importance of a regional innovation system within the capital region outside SDIC. Some small and medium-size firms that are not leading-edge technology firms relocated from the Gangnam area to the Guro area because of the high rental costs in Gangnam. Many firms in SDIC have networks with advanced services in the Gangnam area, suggesting that there is a hierarchical distribution of activities between the Gangnam and Guro areas.

Responding to the recent trend toward strong local and regional networks of R&D and technical services, the National Industrial Complex Management Organization is promoting the development of innovative ICT clusters. For the establishment of innovative clusters, three major strategies are suggested: provision of support programs, improvement of the innovation environment, and leadership creation for cluster formation. Establishment of a center supporting software industry is also suggested for functions such as workforce training, R&D, and the e-learning industry.

Conclusion

This chapter analyzes major characteristics of the dynamics of economic space in the knowledge-based economy of Seoul, focusing on the concentration and restructuring processes of ICT industries in the Gangnam area and the Seoul Digital Industrial Complex.

Four characteristics of the dynamics of economic spaces are identified: (a) the intensified spatial division of labor, (b) the clustering of advanced services and the Internet industry, (c) a globalized network of services, and (d) virtual innovation clusters.

Even in the era of globalization and the Internet, regions are critical for innovation process because regional clustering allows for interfirm networks and collaboration, promotes learning through interactive processes, and provides a territorial dimension. Collective learning processes through formal and informal meetings, interfirm cooperation and competition, intrafirm networks, and interorganizational collaborations are needed for local networks of innovation. The pattern of spatial innovation networks differs, however, depending on the type of innovation system.

Even though the ICT sector is subject to dispersal, advanced knowledge-intensive services tend to concentrate in Seoul, especially in the Gangnam area. Within Seoul, there is a clear trend toward the specialization of each cluster.

Among the four characteristics of the dynamics of economic spaces, the virtual innovation cluster was not discussed in this chapter. In rural areas such as Sunchang and Gochang of southwestern Korea, virtual innovation networks have developed, with collaboration on a national scale through the Internet and periodic face-to-face meetings for sharing knowledge (Park 2004b). The potential exists for creating a virtual innovation cluster in Seoul with international collaboration.

To maintain and regain their competitive advantages, ICT clusters in Seoul need to pursue new strategies. The most important strategy could be the successful development of innovation systems that link local firms to regional, national, and international networks. The local and regional innovation systems can be strengthened by tapping into the global networks of information, knowledge, and technology. Collective learning processes are critical for the development of these innovation systems. To overcome the distance effect, ICT clusters can promote and support virtual innovation systems at the international level. The formation of local networks of innovation and of collective learning processes is critical for the evolution of regional innovation systems. However, the development of regional innovation systems is not limited to the regional dimension or to a closed regional system. Local, regional, national, and global systems are all interlinked in the network of innovation. Innovation clusters in the global spatial economy are linked to each other beyond the regional or national boundary, suggesting that spatial innovation systems beyond the national or regional innovation systems are evolving. Global innovation systems are evolving in the era of the Internet and knowledge-based economy. The dynamic evolution of spatial innovation systems suggests that different geographic configurations should be considered for regional development and regional competitive advantage in a networked world. Workforce training and retraining in the restructuring processes are also important. The government should continue to emphasize education, training, and learning mechanisms for the enhancement of competitive advantages of the ICT clusters.

Local and regional innovation strategies, such as provision of a venture habitat, formation of social capital, enhancement of innovation networks, and promotion of global networks should be considered major strategies for competitive ICT clusters (Park 2001). Overall, the development of the ICT cluster in Seoul should be closely linked to the promotion of a creative city based on local culture, learning festivals, and a club culture for collective learning to ensure the integration of local resources with ICT.

References

Bryson, John R., Peter W. Daniels, and Barney Warf. 2004. *Service World: People, Organisations, Technologies*. London: Routledge.

Castells, Manuel. 2000. *The Rise of Network Society*. Vol. 1 of *The Information Age: Economy, Society, and Culture* (2nd ed.), Oxford, U.K.: Blackwell.

Choi, Ji-Sun. 2003. "Public B2B Electronic Marketplaces: A Spatial Perspective." Ph.D. dissertation, Department of Geography, Seoul National University, Seoul.

Christaller, Walter. 1966. *Central Places in Southern Germany*, Trans. Carlisle W. Baskins. Englewood Cliffs, NJ: Prentice-Hall.

Clark, Gordon L. 1981. "The Employment Relation and the Spatial Division of Labor." *Annals of the Association of American Geographers* 71: 412–24.

Clark, Terry Nichols, and Richard Lloyd. 2000. *The City as an Entertainment Machine*. Chicago: University of Chicago Press.

Daniels, Peter W., Kong Chong Ho, and Tom A. Hutton, eds. 2005. *Service Industries and Asia-Pacific Cities*. London: Routledge.

Gang Nam Gu. 2002. *Analysis of Venture Environment and Long-Term Plan of Teheran Valley*, Gang Nam Gu, Seoul.

Gereffi, Gary, and Miguel Korzeniewicz, eds. 1994. *Commodity Chains and Global Capitalism*. Westport, CT: Greenwood Press.

Glaeser, Edward L., Jed Kolko, and Albert Saiz. 2001. "Consumer City." *Journal of Economic Geography* 1 (1): 27–50.

Hayter, Roger. 1997. *The Dynamics of Industrial Location: The Factory, the Firm, and the Production System*. Chichester, U.K.: John Wiley.

KNSO (Korean National Statistical Office). Various years. "Result of EC Statistical Survey." KNSO, Seoul.

KRNIC (Korea Network Information Center). Various years. "Internet Survey." http://isis.nic.or.kr.

Lösch, Auguste. 1954. *The Economics of Location*. New Haven, CT: Yale University Press.

Maskell, Peter, and Anders Malmberg. 1999. "Localized Learning and Industrial Competitiveness." *Cambridge Journal of Economics* 23 (2): 167–85.

Massey, Doreen. 1984. *Spatial Division of Labor: Social Structure and the Geography of Production*. London: Macmillan.

Nonaka, Ikujiro, and Hirotaka Takeuchi. 1995. *The Knowledge-Creating Company: How Japanese Companies Create the Dynamics of Innovation*. Oxford, U.K.: Oxford University Press.

OECD (Organisation for Economic Co-operation and Development). 1999. *Boosting Innovation: The Cluster Approach*. Paris: OECD.

Park, Sam Ock. 1993. "Industrial Restructuring and the Spatial Division of Labor: The Case of the Seoul Metropolitan Region, the Republic of Korea." *Environment and Planning A* 25 (1): 81–93.

———. 2001. "Regional Innovation Strategies in the Knowledge-Based Economy." *GeoJournal* 53 (1): 29–38.

———. 2002. "Industry in a Networked World: Globalization and Localization of Industry." *Journal of Korean Geographical Society* 37 (2): 111–30.

———. 2003. "Economic Spaces in the Pacific Rim: A Paradigm Shift and New Dynamics." *Papers in Regional Science* 82 (2): 223–47.

———. 2004a. "The Impact of Business-to-Business Electronic Commerce on the Dynamics of Metropolitan Spaces." *Urban Geography* 25 (4): 289–314.

———. 2004b. "Service Worlds and Dynamics of Economic Spaces." Paper presented at the annual residential conference of the International Geographical Union Commission on the Dynamics of Economic Spaces, Birmingham, U.K., August 10–14.

———. 2005. "Network, Embeddedness, and Cluster Processes of New Economic Spaces in Korea." In *New Economic Spaces: New Economic Geographies*, ed. Richard B. Le Heron and James W. Harrington, 6–14. Aldershot, U.K.: Ashgate.

Park, Sam Ock, and Ji Sun Choi. 2005. "IT Service Industries and the Transformation of Seoul." In *Service Industries and Asia-Pacific Cities*, ed. Peter W. Daniels, Kong Chong Ho, and Tom A. Hutton, 301–20. London: Routledge.

Park, Sam Ock, and Kee-Bom Nahm. 1998. "Spatial Structure and Inter-firm Networks of Technical and Information Producer Services in Seoul, Korea." *Asia Pacific Viewpoints* 39 (2): 209–19.

Park, Sam Ock, and James O. Wheeler. 1983. "The Filtering Down Process in Georgia: The Third Stage in the Product Life Cycle." *Professional Geographer* 35 (1): 18–31.

Shin, C. H., B. S. Jeong, C. D. Kang, and R. H. Kim. 2001. *Clustering Information Technology Industries in Seoul*. Seoul: Seoul Development Institute.

Timmers, Paul. 2000. *Electronic Commerce: Strategies and Models for Business-to-Business Trading*. Chichester, U.K.: John Wiley.

Ullman, Edward L. 1957. *American Commodity Flow: A Geographical Interpretation of Rail and Water Traffic Based on Principles of Spatial Interaction*. Seattle: University of Washington Press.

Vernon, Raymond. 1966. "International Investment and International Trade in the Product Life Cycle." *Quarterly Journal of Economics* 80 (2): 190–207.

Yeh, Anthony G. O. 2005. "Producer Services and Industrial Linkages in the Hong Kong–Pearl River Delta Region." In *Service Industries and Asia-Pacific Cities*, ed. Peter W. Daniels, Kong Chong Ho, and Tom A. Hutton, 150–72. London: Routledge.

Zook, Matthew A. 2005. *The Geography of the Internet Industry*. Oxford, U.K.: Blackwell.

CHAPTER 7

Constructing Jurisdictional Advantage in a Mature Economy

The Case of Kitakyushu, Japan

Maryann P. Feldman

Economic growth is a local process, and city-industry clusters are an important economic unit in generating innovation, competitiveness, and prosperity. Local intangible assets are becoming key factors in companies' realized competitive advantage, and a growing body of evidence suggests that firms located near similar and supporting firms enjoy higher productivity growth, are more innovative, grow faster, and pay higher wages. Although these advantages are documented in the literature, they are of more than academic interest. All levels of political jurisdictions—nations, regions, and cities—engage in policy initiatives concerned with generating economic growth, ensuring the stability of their local economies, and guaranteeing the quality of the environment for their citizens. Current economic development theory tends to be descriptive (focusing on the characteristics of clusters) or normative (advocating clusters as an economic growth policy). A prescriptive theory is needed: Given a location in a particular situation with a limited set of given resources, what might the government do to create the conditions supporting economic growth? What strategy should the government pursue to provide long-term sustainable results (Feldman and Martin 2005a, 2005b)? Constructing an appropriate economic development strategy is especially a problem for mature regions with industries facing structural realignment and the loss of jobs because of deindustrialization.

This chapter considers the case of technology-based economic development in a mature economy. Although many candidates, such as Pittsburgh, Pennsylvania; Detroit, Michigan; Cleveland, Ohio; or Manchester, England, come to mind, this chapter focuses on Kitakyushu in Japan. Once a vibrant steel-producing, heavy manufacturing, and shipping center, the region is struggling to reposition itself in an increasingly globally competitive economy. The first section of the chapter adapts the theory of jurisdictional advantage proposed by Feldman and Martin (2005a, 2005b) to mature economies. The second section provides a synthesis of the concept, which considers how communities may position themselves strategically in order to create opportunities for future economic growth. The argument is that every jurisdiction has unique assets that may be built on to construct a coherent set of activities that would be difficult for others to copy. The third section examines the particular problems of mature, deindustrialized regions in general, and the fourth section considers the Kitakyushu region specifically. It is difficult to figure out what useful cluster building is, who the relevant actors are, and—perhaps most importantly—what activities to avoid. The fact that clusters provide economic benefits does not imply that they can be easily built. In some cases, the costs may outweigh the potential benefits or the timelines may be so long that they are politically infeasible. The final section considers how place-specific advantages might be constructed in the Kitakyushu region and in similar declining regions.

What Is Jurisdictional Advantage?

Borrowing from corporate strategy, one could say advantage results either from lower costs relative to the firm's competition or from the production of a set of attributes that are uniquely valued by the market (Porter 1980, 1985). Such advantages are based on the construction of unique activity systems, which are defined as a coherent web of activities. Taken together, these activity sets provide an advantage because the individual activities and components fit well together and actually reinforce each other. Hence, it is difficult, if not impossible, for competitors to replicate a successful firm's strategy. Thus, the essence of strategy is to construct an activity set that allows the firm to perform differently—or to perform different activities—from the competition.

Jurisdictions may benefit from adapting a similar strategic orientation and building an activity system that is unique, not easily replicated, and valuable in producing either a low cost or a differentiation advantage over other places. Feldman and Martin (2005b) identify the Hollywood movie industry and the New York fashion industry as examples of industries that were able to translate an initial cost advantage into a sustained international competitive advantage. These examples are illustrative of high-wage industrial activity based on the employment of highly skilled labor. These industries and others succeeded through the construction of an activity set that yielded an advantage based on differentiation that offered new business models and creative solutions to consumer problems. The literature contains a large number of detailed and carefully constructed case studies about different industries and the genesis of the specific place clusters (see, for example, Braunerhjelm and Feldman 2007).

The current obsession with outsourcing suggests that seeking out locations with low wages is a possible competitive firm strategy; however, there is an important difference between paying low wages and being a low-cost competitor able to achieve greater efficiency. In a global economy where unskilled labor is inexpensive, transportation and communication costs are negligible, and raw materials matter little, skilled human capital, referred to as *talent*, is becoming an important competitive asset for firms and places (Caves 2002; Florida 2000). When talent and human capital are important, relying on lower real wages is not a viable strategy for long-term competitive advantage. Producing talent requires investments in human capital and incentives that motivate individuals to make investment in their own human capital, engage their talents, and be creative. Moreover, talented individuals do not work alone, and innovative activity requires teams of people working together in resource-rich environments. Indeed, talent may be recognized only in specialized settings where genius is encouraged, appreciated, and appropriately rewarded.

What allowed Hollywood and New York to differentiate themselves was the construction of a reinforcing activity set based on talent, professional and trade associations, training programs, and interfirm relationships that both promote and define the industry. Geography provides a platform for organizing economic activity, and the local place is, at its most basic, a collection of those activities. However, when the components fit together, the place is greater than the sum of its parts. That is to say, a coherent and reinforcing set of activities provides advantage. Without engaging a variety of economic agents and supporting institutions, a place may not achieve primacy within an industry. Moreover, rather than simply replicating existing successful clusters, each place must define its unique advantages. The focus should be on things that are not easily replicated, on activities that are reinforcing, and on the coevolution of firms, industries, and resources.

A long-standing literature examines the hierarchy of places and the ordering of locations on the basis of their population size, diversity of the local economy, and specialization in higher-order economic functions (see Henderson 2005 for a review). The world's largest cities, because of their size, have advantages associated with urbanization economies that make it difficult for other places to compete against them. In a knowledge economy subject to increasing returns to scale, the largest cities— Beijing, London, New York, and Tokyo—attract immigrants. Talented individuals are drawn by opportunities in large urban areas; their migration leaves their places of origin at a disadvantage. However, individuals will stay in locations only if there are jobs for them. Places that are suffering net outmigration need to define an advantage. Perhaps one important element of defining advantages and setting realistic goals is an understanding of how a place fits into the national and international urban hierarchy. Unrealistic goals, follower strategies, and bidding wars for firms or talent do not provide a viable long-term strategy.

Jurisdictional strategy is the result of collective choices made over time that shape the local culture, the mix of incentives, and the composition of industries. There is not always a clear and conscious coordination of choices to produce a strategy. Human societies are complex, self-organizing systems: many times outcomes reflect choices made with no coordination or specific outcome in mind or even reflect the unintended consequences of some other, unrelated decision. Nevertheless, over time these choices accumulate to form the basis for what the jurisdiction actually does, and they provide a deep, historical context for understanding what is unique about a place. And as with corporations, strategy is what is actually done, not what is articulated as an objective or corporate motto. Strategy, ultimately, is the result of choices and actions, not proclamations or processes.

The two desired metrics of jurisdictional strategy that are particularly salient for evaluating the success of a place are relative wages and the market value of real estate (Feldman and Martin 2005a). Both are measures of local wealth. A jurisdiction succeeds to the extent that its overall set of choices and actions produces high—and rising—real wage levels and property values. If wage levels are higher than in other comparable places, the jurisdiction is currently translating its human, physical, monetary, and other capital into higher economic output per worker than are other locations. Rising wages indicate an increase in relative effectiveness rather than regression toward the mean. For most of the world's population, equity in a principal residence represents a person's single largest investment asset. The value of jurisdictional amenities and the local quality of life is capitalized into housing prices: more amenities translate into higher property values. When the majority of the population own homes, increases in property values are broadly distributed across the population, and this wealth enables individuals to invest in education and to take risks in starting new companies. Moreover, increases in property values yield higher tax revenues, which, if used judiciously, further increase amenities and increase the attractiveness of a place and attract in-migrants. In this way, virtuous cycles of economic growth are created.

Jurisdictional strategy at the level of the city is particularly important, because the literature on clustering and agglomeration increasingly suggests that smaller and more compact geographic units are critical to the performance of industries (Feldman and Audretsch 1998; Lambooy 2002; Porter 2000). National and state governments, especially in a federalist system, are important contributors to the strategies of cities and provide the institutional framework within which their constituent counties and cities operate. However, if those factors are held constant, the fundamental differences in performance appear to derive from the choices made by actors in the city. As a consequence, the most appropriate focus for questions of jurisdictional strategy is at the city level. Although national and state-level policies are important in setting the stage, the true effect will be at the local level.

The jurisdictional activity system is not the product of any of one actor or class of actors—not firms, not individuals, not governments, not universities. An advantaged jurisdiction contains an activity system that combines multiple, reinforcing and interrelated actors. Moreover, constructing jurisdictional advantage takes the commitment of all the various actors—a consensus vision of what is achievable that is based on the unique context of the place and that acknowledges the strengths and limitations of the actors. Each actor needs to ask what unique contribution it can make to the activity system and then must mobilize resources toward making that contribution. Investments in the local activity set increase the competitiveness of individual firms: entrepreneurs build clusters while they build their firms (Feldman, Francis, and Bercovitz 2005). Governments can play a coordinating role; however, the commitment of firms, industry associations, and other nongovernmental entities is critical. Firms may act opportunistically and simply exploit the jurisdiction, demanding tax breaks and special concessions, only to abandon the place when another jurisdiction makes another bid. However, a firm is better served by being an active partner in creating jurisdictional advantage, rather than a passive exploiter of the jurisdiction's resources.

When firms have a presence in a jurisdiction that is advantageous to their objectives, they have an incentive to build resources to make the jurisdiction better. Proximity makes knowledge spillovers possible. The existence of spatially mediated externalities suggests that firms receive benefits that are outside of the ability of the market to price and efficiently allocate. Although it can be argued that firms pay more taxes as a result of the higher profits they earn on externalities, it can also be argued that firms can and should actively cultivate the sources of the agglomerative benefits by investing in local universities, industry associations, and training programs and by building community and infrastructure so that the jurisdiction proves to be more advantageous for that firm's future activity. Moreover, in many instances these investments are tax deductible and provide a means to make targeted investments in jurisdictions, rather than relying on the process of government budgeting. That is to say, firms may actively build the external resources and infrastructure that benefit their bottom line.

The problem of guiding an economy, especially one that is mature and restructuring, is complex, and there are no quick, easy fixes. Consultants can drop in and advocate a turnkey solution focusing on a limited set of industries that are perceived to be future engines of economic growth. However, these strategies have been sold to other places countless times before and cannot create an enduring advantage. The next section considers the limiting factors that face mature economies and offers some guidelines for crafting jurisdictional advantage aimed at restructuring a local economy.

Constructing Jurisdictional Advantage in a Mature Economy

Regions with mature industries face a multitude of challenges in creating jurisdictional advantage. Older industrial places are characterized by an aging infrastructure and a preponderence of brownfield sites that are difficult to reuse. Such places often face a degraded and polluted natural environment. These problems are exacerbated when prior economic success and expectations about profitability and the scale of activity further inhibit openness to considering new opportunities. Moreover, the immediate needs of ameliorating the effects of job loss and the erosion of the economic base take precedent over long-term strategic thinking. Pittsburgh, Pennsylvania; Buffalo, New York; Detroit, Michigan; Cleveland, Ohio; Glasgow, Scotland; and Manchester, England are often-used examples of industrial cities that have faced economic restructuring (Lever 1991; Rappaport 2003). These cities are associated with their prior industrial successes, and changing a city's image or brand has proven difficult.

The essence of strategy, most simply, is turning a weakness into a strength and a threat into an opportunity. It requires an inventory of the activities in a place and an understanding of how these activities fare and what factors limit their future potential.

Strategy is more about adaptation and process than about rigid adherence to plan. Having a plan is important, because it provides structure and allows dialogue, networking, and construction of consensus about a shared future. However, it is difficult to anticipate the future direction of new technologies and market changes, and the best that a jurisdiction can do is to be prepared to act when an opportunity presents itself. In a mature economy, the activities that previously provided success can prevent change (Grabher 1993; Kaufmann and Tödtling 2000; Tödtling 1992). This is a classic case of path dependency and lock-in, which may inhibit change (Arthur 1994; David 1997). The concept of path dependency, while at first glance deterministic, may be reconceptualized as a source of advantage to build on. Such reconceptualization is the essence of constructing advantage. Douglass North (1990: 98–99) argues, "At every step of the way, there are choices—political and economic—that provided real alternatives. Path dependence is a way to narrow conceptually the choice set and link decision-making through time. It is not a story of inevitability in which the past neatly predicts the future." The history of the place and its trajectory define what is unique about that place that might become the source of jurisdictional advantage—something that will not be easily duplicated by other places and that provides a basis for economic growth.

Restructuring may require a significant change in expectations about profit margins, labor relationships, skill requirements, and the use of strategic alliances. Though many places have made concerted efforts to stop their economic decline—using a mixture of urban renewal and rebranding strategies to attract new residents, offering economic incentives to attract new businesses, and addressing environmental problems left by heavy industry—successfully transforming a declining city requires a long, sustained commitment. Pittsburgh, for example, has been working to revitalize and diversify its economy since the steel mills closed in the early 1980s. Nonprofit development organizations have been established to promote new employment opportunities through education and retraining, and significant resources have been oriented toward industrial redevelopment and improving housing (Yeum 2004). Local universities—notably Carnegie Mellon—have engaged in developing science parks and incubators with good results. Despite these efforts and pockets of success, Pittsburgh's population continues to decline (Rappaport 2003), and the city's median household income—US$28,588—remains well below the national average of US$41,994. Still, Pittsburgh has fared better than similar cities in what is colorfully known as the U.S. rust belt.

Around the world, policy makers seem to be enamored with entrepreneurship, and the dialogue on restructuring often emphasizes entrepreneurs who seize emerging opportunities and start new firms, thereby creating jobs and contributing to economic growth. The success of the U.S. economy leads many others to try to emulate the success of Silicon Valley and other technology-based places in the United States. Although entrepreneurship has captured the imagination of economic development officials, transferring it to other areas of the United States has proven difficult, and while successful entrepreneurial centers look similar, the process that creates their success emphasizes different attributes.

There are some additional problems with entrepreneurship in mature economies. Entrepreneurs tend to start firms in places where they previously worked and in the same or similar industries. Regions with mature manufacturing industries may have difficulty relying on entrepreneurs, as their employment was in an economically disadvantaged sector facing declining demand. Moreover, mature manufacturing industries frequently have high barriers to entry, and even if niche markets such as specialty steel may be identified, it is difficult for entrepreneurs to enter those industries. There have been successful adaptations to specialty steel using minimills technology in mature regions that previously had successful steel industries based on blast furnaces; however, these cases required large public sector investments (D'Costa 1999).

It is difficult to imagine that American-style entrepreneurship would be easy to motivate in more traditional and collective societies such as Japan. Entrepreneurship is about risk taking and the potential of supranormal returns that motivate the effort required. Often left unmentioned are the costs of entrepreneurship, which are borne by individuals and their families. If the endeavor succeeds, the entrepreneur is amply compensated;

yet it is well known that most new ventures fail: only 1 in 10 is expected to grow and be in existence within four years. It is difficult to envision American-style entrepreneurship in a society that does not embrace failure as a routine outcome. There may be other more efficient and socially harmonious ways to organize innovative effort in a place that has collective views of society. A new variety of entrepreneurship is needed that exemplifies the appreciation of differences among places—differences described in the literature on adapted varieties of capitalism (Hall and Soskice 2004). It should be possible to have varieties of entrepreneurship that build on societal values and cultural traditions. Moreover, the emphasis on entrepreneurship typically ignores the potential to revitalize existing firms and to encourage established firms to grow and find new markets, activities that are equally entrepreneurial and potentially offer high-growth opportunities.

The next section examines the specific case of the Japanese city of Kitakyshu to see how restructuring is taking place in one mature local economy and to offer an example of how the sources of advantage may be inventoried and investigated.

Constructing Advantage in Kitakyushu

Kitakyushu, located in the north of the most western of the four main islands of Japan, was formally established in 1963 with the merger of five smaller towns: Moji, Kokura, Yawata, Wakamatsu, and Tobata. In this manner, a series of small contiguous cities, recognizing their mutual dependence, formed a larger and more coherent economic unit that would promote their mutual interests as a modern industrial city with an important port. At the core of the region, a dynamic and prosperous steel industry developed during the first half of the 20th century. At the center of the industry and region was the Yawata Steel Works, which was established in 1901 by the government of Japan, merged with other private firms in 1934, and later renamed Nippon Steel.

Steel and later chemicals were the traditional twin industrial pillars of the region. In the 1970s, the newly emerging semiconductor industry was drawn to Kyushu by the availability of lower-cost labor, abundant water resources, reliable and cheap hydropower, and convenient access to air transport through five well-serviced airports. Producers of wafers, dynamic random access memories (DRAMs), and later integrated circuits (ICs) and their supporting firms spread all across Kyushu, which then came to be known as Japan's Silicon Island. This industry remains a major force, although DRAM production has long since departed to other East Asian countries, and Japan's share of wafer fabrication is a fraction of what it once was.

A third industry began moving into Kyushu during the 1980s: automobiles. The automobile industry also was attracted by lower wage and rental costs and the relative ease of shipping to overseas markets through Kitakyushu and other ports. This industry also has expanded, and local firms have diversified into auto parts production from their core businesses in electronics or metallurgy because the auto industry increasingly requires their expertise to make lighter, smarter, more fuel-efficient cars.

Green Technologies

A fourth new industry that is striking roots might arguably have the most potential over the longer term and could spawn a cluster in Kitakyushu by harnessing the industrial capabilities that have been accumulated by the electronics industry and by firms servicing the auto assemblers and the traditional heavy industries. This industry is green technologies, including renewable energy and environmental remediation. The green technologies industry owes its rise to circumstances specific to Kitakyushu and the surrounding neighborhood, and it is a good example of building local capabilities to address a pressing need. Arguably, green technologies could provide firms in Kitakyushu with a lucrative niche in global markets, and the prospective technological possibilities and demands are such that there are ample opportunities for existing firms to diversify and for new firms to enter, as is explored in more detail by Nabeshima and Yamashita in chapter 8.

The steel industry, which brought economic prosperity to Kitakyushu, also created environmental pollution. By the 1960s, Kitakyushu had heavy air pollution, contaminated water, and toxic industrial waste sites, and it was considered one of the most polluted cities in Japan (Fujikura 2001; Sueyoshi 1994). In the early 1970s, the citizens of Kitakyushu began to exert political pressure on the local government to address environmental concerns, reflecting a strong history of cooperation between industry, the city government, and the citizens of Kitakyushu. The citizens were respectful of the economic importance of the steel mills and sought to find a workable mechanism (Fujikura 2001; Yeum 2002). Public officials were able to use scientific data collected by the Ministry of International Trade and Industry to identify the most egregious polluters (Fujikura 2001). The solution was a prolonged public debate that resulted in a series of actions that provided an incentive for firms to limit effluents. These actions succeeded in ameliorating environmental problems (Fujikura 2001; Sueyoshi 1994).

Kitakyushu has been able to clean up its local environment following the Kitakyushu Renaissance Master Plan, which dates to 1987, when Koichi Sueyoshi was elected mayor on a platform of economic renewal. The plan encompassed a short-term redevelopment of the city, as well as a longer-term development of an infrastructure that would support innovation and economic diversity (Sueyoshi 2001). In many ways, Kitakyushu modeled its revitalization efforts on its sister city, Pittsburgh (Yeum 2004). One striking difference, however, is the extent to which industry partners, local residents, and the government worked together in Kitakyushu to create a vision for revitalizing the city's economy. For example, Nippon Steel, a prominent anchor firm in the region, made significant investments both financially and as a participant in the strategic planning process, including playing a major role in developing Space World, a theme park that opened in 1990 (Shapira 1993).

Kitakyushu, over time, turned a disadvantage into a unique expertise that has great growth potential. The International Kitakyushu Training Association was established in 1980 to leverage the city's experience and knowledge in environmental renewal and to transfer this knowledge to other cities struggling with pollution. The municipal government also established a public-private partnership named Eco-Town to promote the development of an industry focused on environmental issues, pollution control, and remediation. Kitakyushu has produced a number of firms focused on environmental consulting, recycling, and industrial waste management—a new and emerging industry based on expertise that did not exist anywhere in the world 30 years ago. This expertise was not developed with the intention of creating an industry or even promoting economic growth. It was just the outcome of mutually beneficial cooperation to address a pressing local problem. Indeed, it was initially feared that aggressive pro-environmental activism would place the local steel industry at a disadvantage as that industry declined because of the pressures of globalization. However, the seeding of a new industry was in place. The market for industrial remediation and environmental services is rapidly growing, reflecting shifting global priorities (Steffen 2006).

Kitakyushu appears to be in a unique position to build an internationally competitive industry in the emerging sector of green or clean technology. As with any emerging sector, many possible scenarios may be realized and many specialized segments are likely to emerge. Kitakyushu's experience in environmental remediation provides unique and not easily replicated expertise. Although it is impossible to predict the future, almost certainly there will be a demand for green technologies and environmental remediation. Kitakyushu could build on its experience to provide services and equipment for pollution abatement and environmental integrity.[1] Moreover, the city's experience in public-private partnerships provides a potential mechanism for future coordinated action to engage the process of creating a sustainable cluster.

Although the environmental cleanup and recycling industry offers one focus for cluster development, even more promising is the industry producing alternative, renewable energy solutions—in particular solar cells—a field in which Japan is already a leader and one that is being heavily promoted by the national government.

The Solar Cell Industry

Japanese firms have close to 50 percent of the world market share in photovoltaic (PV) modules (see table 7.1). Total production in 2005 was 884 megawatts, of which 579 megawatts (60 percent of the production) was exported, mainly to Europe.[2] With the expectation of a growing market, firms are investing both in expanding existing facilities and in setting up new establishments. In addition, a steady trickle of new entrants is adding to the capacity by introducing new technologies[3] and providing complementary services to the mainstream producers (see table 7.2).[4]

The bulk of the expansion is in the Kansai area, while new establishments are mainly in Kyushu. Currently, two types of PV modules are being manufactured: one based on crystalline silicon modules and the other on rigid or flexible thin-film modules. The crystalline silicon module is the most common form, with a global share of close to 90 percent. In contrast, the thin-film module is a newcomer. One advantage of the

---

1 Emerging clusters of expertise are developing around green technologies such as alternative fuels in Denver, Colorado; fuel-efficient and sustainable housing in Denmark; and sustainable agriculture in Italy.

2 In 2006, the total output of the global solar equipment industry amounted to US$20 billion, and it is projected to increase to US$90 billion by 2010, increasing the demand for silicon from 40,000 metric tons to 120,000 metric tons (Marsh 2007).

3 On the horizon are organic photovoltaics that use carbon-based dies and polymers, string ribbon technology that conserves silicon, ultra-thin film cells that conserve the indium phosphide substrate by replacing it with less expensive oxidized wafer silicon, spherical solar cells, and printed cells (Bradford 2006; Dumé 2007; Fairley 2005).

4 Although the entry is recent, these firms have been researching the solar technology since the oil shocks of the 1970s (DBJ 2007).

Table 7.1. Global Market Share of Photovoltaic Modules, 2004

Firm	Market share (%)
Sharp	27.1
Kyocera	8.8
BP Solar (United States)	7.2
Mitsubishi Electric	6.3
Q-Cells (Germany)	6.3
Shell Solar	6.0
Sanyo	5.4
Others	32.9

Source: DBJ 2007.
Note: Worldwide production was 1,195 megawatts in 2004.

Table 7.2. Recent Investments in Photovoltaic Module Production in Japan, 2003–07

Firm	Location	New or expansion	Annual production capacity (megawatts)
2005			
Sanyo	Osaka	Expansion	70.0
Sharp	Nara	Expansion	85.0
Mitsubishi Electric	Nagano	Expansion	45.0
Kyocera	Shiga	Expansion	40.0
2006			
Fuji Electric Systems	**Kumamoto**	**New**	**12.0**
2007			
Showa Shell	**Miyazaki**	**New**	**20.0**
Mitsubishi Heavy Industry	**Nagasaki**	**New**	**40.0**
Honda	**Kumamoto**	**New**	**27.5**
Kaneka	Hyougo	Expansion	25.0
Fuji Pream	Hyougo	New	12.0

Source: DBJ 2007.
Note: Investments in Kyushu are in **bold**.

thin-film module is that the base material is not crystalline silicon, which is in short supply because of demand from the semiconductor industry. Other advantages include thinness and the shorter payback time, although the energy conversion rate is lower than that of crystalline silicon (see table 7.3). Rigid thin-film modules are created directly on glass

Table 7.3. Comparison between Crystalline Silicon and Amorphous Silicon

Characteristic	Crystalline silicon	Amorphous silicon
Base material	Silicon crysta	Silane gas (and other gases)
Thickness	250 micrometers	3 micrometers
Color	Blue	Black
Energy payback time	3 years	2 years
Conversion efficiency	12–14%	6–11%

Source: DBJ 2007.
Note: Energy payback time is longer for crystalline silicon because of the energy requirement in at the beginning of the crystallization process.

substrate, whereas flexible ones are created on plastic. The common technologies used for thin-film PV modules are amorphous silicon, micromorphous silicon (alone or tandem), and copper indium gallium selenide (DBJ 2007).

Consumer electronics firms (such as Sharp, Sanyo, and Kyocera) make the PV modules from crystalline silicon, whereas thin-film modules are made by firms in the chemical industry, by equipment manufacturers, and by an auto firm (Honda) (DBJ 2007).

About 40 researchers are working on solar power–related projects throughout Kyushu. Some of the firms producing in the area are actively collaborating with local universities. For instance, Mitsubishi Heavy Industries has a research and development facility at its Nagasaki factory, and it is collaborating with Nagasaki University in solar power–related research. Similarly, Fuji Electric Systems is collaborating with Kumamoto University (DBJ 2007).

The main reason new establishments are located in Kyushu is that the production process for thin-film modules is similar to that of semiconductor products. For this reason, it is easier to recruit workers (both semiconductor and thin-film module makers have a three-shift, 24-hour operation). The presence of supporting industries in Kyushu is another plus. Makers of PVs need the raw silicon made by ingot producers, but the technology now allows them to make use of wafers discarded or sold by IC manufacturers, which are numerous in Kyushu.

PVs are combined with glass, frames, and junction box fuses—all of which are present near Kitakyushu—to make a complete solar cell module. Over time, the area has also pulled in the suppliers of inverters, batteries, and wiring as well as the distributors, designers, architects, engineers, and installers who integrate PV modules into homes, buildings, and production facilities. The entire value chain—which includes financiers—is long,

Figure 7.1. Photovoltaic Industry Production Chain and Various Support Services

PV production chain	Solar component and equipment manufacturers	Solar PV product manufacturers	Wholesalers and distributors	Installers and roofers	End users
	Architects, consultants, engineers, and project managers				
	Financial services and subsidies				
Support services	Utilities				
	Research and development				
	Supporting trade associations (such as the installers' association)				

complex, and labor intensive, which is attractive, because such a cluster can generate many jobs (see figure 7.1).[5] Moreover, because the technology is still evolving—with printable modules offering unparalleled flexibility—the links with universities are strong.

As a market, Kyushu has several positive features. In the first place, cities in Kyushu are sunnier than other cities in Japan. In addition, single-unit dwellings (60 percent of the market) are much more common in Kyushu than in other areas (50 percent in Tokyo). More households in Kyushu have adopted solar water heaters than households in other cities. And the current trend is to replace solar water heaters with solar power panels. These conditions, both in production and demand, favor Kyushu—and in particular Kitakyushu—as the prime location to establish PV module manufacturing (DBJ 2007).

Innovation Capability
To what degree is cluster formation in the Kitakyushu area based on new industries and to what extent is it based on the deepening of existing industries, such as electronics and autos, which are supported by increasing innovation capability? Such innovation capability, while not critical to cluster formation, certainly contributes to the cluster's growth and resilience, as noted by Kenney in chapter 2 and Chen in chapter 3. One way to examine the innovation capability of the local cluster is to generate a list of U.S. patents that designate Kitakyushu as the city location of the patent inventor or patent assignee. Patent applications in

---

5 Portland, Oregon, is growing a PV cluster, as is Freiburg in Saxony, Germany.

the United States demonstrate a desire for international intellectual property protection, which indicates the likelihood that the patents are related to products or services aimed at the global marketplace. While there were many more Japanese patents originating from Kitakyushu, focusing on U.S. patents captures activity that has the potential to generate competitive global advantage. Although other possible indicators, including new start-up companies, the amount of external investment, the rise in per capita income relative to local investment and gross national product, and the demographics of the labor force, including the retention of science and technology graduates, are also relevant, these data were not available. Patents, however, are easily accessed and analyzed to provide a window on innovation activity in Kitakyushu. This analysis allowed examination of companies engaged in inventive activity. In addition, the number of patents received by the Kitakyushu Foundation was analyzed, indicating the focus of the academic research within Kitakyushu and the strength of the international commercialization potential of these patents.

The 1987 Kitakyushu Renaissance Master Plan included plans for a science and research park to bring industry, academia, and government together to promote innovation. This strategy is used around the world to encourage technology-intensive economic development. Unfortunately, many times these science parks are little more than real estate deals. What appears to matter most are the internal dynamics of the science park and the larger cluster—the focus of the researchers and their ability to work together and to be relevant for local activity. The Kitakyushu Science and Research Park opened in 2001, and the details of the construction are instructive (Sueyoshi 2001). It may strike the reader as odd that the park opened 14 years after the plan was announced—a rather long time in politics. The reason was that Kitakyushu did not have a research university to anchor the effort. The municipal University of Kitakyushu focused on teaching and did not have the scientific expertise needed to build the desired research collaborations. At the time, the Kitakyushu Foundation for the Advancement of Industry, Science, and Technology (FAIS) was created with the mandate of attracting researchers to work in the park and creating strategic alliances that would augment local efforts (Sueyoshi 2001). The previous absence of a research university in Kitakyushu, coupled with deliberate efforts to bring external universities to the Kitakyushu Science and Research Park, means that the academic innovative activity in Kitakyushu is concentrated within the park. Japanese science and research parks assume the central administrative and technology transfer roles that universities would normally play in the United States (Bass 1998). There are 200 researchers working at the park, focused primarily on environmental sciences, life sciences, engineering, and information technologies. Academic innovation at the park appears to place far greater emphasis on (a) biomedical engineering and pharmaceuticals and (b) computers and data imaging than industry in Kitakyushu does at this time.

Table 7.4 summarizes the inventive strength of firms in Kitakyushu, as measured by the number of U.S. patents. The patents were grouped

Table 7.4. Inventive Strength in Kitakyushu

General classification	Number of U.S. patents filed from Kitakyushu	Companies that patented most frequently
Metal products and processing	96	Nippon Steel (44) Catalyst and Chemicals Industries (11) TOTO (10) Asahi (5) Sumitomo (5) Mitsubishi (4)
Chemical products or processing	58	Mitsubishi (19) Nippon Steel (10) Catalyst and Chemicals Industries (7) Asahi (5)
Electrical systems and equipment	51	Yaskawa Denki (31) Toshiba (5) Catalyst and Chemicals Industries (4)
Consumer products	46	TOTO (43)
Mechanical systems and equipment	37	Nippon Steel (9) TOTO (4) Yaskawa Denki (4)
Optics, lasers, electronics, and semiconductors	32	Toshiba (17) Mitsui (5) Yaskawa Denki (4)
Robotic devices and control systems	29	Yaskawa Denki (23) Japan Tobacco (3)
Computers, data processing, or image storage and transmission	13	Matsushita Electric Industrial (6)
Nonmetallic products and processing	12	Nippon Steel (3) Mitsubishi (3)

(continued)

Table 7.4. Inventive Strength in Kitakyushu (continued)

General classification	Number of U.S. patents filed from Kitakyushu	Companies that patented most frequently
Biomedical engineering or pharmaceuticals	11	Catalyst and Chemicals Industries (3)
Transportation vehicles and products	4	
Miscellaneous	4	
Total	393	

Source: Created by Beth-Anne Leech, University of Georgia, Athens, GA, October 2006.

into 12 categories that allow comparisons with the industrial and economic data provided by the city of Kitakyushu. Companies in Kitakyushu received 393 U.S. patents between 1998 and 2006. These patents do not comprise all of the innovative activities for the companies; many of the highly innovative multinational companies have research facilities in other locations. For example, TOTO, which is headquartered in Kitakyushu, has a total of 335 U.S. patents for all years, but only 171 list Kitakyushu as the inventor city. Nippon Steel, also headquartered in Kitakyushu, has a total of 2,113 U.S. patents for all years, but only 489 list Kitakyushu as the inventor city. A majority of the U.S. patents were in the metal, chemical, and electrical products and processing industries. These industries have historically provided the region's economic base and still account for the largest share of exports. Since its founding in 2001, FAIS has applied for 157 Japanese patents. FAIS's inventive activity also focused on the Japanese market, rather than international markets, as FAIS has only been granted one U.S. patent to date.

Table 7.5 presents a more comprehensive view of the inventive work in Kitakyushu. The number of U.S. patents is listed along with the number of Japanese patents. The number and percentage of patents are compared to the percentage of exports and imports, as well as the percentage of employees, by sector. Although there is some inventive activity in the electronics and high-technology sectors, this activity has not yet translated into either exports or employment. Likewise, many of FAIS's inventive activities are still in their infancy; however, the focus at this broad level of aggregation does not appear complementary ($\rho = 0.214$). This finding suggests that FAIS is trying to move into new sectors and to emulate the success of Carnegie Mellon University in Pittsburgh, with its emphasis on robotics, computer science (especially search engines), and biomedical

Table 7.5. Are Private and Public Sector Activities Complementary?

General classification	Number of U.S. patents filed from Kitakyushu[a]	Number of Japanese patents filed from Kitakyushu FAIS[b]	Percentage of U.S. patents filed from Kitakyushu	Percentage of Japanese patents filed from Kitakyushu FAIS	Percentage of exports by item through the port of Kitakyushu[c]	Percentage of imports by item through the port of Kitakyushu[c]	Percentage of employees in Kitakyushu's industries[c]
Mechanical systems and equipment	37	14	9.4	8.9	43.4	16.0	10.0
Chemical products or processing, including fuels	58	33	14.8	21.0	16.8	25.6	0.0
Electrical systems and equipment	51	33	13.0	21.0	0.0	0.0	13.5
Computers, data processing, or image storage and transmission	13	21	3.3	13.4	0.0	0.0	0.0
Biomedical engineering or pharmaceuticals	11	22	2.8	14.0	0.0	0.0	0.0
Consumer products, including food products	46	0	11.7	0.0	0.2	10.4	17.3
Metal products and processing	96	7	24.4	4.5	24.5	6.3	27.1
Nonmetallic products and processing	12	10	3.1	6.4	2.2	0.1	0.0
Transportation vehicles and products	4	0	1.0	0.0	0.0	0.0	0.0

(continued)

Table 7.5 **Are Private and Public Sector Activities Complementary?** *(continued)*

General classification	Number of U.S. patents filed from Kitakyushu[a]	Number of Japanese patents filed from Kitakyushu FAIS[b]	Percentage of U.S. patents filed from Kitakyushu	Percentage of Japanese patents filed from Kitakyushu FAIS	Percentage of exports by item through the port of Kitakyushu[c]	Percentage of imports by item through the port of Kitakyushu[c]	Percentage of employees in Kitakyushu's industries[c]
Optics, lasers, electronics, and semiconductors	32	11	8.1	7.0	0.0	0.0	0.0
Robotic devices and control systems	29	4	7.4	2.5	0.0	0.0	0.0
Miscellaneous	4	2	1.0	1.3	12.9	41.6	32.1[d]
Total	393	157	100.0	100.0	100.0	100.0	100.0

Source: Created by Beth-Anne Leech, University of Georgia, Athens, GA, October 2006.

a. Data from the U.S. Patent Database.

b. Data from the Japanese Patent Database.

c. Data provided by the city of Kitakyushu for 2003.

d. Includes raw materials.

engineering. A logical next step would be to inventory the inventive firms and individuals and to delve in greater detail into the types of activities that are granted patents to discern developing expertise. Interviewing local inventors would be a logical first step toward understanding their activities. This call for research represents a departure from the traditional model of economic development by emphasizing local activity and home-grown firms.

Inventive activity, as reflected in the patents, appears limited and diffuse, with little complementarity between public research organizations and private companies. Certainly the premise that Kitakyushu could position itself as a global leader in environmental remediation technology or PV technology is not reflected in the patent data. Current efforts directed toward innovation do not appear to be contributing, thus far, to the growth of a globally competitive green cluster or, for that matter, any other cluster. One recommendation that follows from this analysis is a more focused public-private effort to encourage innovation in green technologies, which is discussed further by Nabeshima and Yamashita in chapter 8. A first step would be to identify the entrepreneurs and companies working with these technologies, to assess their capabilities and performance, and then to evaluate what additional resources they might need. There may already be a local industry association or community developing, but the efforts of an early-stage or nascent cluster are typically hidden in the shadows of established larger companies. Although it is advisable to see what other jurisdictions are doing to encourage environmental remediation and green technology to learn what has been tried elsewhere in the world, the task is to adapt existing policies to local conditions, to innovate rather than copy, and to be cognizant of local conditions. Although government cannot dictate the formation of a vibrant industrial cluster, it is possible to provide incentives for inventive activity and to encourage collaboration.

Kitakyushu has been working to create an environment in which firms can prosper and compete in the global economy. Progress has been made, and certainly the citizens, government, and local industry have demonstrated a sustained and committed effort to move their local economy forward. Similar places around the world are struggling to restructure, and with increased globalization, it is likely that more places will find themselves with a similar need to reorganize their local economies. Industrial revival through clustering is a desirable strategy for Kitakyushu and similar places, but danger lies in the fact that existing activity is persistent, especially when it has previously been successful.

Perversely, many places cling to declining industries without diversifying their economic base until the cycle of decline is entrenched and pervasive. Just as investors have a balanced portfolio, places need to promote the activities of both large and small firms, specialized activities, and related diversification. Most of all, they need to promote innovation and the pursuit of opportunity. This area is certainly fruitful topic for further academic study and a fruitful laboratory for public policy, public-private partnerships, and societal innovation.

Conclusion

Crafting an appropriate place-based strategy for economic growth may be the ultimate local innovation. Two extreme philosophies are available to jurisdictional policy makers in matters related to economic development. One approach advocates aggressive planning toward a targeted industry. There are myriad examples of politicians and civic leaders focusing on a particular emerging, high-growth industry with great fanfare. Most of these examples will not succeed in achieving the promised result. Even when efforts are successful at generating start-up companies, it is difficult for a jurisdiction to garner long-term benefits if complementary assets are lacking.

The counterargument may appear to be a simple laissez-faire philosophy: letting market forces determine the allocation of resources. The underlying rationale is that industrial clusters that are part of successful cities arise for a variety of historically contingent or serendipitous factors that are not easily replicated. Firms locate and invest in particular cities for reasons that are not well understood, much less predictable and controllable. This view suggests that the most constructive thing a jurisdiction can do is to let market forces determine its future.

However, laissez-faire is an increasingly dangerous argument. In the knowledge-based economy, there are numerous market failures that lead to underallocation of the very goods that provide advantage. After all, market failure is one of the classic reasons for government provision of infrastructure, government funding of basic research, and government promotion of public goods such as education. Those resources, which are associated with market failure, take on new importance in the emerging knowledge-based economy and suggest that there may be a role for collective action and government participation. Given the challenges of collective jurisdictional decision making, the laissez-faire approach has appeal, but because industrial development demonstrates high levels of path dependency and increasing returns, if a city misses out on an important trend, such as new technology or infrastructure, it may miss out for a very long time.

A jurisdictional activity system is not the product of any one class of actors—not firms, not individuals, not governments, not universities. It is hard to find a highly competitive cluster—and therefore, highly advantaged jurisdiction—that does not have an activity system that is a combination of multiple actors. Moreover, constructing jurisdictional advantage takes the will of all the actors—a consensus vision and vision of uniqueness. Each party needs to ask what unique contribution it can make to the unique activity system. The government can play a coordinating role. The case of Kitakyushu shows how a city can leverage its actors to work together toward economic restructuring. Kitakyushu has established a history of cooperation among industry, the government, higher education, and the local citizens to promote economic revitalization and an environment in which its local firms can compete globally. This history may reflect a particular variety of capitalism that is more community based and consensus seeking. Certainly there are some useful lessons.

The idea that firms act as solo players is a romantic image that just does not seem to hold. Free-market advocates tend to point to high-tech industries like software in which there are lots of new companies and lots of cut-throat competition. However, software is one of the industries most dependent on—and linked into—the U.S. higher education system. The industry would not function without it. The same holds for pharmaceuticals, medical devices, aircraft, and any new potentially high-growth emerging industry. Strategy is choice, and closer inspection reveals that each of these industries has benefited from a jurisdictional activity set that coordinates the actions of various categories of actors. Hence, having a goal (high and rising wages) and a structure for thinking about achieving that goal (differentiation or low cost) and a tool for guiding the strategy (a distinctive activity system) may be useful.

References

Arthur, Brian. 1994. *Increasing Returns and Path Dependence in the Economy*. Ann Arbor, MI: University of Michigan Press.

Bass, Steven J. 1998. "Japanese Research Parks: National Policy and Local Development." *Regional Studies* 32 (5): 391–403.

Bradford, Travis. 2006. *Solar Revolution: The Economic Transformation of the Global Energy Industry*. Cambridge, MA: MIT Press.

Braunerhjelm, Pontus, and Maryann P. Feldman, eds. 2007. *Cluster Genesis: The Origins and Emergence of Technology-Based Economic Development*. Oxford, U.K.: Oxford University Press.

Caves, Richard E. 2002. *Creative Industries: Contracts between Art and Commerce*. Chicago: University of Chicago Press.

David, Paul A. 1997. "Path Dependence and the Quest for Historical Economics: One More Chorus of the Ballad of QWERTY." Discussion Paper in Economic and Social History 20, Oxford University, Oxford, U.K.

D'Costa, Anthony P. 1999. *The Global Restructuring of the Steel Industry: Innovations, Institutions, and Industrial Change*. London: Routledge.

DBJ (Development Bank of Japan). 2007. "Emergence of a New Industrial Cluster: Rapid Investment in Photovoltaic Module Production in Kyushu." DBJ, Fukuoka.

Dumé, Belle. 2007. "Exfoliation Produces Lighter, Cheaper Solar Cells." *New Scientist*, July 13, 17.

Fairley, Peter. 2005. "The Greening of GE." 2005. *IEEE Spectrum* 42 (7): 28–33.

Feldman, Maryann P., and David B. Audretsch. 1998. "Innovation in Cities: Science-Based Diversity, Specialization, and Localized Competition." *European Economic Review* 43 (2): 409–29.

Feldman, Maryann P., Johanna Francis, and Janet E. L. Bercovitz. 2005. "Creating a Cluster While Building a Firm: Entrepreneurs and the Formation of Innovative Clusters." *Regional Studies* 39 (1): 129–41.

Feldman, Maryann P., and Roger Martin. 2005a. "Jurisdictional Advantage." In *Innovation Policy and the Economy*, vol. 5, ed. Adam B. Jaffe, Josh Lerner, and Scott Stern, 57–85. Cambridge, MA: MIT Press.

———. 2005b. "Constructing Jurisdictional Advantage." *Research Policy* 34 (8): 1235–49.

Florida, Richard. 2000. "Competing in the Age of Talent: Quality of Place and the New Economy." Report Prepared for the R. K. Mellon Foundation, Pittsburgh, PA.

Fujikura, Ryo. 2001. "A Non-confrontational Approach to Socially Responsible Air Pollution Control: The Electoral Experience of Kitakyushu." *Local Environment* 6 (4): 469–82.

Grabher, Gernot. 1993. "The Weakness of Strong Ties: The Lock-in of Regional Development in the Ruhr Area." In *The Embedded Firm: On the Socio-economics of Industrial Networks*, ed. Gernot Grabher, 255–77. London: Routledge.

Hall, Peter A., and David Soskice. 2004. "An Introduction to Varieties of Capitalism." In *Varieties of Capitalism: The Institutional Foundations of Comparative Advantage*, ed. Peter A. Hall and David Soskice, 1–70. New York: Oxford University Press.

Henderson, J. Vernon. 2005. "Growth of China's Medium-Size Cities." In *Brookings-Wharton Papers on Urban Affairs: 2005*, ed. Gary T. Burtless and Janet Rothenberg Pack, 263–303. Washington, DC: Brookings Institution Press.

Kaufmann, Alexander, and Franz Tödtling. 2000. "Systems of Innovation in Traditional Industrial Regions: The Case of Styria in a Comparative Perspective." *Regional Studies* 35 (1): 29–40.

Lambooy, Jan G. 2002. "Knowledge and Urban Economic Development: An Evolutionary Perspective." *Urban Studies* 39 (5–6): 1019–35.

Lever, William F. 1991. "Deindustrialisation and the Reality of the Post-industrial City." *Urban Studies* 28 (6): 983–99.

Marsh, Peter. 2007. "Solar Energy Demand Soars." *Financial Times*, April 4.

North, Douglass C. 1990. *Institutions, Institutional Change, and Economic Performance.* Cambridge, U.K.: Cambridge University Press.

Porter, Michael E. 1980. *Competitive Strategy: Techniques for Analyzing Industries and Competitors.* New York: Free Press.

———. 1985. *The Competitive Advantage: Creating and Sustaining Superior Performance.* New York: Free Press.

———. 2000. "Location, Competition, and Economic Development: Local Clusters in a Global Economy." *Economic Development Quarterly* 14 (1): 15–34.

Rappaport, Jordan. 2003. "U.S. Urban Decline and Growth, 1950 to 2000." *Economic Review* (Third Quarter): 15–44.

Shapira, Philip. 1993. "Steel Town to Space World: Restructuring and Adjustment in Kitakyushu City." In *Japanese Cities in the World Economy*, ed. Kuniko Fujita and Richard Child Hill, 224–54. Philadelphia, PA: Temple University Press.

Steffen, Alex. 2006. *Worldchanging: A User's Guide for the 21st Century.* New York: Harry N. Abrams.

Sueyoshi, Koichi. 1994. "From Sea of Death to International Environmental Leadership: The Case of Kitakyushu City." *Marine Policy* 18 (2): 195–98.

———. 2001. Presentation at the First International Conference of the Anglo-Japanese Academy, Macclesfield, Cheshire, U.K., September 8.

Tödtling, Franz. 1992. "Technological Change at the Regional Level: The Role of Location, Firm Structure and Strategy." *Environment and Planning A* 24 (11): 1565–84.

Yeum, Mi Gyeung. 2002. "Partnership, Participation, and Partition in Urban Development Politics in Kitakyushu, Japan." *Asian Perspective* 26 (2): 157–78.

———. 2004. "Corporate Governance Regimes, Industrial Restructuring, and Community Responses: A Comparison between Kitakyushu and Pittsburgh." *Asian Perspective* 28 (2): 135–69.

CHAPTER 8

Kitakyushu

Desperately Seeking Clusters

Kaoru Nabeshima and Shoichi Yamashita

Successful industrial regions are those that can shift directions during the course of their life cycle in response to or in anticipation of changing circumstances, particularly the changing role of a major economic driver. The city of Kitakyushu is now faced with the need to find additional drivers of growth as its traditional industries decline. Industrialization of the area commenced when the first iron and steel mill (Yawata Steel) was constructed in 1901, leveraging the region's geographic advantages of having ports close to China (from which coal was imported at that time) and being relatively earthquake free. Northern Kyushu became one of four major clusters in Japan for the heavy industries and the chemical industry.

Those industries account for 50 percent of the manufacturing sector in value. However, in terms of employment, their share is declining. The steel industry employed about 40,000 workers in 1971, but the number dwindled to 16,000 in 1991 and to only 7,000 in 2003. Economic activities in the city of Kitakyushu and in Kyushu area in general shifted to processing- and assembly-oriented activities, especially relying on the semiconductor and automobile industries for their growth in the latter half of the 20th century. In the late 1960s, Kyushu emerged as a major center in Japan for semiconductor production. At one point, semiconductor production in Kyushu accounted for more than 40 percent of all semiconductor production in Japan. In the mid-1980s, Kyushu ranked third in the world in terms of semiconductor production after Silicon Valley and the Dallas area in Texas (Sargent 1987). However, as the competitiveness of the neighboring economies such as China, the Republic of Korea, and Taiwan (China) increased, the production of semiconductors in Kyushu dropped rapidly and that of dynamic random access memories (DRAMs) ceased altogether. Although Kyushu has been able to sustain its competitiveness in other semiconductor products, such as ASICs (application-specific integrated circuits), Kyushu's share of semiconductor output within Japan and the world is falling. The retreat of both the heavy industries and the electronics industry is being partially offset by the expansion of firms serving the automotive industry and the so-called green sector.

Automobile firms came to Kyushu in the late 1970s, looking for a cheaper production site within Japan to complement their overseas expansion, and their presence in Kyushu grew in 2000s.[1] Because of the pollution associated with the concentration of heavy and chemical industries in Kyushu, a number of firms specializing in pollution abatement technologies and green technologies have emerged. Some of the leading firms have a large number of subcontractors with substantial technological capabilities in advanced materials, processing, and finishing, all of which can serve as a nuclei of future cluster development.

In the interests of long-term economic development, the Kyushu area and Kitakyushu are seeking to transform Kyushu's economic structure and to revitalize its local economy by drawing on accumulated experience and skills. As previous chapters have noted, a region cannot rely on a particular industry for long. The resilient regions are those that can diversify their economic activities as the external environment and comparative advantages change and that can shift their focus to embrace promising new industries, as discussed in chapter 2 by Kenney. Gradually, the economic drivers in Kyushu are shifting toward the advanced semiconductor and automobile industries, as well as industries specializing in green technologies. Kitakyushu and the northern Kyushu area will play a significant role in future development of these industries

---

1 With the arrival of semiconductor and automobile manufacturing, Kyushu has become more integrated with the rest of Japan. Before then, much of its growth depended on the final demand in Kyushu. Furthermore, after 1985, Kyushu became more integrated to foreign markets, especially to East Asia (Akita and Kataoka 2002).

because the area is the center of research- and knowledge-intensive activities in Kyushu.

The post–World War II period of growth in Kitakyushu was led by major Japanese electronics firms such as Mitsubishi, NEC, and Sony. They came to Kyushu because of relatively cheaper production costs and easier access to clean water and energy. The initial development of the automobile industry in Kyushu was spearheaded by Toyota and Nissan. Unlike the case in some developing countries, where the presence of major foreign firms has not led to backward and forward links, firms in Kitakyushu were able to link with these lead firms. When they saw the opportunities, many of the local small and medium-size enterprises diversified from their traditional business lines into the semiconductor and automobile industries. A major local firm was also a good source of spinoff firms that catered to the semiconductor industry. Yaskawa Electric spun off 28 firms, many of them specializing in specific intermediate products and processes. Similarly, many local small and medium-size enterprises were able to diversify to meet the needs of the automobile sector.

Although firms in Kitakyushu—and Kyushu more broadly—were able to take advantage of the entry of large firms, questions remain whether firms in Kitakyushu can maintain the momentum. Manufacturing activities in Kyushu tend to be dominated by the subsidiaries and branches of major firms with headquarters elsewhere. Local firms tend to be the subcontractors to these subsidiaries and branches of major firms. The decisions are made by the headquarters (typically located in Tokyo or Osaka), and production is carried out in Kyushu. This type of situation is often referred to as a *branch economy*.[2] The danger of branch economies is that their fate is in the hands of the lead firms. There is always a possibility that the lead firms may decide to move to other locations. If the local economy is not dynamic and is unable to nurture indigenous firms, it will have difficulty filling the void created by the departure of these branches and subsidiaries. To sustain its dynamism, a local economy needs a build-up of local suppliers linked to major national electronics and automobile producers or to large local firms that are less likely to relocate, rather than to branches and subsidiaries of nonlocal firms.

This chapter explores the various possibilities for industrial development that exist for Kyushu in general, the roles played by firms in

---

2 The situation bears similarity to branch economy and enclave industrialization in developing countries, in which multinational corporations take the lead with respect to decision making and the lead (foreign) firms often display a footloose attitude.

Kitakyushu in such development, and the policies that are in place to stimulate the clustering of knowledge- and research-intensive activities in Kitakyushu. Some possible areas for development are electronic components (including semiconductors), automobiles (especially embedded electronics), and green technologies.

The Birth and Development of the Silicon Island

To understand the challenges and opportunities facing Kyushu today, one must first understand how it came to be known as the Silicon Island and also how local capabilities have been nurtured.

The Early Days

The first semiconductor factory in Kyushu, owned by Mitsubishi Electric, started operating in Kumamoto prefecture in 1967. It was followed by the NEC Kyushu factory in Kumamoto, which opened the following year. At that time, the NEC factory was the largest semiconductor factory in the world. Other major Japanese electronics firms such as Toshiba, Sony, ROHM, and Oki Electric also established semiconductor factories throughout Kyushu, and the island of Kyushu was soon nicknamed "Silicon Island."

During the early days of semiconductor manufacturing, Kyushu enjoyed a number of advantages over other regions. The first was the plentiful supply of clean water. Initially, the cleaning process of silicon wafers was a wet process, requiring a large quantity of pure water. Similarly, the etching process required a large quantity of pure water. The spring water from the foot of Mount Aso provided more than enough fresh, pure water for factories. Second, because of the rainfall and the geographic features of Kyushu, hydropower provided Kyushu with steady and inexpensive electrical power. Third, an ample supply of women were willing to work at the semiconductor factories. Fourth, because many semiconductor products are highly valued but small and light, they can be easily transported by air. With five regional airports all served by jet airplanes (airports in Kyushu were among the first to be served by jet airplanes in Japan because of the distance from Tokyo), Kyushu was in a good position to benefit from the logistic advantages conferred by air transportation.[3]

---

3 The development and improvement of the airports in Kyushu was a result of an earlier boom in tourism industries in Kyushu. This boom also led to the building of a road network catering to tourists (Sargent 1987).

Finally, Kyushu was attractive to many new firms—mainly subsidiaries of major electronics firms—because of the tax incentives provided by the central government's Technopolis initiative through the local governments.[4] These subsidiaries began to form networks with existing local firms and to create a smaller version of a *keiretsu* within Kyushu. This *keiretsu* spanned the entire value chain within each group, from wafer fabrication to wafer testing to packaging. Because these firms were linked vertically within a group, they shared technologies among the member firms, and incremental innovations were frequent. Technologies developed within the group were shared widely among the member firms, and the lead firm provided training and technical assistance to subcontractors. The form of the production network and the organization of innovation adopted by electronics firms are similar to those of the automotive industry.[5]

Changing the Global Landscape

The strength of Silicon Island derived from the emergence of the entire value chain in Kyushu. Currently, 15 wafer process factories are operating in Kyushu, including those owned by Sony, NEC, Renesas, and Toshiba. The number of semiconductor-related firms in Kyushu increased from 230 firms in 1990 to 650 firms in 2005 (Kyushu Economic Research Center 2007). Many local firms have diversified into the semiconductor industry.[6] Japan entered the DRAM market and quickly became a major producer. By the late 1970s, Japan had become the largest and most advanced producer of DRAMs. When the capacity of DRAMs was 1 megabit or lower, Japanese firms had close to 100 percent of the global market share.[7] However, with the shift from the mainframe computer to the personal computer (PC), Japanese firms began to lose their competitive edge against newcomers, especially Korean firms, which were able to produce DRAMs of adequate quality for PC use at a competitive price. The high-quality DRAMs produced in Japan were aimed at mainframe

---

4 These tax incentives were introduced in 1983 to stimulate clustering of high-tech industries in inland areas near major transportation hubs (airports and highway exchanges) (Kyushu Economic Research Center 2007).

5 The automotive clusters in Nagoya, Kanagawa, and Hiroshima had been around for a much longer time and are much larger in scale.

6 For instance, Hano Manufacturing began as a nameplate maker. When the semiconductor factories began to appear in Kyushu, Hano Manufacturing diversified into printed circuit board manufacturing, using its technological capability in etching (IST and DBJ 2003).

7 In the overall integrated circuit market, Japan's world share peaked at 16 percent in 1989 (Tomokage 2005).

computers that were not replaced frequently. As the PC gained in dominance, the replacement cycle became much shorter and the quality of DRAMs became less of an issue, opening up a window of opportunity for newcomers like the Korea firms to enter the market. As a result, Japanese firms began to lose their market share since then (Yunogami 2004).

As product and production technologies advanced, many of the advantages enjoyed by Kyushu disappeared. For instance, etching moved from the wet process to the dry process, eliminating the need for pure water. With miniaturization, dust became a major concern during the manufacturing process. The largest source of dust is the workers themselves. To overcome this problem, manufacturers have moved much of their production to clean rooms equipped with assembly robots, greatly reducing the need for inexpensive labor such as that found in Kyushu. In terms of transportation, most airports are now being served by jet airplanes, again eroding a competitive advantage that Kyushu enjoyed by having five regional airports.

Furthermore, a new model of the production process emerged with the establishment of silicon foundries such as Taiwan Semiconductor Manufacturing Corporation (see chapter 3 by Chen). This development led to the emergence of fabless integrated circuit (IC) design houses and other firms catering to particular segments of semiconductor manufacturing. Such a division of labor among different firms was quite the opposite of the vertically integrated production system in Japan.

With these changes in the market dynamics, along with the miniaturization of the IC, advances in production processes, a stronger yen, and the changing organization of production, all of the DRAM factories in Kyushu closed.

Prospects of Semiconductor Industry in Kyushu
Most semiconductor firms in Kyushu have shifted their focus to ASICs. Although Kyushu's share of semiconductor production in Japan has declined to 30 percent, northern Kyushu is still competitive in design and software. Its proximity to East Asia,[8] especially the growing market of China, is an advantage for export-oriented firms. The share of semiconductor exports from Kyushu to East Asia has been increasing and is now about 55 percent of total exports from Kyushu. Many firms are diversifying their operation to other semiconductor products. For instance, Sony is

---

8 The economic center of gravity is moving toward Asia, helped by the rapid growth of China and India (Grether and Mathys 2006).

investing more than ¥60 billion to expand its Kumamoto factory's production of CMOSs (complementary metal-oxide semiconductors) for digital cameras and camera phones. This investment represents a 20 percent increase in production capacity. Similarly, other firms are investing in CMOS, new cell phone development, and LCD (liquid crystal display) and plasma television production.[9] Fifteen percent of the world's shipment of silicon wafers still originates from Kyushu (Kyushu Economic Research Center 2007).

However, ICs are still relatively low-value items. Because of the IC's shorter product life, recouping investment in IC production is becoming much harder. For instance, ICs for cell phones are different for each model of handset. Although it takes 18 months for design and development, the product life of the average cell phone handset in Japan is only three months. Hence, the production run is quite limited also. Unless ICs are either high value-added products (for instance, Intel's central processing units) or memories (sold in bulk), many firms struggle to make profits (Kyushu Economic Research Center 2007).

Faced with difficulties in production, the current policy emphasis is to nurture large-scale integration (LSI) design capabilities in the Kyushu area. About 120 design-related firms are in Kyushu—many of them spin-offs from major electronics firms (Kyushu Economic Research Center 2007). These firms are clustered around the cities of Fukuoka and Kitakyushu, especially around the Institute of System LSI Design located in the Momochi area of Fukuoka city. Established by the Fukuoka prefecture, the institute has been managed by the Fukuoka Industry, Science, and Technology Foundation to make northern Kyushu a hub of LSI design in East Asia. So far, the institute has successfully attracted a number of design firms and skilled workers to the area. The institute also acts as the focal point for university-industry links, hosting Fukuoka Laboratory for Emerging and Enabling Technologies of SoC (system-on-a-chip),[10] System LSI Research Center of Kyushu University, and User Science Institute of Kyushu University. The institute also has an incubation facility that hosts more than 50 firms and a System LSI college to train the next generation of the engineers.

---

9 The Cell chip used in Sony's PlayStation 3 is also made in Kyushu, although manufacturing will be transferred from Sony to a new joint-venture firm between Sony and Toshiba (Sony Corporation 2007).

10 At the end of March 2007, it ceased the operation following the closure of Knowledge Cluster projects by the Ministry of Education, Culture, Sports, Science, and Technology.

Although a number of software firms are located beside design firms in northern Kyushu, most of them are branch offices of major U.S. and Japanese firms. For instance, there are branches of Yahoo!, Google, Apple, au, NTT DoCoMo, SoftBank, and Rakuten, but these branches do not conduct any of the key development work. Such work is done in the firms' headquarter locations, mainly in Tokyo. SoftBank has two branches, one in Fukuoka city and another in Kitakyushu, but these branches are the locations for data and call centers.[11] Firms in the software industry in Fukuoka city tend to write code for programs that are used internally by large firms. For instance, Fujitsu and NEC outsource their software development work to their branches in Fukuoka city. Many software firms in Fukuoka city serve as the software factories for large firms located in Tokyo, much like in the manufacturing industry. In contrast, software firms in Kitakyushu are spinoffs of large local companies and tend to work mainly with those companies. Nippon Steel, TOTO, and Yaskawa Electric initially relied on in-house software development for their needs and later spun off those development sections as separate firms, forming Nippon Steel Solutions, TOTO Info, and Yaskawa Information Systems, respectively. For example, half of the business of Yaskawa Information Systems is with its parent firm. The remainder of its business is with other firms, and it hopes to expand that business. Unlike the branch firms in Fukuoka city, firms located in Kitakyushu have headquarters there (although many are still affiliated with the parent firm), and they have the management autonomy to decide into which areas to expand. These software firms can be the nuclei of cluster development in Kitakyushu if they are successful in expanding their business lines beyond those of their parents. This possibility is even greater if the expansion takes place in areas related to other industries that are emerging in northern Kyushu.

Commercial and embedded applications (especially for controls) can be promising areas for firms in Fukuoka and Kitakyushu. However, for this development to become a reality, research on encryption, image processing and analysis, and data mining that is ongoing in local universities must yield commercially successful algorithms. Absent new discoveries, the likelihood of developing a software cluster in Kitakyushu is slim. Chances are the same for a hardware cluster of mobile phones and other portable communication and computation devices.

---

11 Other call centers are located throughout Kyushu, mainly in prefectural capital cities where workers are easier to recruit. In general, lower wages in Kyushu have attracted call centers (Kyushu Economic Research Center 2007).

Roads to Becoming an Automobile Island

Kyushu's initial entry into the automobile industry began with the establishment of a Nissan factory in Fukuoka prefecture in 1975 to produce a Datsun truck. In the following year, Honda established its motorcycle factory in Kumamoto.[12] Gradually, other automobile firms followed (see figure 8.1). In 1992, Toyota established its first factory in Kyushu. In the same year, Nissan invested heavily to expand the production capacity of the original factory. In 2004, Daihatsu established its own factory in Kyushu. Toyota established an engine factory in 2005, making Kyushu the first location of a Toyota engine factory outside of the Aichi area. Already Toyota is planning to double the production capacity of engines from 220,000 units to 440,000 units by spring 2008 (Invest Fukuoka 2007).[13] Although the strategy of the automobile industry is to produce in the destination country, the demand for Japanese automobiles is outstripping the ability of firms to expand their overseas operations, and they are looking for places where they can expand the domestic production capacity. In addition, because the major clusters of automobile production are in the Kanto and Chubu areas, automobile firms are looking for other regions in Japan for purposes of risk diversification (DBJ 2005).[14] The factors that have attracted automobile firms to Kyushu are almost the same those that drew electronics firms to the island: the wage level is lower in Kyushu than in other areas in Japan, Kyushu has a number of ports available for exporting (and for domestic shipping between Kyushu and the Kanto and Chubu areas),[15] and it has a good internal transportation system.

---

12 Beginning in 2008, the Kumamoto factory will become Honda's flagship motorcycle factory in Japan. It will also serve as a parent plant for factories outside of Japan (Kyushu Economic Research Center 2007).

13 The new engine factory is located near the new airport, which opened in 2006. Kitakyushu is planning to convert the old airport into an industrial estate that caters to automotive firms.

14 One of the major concerns is the possibility of earthquakes. Both Kanto and Chubu are prone to earthquakes, and a major earthquake is expected to hit Tokai (situated in the middle of the Kanto and Chubu areas) in the future. The earthquake in Niigata in 2007 highlighted the risks associated with a just-in-time system. Even though the earthquake caused only minor damage to the factory, the lack of energy and water halted the production of piston rings, causing stoppages at several automobile firms that relied on those parts.

15 Nissan Kyushu exports 60 percent of its production directly to North America, whereas Toyota Kyushu sends 80 percent of its finished cars to Nagoya before exporting them to North America (DBJ 2005).

Figure 8.1. Automobile Production in Kyushu, 1993–2005

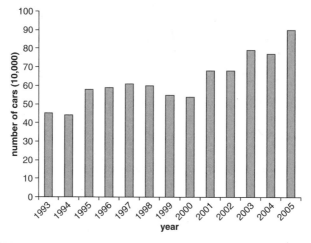

Source: KIAC 2006.

A number of small and medium-size enterprises have diversified from their existing businesses to enter the automotive parts sector. Currently, there are about 340 local automotive parts firms, mainly in Fukuoka prefecture (KIAC 2006). However, many of them are still second- and third-tier suppliers. Although the location of Kyushu is an advantage from the perspective of assemblers because they can diversify risks, it is a disadvantage from the point of view of local automotive parts firms that are trying to move up the value chain to become first-tier suppliers. Japanese automobile firms tend to involve major first-tier suppliers when designing new models. Typically, the lead firm is responsible for 30 percent of the car (mainly engines and assembly), while the first-tier suppliers are responsible for the remaining modules and components. In many cases, parts necessary for modules and components are further subcontracted to the second- and third-tier suppliers, organized by the first-tier suppliers (KIAC 2006).[16] In this arrangement, the lead firms need to negotiate with only a few firms. Firms in Kyushu tend not to be involved in the earlier stages because of their distance from the

---

16 Automobiles are among the most complex products, requiring anywhere from 30,000 to 50,000 parts, and the lead firm does not have the necessary resources to deal with each supplier. In the case of Toyota, there are 205 first-tier suppliers. One of the first-tier suppliers, Denso has 81 first-tier (second-tier from the perspective of Toyota) suppliers of its own (KIAC 2006).

Table 8.1. Rates of Automotive Parts Procurement

Area	Parts procurement rate within area (%)
Kanto	84
Chubu	84
Kinki	68
Chugoku	67
Kyushu	51

Source: KIAC 2006.
Note: Major firms are Honda and Nissan in Kanto, Toyota in Chubu, Daihatsu in Kinki, and Mazda and Mitsubishi in Chugoku.

headquarters of the major automobile firms (in the Kanagawa and Nagoya areas). Because of this circumstance, first-tier suppliers, although some are located in Kyushu,[17] focus their activities on production and do not have any research and development (R&D) activities in Kyushu (Kyushu Economic Research Center 2007).

Furthermore, the number of parts produced within Kyushu is low, relative to other major automobile clusters in Japan. For instance, more than 80 percent of parts can be procured in the Chubu area (where Toyota has its headquarters) and Kanto area (where Nissan is located), but only about 50 percent can be sourced within Kyushu (see table 8.1).[18] A worrisome trend is the slower pace of growth of automotive parts production relative to the number of automobiles assembled in Kyushu, especially after 1993. Although the number of automobiles assembled in Kyushu doubled in the past decade to reach more than 1 million cars, the automotive parts production in Kyushu has increased from ¥481 billion in 1993 to only ¥584 billion in 2003 (KIAC 2006) (see figure 8.2). Clearly, the growth of automotive parts production in Kyushu has slowed since 1993. This decline is in stark contrast to the automotive parts shipments from Aichi area, where many of the traditional suppliers to Toyota are located. Although overall domestic automobile production in Japan has

---

17 Kyushu has 122 first-tier suppliers, of which only 7 are local firms. More than 40 percent of subsidiaries and branches of first-tier automotive parts manufacturers are located in Fukuoka prefecture. Similarly, 43 percent of equipment manufacturers are located in Fukuoka prefecture (KIAC 2006).

18 However, this amount is an improvement from 30 percent in 1993. With the establishment of the engine factories, the expectation is that procurement within Kyushu will reach 60 percent in the near future (KIAC 2006).

Figure 8.2. Trends in Automotive Parts Production in Kyushu, 1981–2003

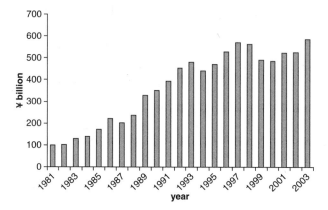

Source: KIAC 2006.

been hovering at about 10 million cars for the past 10 years, automotive parts shipments from Aichi area have been expanding, mainly for the export market (KIAC 2006).

Part of this slow growth of the automotive parts industry may be attributable to the higher capabilities required by first-tier suppliers and assemblers. In essence, the second- and third-tier parts manufacturers must have design capabilities in addition to efficient manufacturing capabilities. This requirement is specific to Japanese automobile makers. European and U.S. automotive parts firms tend to adopt an original equipment manufacturer approach to subcontracting in which subcontractors produce parts based on the blueprints provided by the lead firms. Under this arrangement, only efficient manufacturing capability is required. In contrast, most Japanese automotive parts firms (assemblers and first-tier suppliers) will provide only the necessary specifications, leaving the subcontractors to come up with their own designs. This system requires higher technological capabilities on the part of the subcontractors. In addition, the time necessary to develop new products is becoming shorter. In the past, the typical duration between model changes was 24 months, but model changes every 18 months are now becoming common. For new models that are derivatives of existing models, the duration is only 12 months. Within these periods, subcontractors need to design and develop parts and meet the cost and quality requirements. Typically, engineers from subcontractors are involved as guest engineers with lead firms during the initial development stage.

For that reason, being isolated from this stage is a major disadvantage (KIAC 2006).[19]

Nonetheless, firms in Kyushu are beginning to supply some advanced parts and components, such as those for hybrid engines. The presence of steel firms is helpful, particularly producers of specialized steel. At the Yawata factory, Nippon Steel makes electromagnetic steel, which is an essential component of motors for hybrid engines. The quality of this steel and its processing are said to influence the performance of the hybrid engines. The processing of this steel for hybrid engines is done in Kitakyushu by firms such as Mitsui High-tec, which makes the motor core used in the hybrid engine (Kyushu Economic Research Center 2007).[20] As the parts and components in the automobile industry become more complex and sophisticated, processing technologies that in the past were not within the main technological domain of automotive industry or did not require the precision of the semiconductor industry are becoming necessary (DBJ 2005). Some local firms have entered the automotive parts industry because they possess technological capabilities such as metal processing and die casting that were nurtured in the semiconductor industry.[21] Moreover, the models being assembled in Kyushu are becoming more sophisticated. Although in the past firms in Kyushu were responsible for assembling and producing parts for inexpensive models, in recent years they have supplied more parts for the top-of-the-line models, where higher quality (of similar parts) is required, suggesting that firms in Kyushu are accumulating the technological expertise and capabilities. For instance, Toyota's Lexus line production in Kyushu began in 2005 with a capacity of 230,000 cars a year, and production is expected to increase to 500,000 soon (Nishinihon Shimbun 2007). Although this trend suggests that firms in Kyushu have sufficient capability to produce high-quality parts used in luxury models, many firms in Kyushu are still finding it harder to

---

19 From the first-tier suppliers' point of view, unless the transportation cost is more than 1 percent of the price of the part, they will still rely on their traditional suppliers located outside of Kyushu (KIAC 2006).

20 Mitsui High-tec developed its capabilities in this area by providing the motor cores for consumer electronics firms (DBJ 2005).

21 Similarly, some automotive parts firms are entering semiconductor equipment manufacturing. Because the semiconductor industry is highly cyclical, the orders for equipment are also subject to large swings. Semiconductor equipment manufacturers need to find parts manufacturers that can respond quickly and manufacture parts and components that are based on their blueprints. Some automotive parts firms are leveraging their capabilities in welding and flexible manufacturing—nurtured through the creation of prototypes on short notice for the automotive industry—to enter this market (DBJ 2005).

Figure 8.3. Targeted Areas of Semiconductor Firms in Kyushu, 2003–05

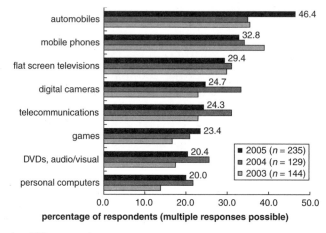

Source: Tomokage 2005.

branch out from their existing product lines for automobiles and also to become first-tier suppliers.

The ever-increasing trend in embedded electronics in automobiles is opening up a window of opportunity to firms in Kyushu. Close to 30 percent of the value added of an automobile now comes from the embedded electronics such as the car navigation system and sensors. The share of semiconductor outputs in Japan used in the automotive sector was 8 percent in 2002. The expectation is that 30 percent of the semiconductor output will be absorbed by the automotive sector by 2010 (DBJ 2005). In fact, the automobile industry is identified as one of the focus areas by semiconductor firms in Kyushu (see figure 8.3). One estimate puts the potential market for electronics in cars to be ¥50 billion to ¥100 billion in Kyushu alone. Safety and liability concerns induce automobile firms to source their semiconductor components from integrated producers rather than to outsource them.[22] Kyushu has the largest number of integrated firms, making Kyushu an attractive location for automobile firms (DBJ 2005). Kitakyushu is home to Zenrin, the largest supplier of digital maps and software for car navigation systems in Japan.[23] The new models of cars that incorporate a number of features and functions made possible by

---

22 The main reason behind this preference toward an integrated manufacturer is to ensure the quality of the components and the clear assignment of responsibility in case of vehicle malfunction (DBJ 2005).

23 Zenrin is the map provider for Google Maps in Japan, and it is also expanding overseas.

electronics, especially information technology, require customized semi-conductor products. This trend represents a great opportunity for the existing semiconductor-related firms specializing in ASICs. Kyushu NEC makes on-board computers for automobiles, and Mitsubishi Electric makes power devices used in hybrid engines in its Kumamoto factory (Kyushu Economic Research Center 2007).

One worrisome factor is that the wave of entry by local firms was largest in the 1970s and 1980s and relatively few new firms have entered the industry since then. The growth of establishments, in recent years, has been mainly driven by subsidiaries and branches of firms located outside of Kyushu.

Many local automotive parts firms have entered the automobile indus-try as a part of their diversification strategy.[24] Hence, the share of automo-tive parts in their revenue is lower compared with that of subsidiaries and branches. For instance, of all the local firms that manufacture automotive parts, only 13 percent derive all of their revenue from automotive-related activities, while 44 percent of subsidiaries and branches derive such revenue. Similarly, 42 percent of local firms derive less than 60 percent of their revenue from automotive parts, while less than 20 percent of subsidiaries and branch firms do so (KIAC 2006).

The major problem facing the local firms is the need to improve their production processes. To meet the quality and cost requirements, many firms see improvements in their production processes as the only way of remaining competitive because they have reached the limit in terms of lowering material and wage costs. However, making such improve-ments requires additional investment. Many local firms in Kyushu are too small physically, because their activities are mainly geared toward the consumer electronics sector, where each part is small. In the case of automobiles, parts and the equipment needed to produce them are much larger, especially dies, press machines, and jigs. Making the dies for the automotive industry requires equipment that can handle much larger and heavier parts. Firms entering the industry need not only new equip-ment, but also a larger factory. Many of the small and medium-size enterprises cannot undertake such massive investment (a minimum of US$1 million). However, without such investment, there is a limit to the

---

24 Even though the entry requirement is high, the automotive parts industry is attractive because after the parts are approved, they are used for the duration of the model (which is three to four years). This circumstance is welcome compared with the rapid product changes (every few months) in the electronics industry.

types of parts and equipment that they can produce, thereby constraining their expansion opportunities (KIAC 2006).

In addition, although the Kyushu area was favored for some time as a production site because of the ease of securing workers, with expansion in production capacity, firms are beginning to face shortages of skilled workers. This shortage most deeply affects the local small and medium-size enterprises, which are losing experienced midlevel skilled workers to subsidiaries and branches of larger firms.

Eco Island?

The intense concentration of heavy and chemical industries in Kitakyushu in particular and Kyushu island more generally gave rise to serious environmental problems beginning in the late 1960s. The air and water were heavily polluted and caused serious health ailments—in some cases death—mainly because of untreated industrial waste.[25] In 1967, the government passed a law clarifying the responsibilities of firms, local governments, and the central government in an effort to curb industrial pollution. However, the law did not prescribe any environmental regulation, which was left to the local governments (Welch and Hibiki 2003). In Kitakyushu, a civic group pressured the local government to strengthen pollution abatement efforts by private industries.[26] Leading firms in the area, such as Nippon Steel, cooperated with local governments to improve their pollution abatement efforts and lessen the negative impact of industry on the environment. After the second oil shock, manufacturing firms invested heavily in energy-saving technologies and pollution abatement technologies. Currently, heavy users of energy, such as steel and cement firms, are leading the charge in reusing industrial waste as an alternative fuel source (Kyushu Economic Research

---

25 Four major pollution-related diseases were identified in the 1960s: Minamata disease (in Kumamoto prefecture and Kyushu), Niigata Minamata disease, itai-itai disease, and Yokkaichi asthma.

26 Unlike Europe or the United States, pollution control in Japan is highly decentralized. Local governments can set their own emission and pollution control targets. These targets were agreed to by the firms before they obtained licenses for establishments and operations. The enforcement was done by way of periodic monitoring and assessments of targets. Noncompliance was punished by warnings and revocation of licenses. This particular arrangement was feasible in Japan because the production system occurred within closely related firms linked to a lead firm. Hence, the local governments needed to negotiate only with the lead firms, which would then communicate with the lower firms (Welch and Hibiki 2003).

Center 2007).[27] In response to this demand for reuse of industrial waste, a number of firms sprang up in the Kyushu area—mainly firms in the plant engineering industry. Many of these firms are spinoffs from the existing large firms. For instance, Nittetsu Yawata Engineering and Yoshikawa Kogyo spun off from Nippon Steel, Shinryo from Mitsubishi Chemical, and Mishima Kosan from Asahi Glass. This industry accounts for close to 10 percent of manufacturing employment in Kyushu. Through these efforts, almost half of industrial wastes are reused annually, mainly as solid fuels for energy-intensive industries. Some firms are specializing in recycling products and inputs used in Kyushu, such as automobiles, building materials, silicon wafers, and nonferrous metals (Kyushu Economic Research Center 2007).

Building on the experience, Kitakyushu city pioneered a plan to create an Eco-Town by hosting a number of recycling firms so as to develop an environmental business cluster in Kitakyushu.[28] The aim is to promote recycling by local industry and residents and a reduction of waste generation. As one of the pioneers in this area, Kitakyushu Eco-Town attracts more than 30,000 observers a year (Kyushu Economic Research Center 2007). The accumulated knowledge and technical expertise have also helped improve the environment in Kitakyushu's sister city, Dalian, in China.[29] Kyushu island itself was selected for the Kyushu Recycling and Environmental Industry Plaza Initiative, a policy established by the Ministry of Economy, Trade, and Industry (METI) in 2006 to develop an environmental industry cluster.[30]

Kitakyushu can build on the existing knowledge of pollution abatement to move toward green technology. For some time, the central government has been actively supporting alternative energy sources to lessen dependence on fossil fuels because of energy security reasons and concerns about

---

27 Kyushu was one of the first areas to adopt cleaner production technologies.

28 The central government identified 26 cities and areas for the Eco Town initiative and Kitakyushu is one of them. Kitakyushu thus receives fiscal support from the central government. Other Eco-Towns also tend to be located in the former heavy and chemical industrial zones (http://www.meti.go.jp).

29 The collaboration with Dalian municipal government began in 1993. Four local firms participated in this collaboration to transfer clean production technologies. By the end of the formal collaboration in 2000, the livability in Dalian had greatly improved. For instance, carbon dioxide emission per square kilometer decreased from 39 in 1997 to 26.4 in 2000, and almost all the wastewater was treated by 2000 (Shin 2007).

30 Kyushu was also identified by METI as a cluster for semiconductor production. See http://www.cluster.gr.jp/ for the list of cluster projects supported by METI.

global warming.[31] Local governments have also done so. In recent years, the central government has redoubled its effort to develop a renewable energy sector. The global market for clean energy was US$55 billion in 2006, and the market is estimated to grow to more than US$200 billion by 2016 (Makower, Pernick, and Wilder 2007). Currently, Japan is the only country in which solar energy is commercially viable without any subsidies from the government, and Japanese firms have nearly half of the world output in photovoltaic modules (see table 7.1 in chapter 7) (DBJ 2007). Traditionally, the production of photovoltaic modules was concentrated in the Kansai area, where Sharp, Kyocera, and Sanyo are located, and those firms are expanding their production capacity. Much of their product is based on crystalline silicon modules. Kyushu is attracting new investments in photovoltaic modules, especially thin-film photovoltaic modules, which are second-generation technology (see table 7.2 in chapter 7).[32] The attractiveness of the thin-film module is its lower cost of production compared with that of the crystalline silicon module. Almost half of the cost of crystalline silicon modules comes from materials—silicon—and wafer processing. Thin-film modules use much less material, and the panel size can be larger, making them cheaper to produce.

The critical issue facing solar power is the low efficiency in energy conversion. Improvements in energy conversion efficiency are needed to make solar power more competitive, not only in Japan but also in the global market. Such improvements require greater research. Some of the new firms are actively collaborating with local universities. For instance, Mitsubishi Heavy Industries has an R&D facility at its Nagasaki factory, and it is collaborating with Nagasaki University in solar power–related research. Similarly, Fuji Electric Systems is collaborating with Kumamoto University (DBJ 2007).

The question is whether Kyushu, especially Kitakyushu, can capitalize on this emerging opportunity. With the technology shifting from crystalline silicon modules to thin-film modules, there is a window of opportunity. The production process for thin-film modules is similar to that of

---

31 The research on solar power began with the Sunshine Project, launched in 1974 by the Ministry of International Trade and Industry (now METI) (Nagamatsu, Watanabe, and Shum 2006). This project was followed by the creation of the New Energy and Industrial Technology Development Organization in 1980. Subsidies for residential solar power were introduced in 1994 and for wind in 1998 (Maruyama, Nishikido, and Iida 2007).

32 Currently, two types of photovoltaic modules are commercially produced around the world. See chapter 7.

semiconductors. Hence, Kyushu has an edge, as it is the largest producer of semiconductor products in Japan. On completion of all the planned establishments, Kyushu will be producing 10 percent of all photovoltaic modules manufactured in Japan. Whether Kyushu can continue to expand will depend on the ability of the local firms and research institutes to advance the technological frontier in solar energy.[33]

Wind energy is another promising area.[34] According to one estimate, 7 to 10 percent of current energy use in Japan could be generated through wind. A number of power companies are already generating electricity using wind energy. For instance, NS Windpower Hibiki has 10 wind power turbines (General Electric turbine, 1,500 kilowatts) (Kyushu Economic Research Center 2007). The company is expected to produce 35 million kilowatts per hour per year—enough to supply energy to 10,000 households. The technology involved in producing efficient wind turbines is complex, with ample scope for further refinement. Firms affiliated with the heavy and automobile industries may be able to diversify into this area.[35]

Although recycling can be an effective way to reuse the resources, another track is to adopt more environmentally friendly production processes and materials.[36] The existing chemical industry can contribute

---

33 Many regions, such as the Portland area in Oregon, Taiwan (China), and Korea, are also looking at the photovoltaic modules as an industry to enter so as to leverage their experience in semiconductor production. Even those locations with other capabilities, such as Toledo, Ohio, with its glass making (an important component to the module), are diversifying into this area. The development of photovoltaic modules in Toledo is also supported by the research efforts of nearby university and corporate research labs (Calzonetti 2007).

34 The target set by the Japanese government is to generate 3 gigawatts from wind power by 2010. In 2007, the total capacity installed was little more than 1 gigawatt (Maruyama, Nishikido, and Iida 2007).

35 Another natural source of energy that Japan can tap is the geothermal energy. In Iceland, which shares a number of characteristics with Japan, about 90 percent of homes are heated by geothermal energy, whereas in Japan, the percentage is insignificant (*Nikkei Weekly* 2007). Japan has fewer than a dozen geothermal power plants, mainly because the most efficient sites are already designated as national parks and major tourist destinations (for hot springs). Of these power plants, half are in Kyushu and the other half in Hokkaido.

36 Another expanding area is the market for secondhand goods. This market is stimulated in part by the stagnant economy in Japan. The growth of the secondhand goods market also spurred the development of various auctions and e-commerce trading sites in Japan. In addition, to save on the materials cost, many firms are now engaging in refurbishing parts, especially in the automobile industry (Kyushu Economic Research Center 2007).

to this area as well as to material sciences and, in the future, to nanotechnology for the development of safer materials, which can be a growth area in future.[37]

Directions toward Development of Clusters in Kitakyushu

The economic structure in Kyushu has been changing, moving away from the heavy industries and the chemical industry to the assembly and processing industries, especially the semiconductor, automotive, and green industries. Northern Kyushu—especially Fukuoka city and Kitakyushu city—has played a significant role in this transition. Fukuoka city is the favored location for the regional headquarters of major Japanese firms. Many firms in Kitakyushu have diversified into these growing industries, and some of the knowledge-intensive activities are located in Kitakyushu. However, for Kitakyuhsu to move more into knowledge-intensive activities, it must increase local research activities by both public entities and private entities.

Kitakyushu Science and Research Park

In an effort to improve its knowledge-generation capabilities, Kitakyushu has created the Kitakyushu Science and Research Park (KSRP), and major universities have begun to locate satellite campuses within KSRP. Among the universities that have been attracted to KSRP are Kyushu Institute of Technology, City University of Kitakyushu, Waseda University, and Fukuoka University. Each of these universities has established graduate schools within the science park, such as the Graduate School of Life Science and Systems Engineering at the Kyushu Institute of Technology; the environmental engineering school at the City University of Kitakyushu; the Graduate School of Information, Production, and Systems at Waseda University; and the engineering school at Fukuoka University.[38] Private research institutes are also located within the park. KSRP provides a public space where university

---

37 In the United States, more than 3,000 patents were granted to green chemistry from 1983 to 2001. Currently, the United States is leading the field (with 65 percent of green chemistry patents), followed by Europe (24 percent) and Japan (8 percent). Although the granting of patents in this area to U.S. and European residents seems to be leveling off since 1983, the trend is still increasing for Japanese residents (Nameroff, Garant, and Albert 2004). See Glavic and Lukman (2007) for the definition of *green chemistry* and Manley, Anastas, and Cur (forthcoming) for some examples.

38 As of April 2007, these four universities had 160 faculty members and 2,173 students, of which 305 are in doctoral courses and 792 are in master's courses.

faculty members, researchers, professionals from private industry, and entrepreneurs can exchange ideas and engage in networking activities. With the strong support from Kitakyushu, incubator facilities are also located within the park.[39]

The construction of the Science City project commenced in 1996, and in April 2001, KSRP opened. Support for the park also came from the Ministry of Education, Culture, Sports, Science, and Technology (MEXT) through the knowledge-cluster development projects.[40] Northern Kyushu was identified by MEXT as a focus of its knowledge-cluster policy. Accordingly, the area received ¥500 million for the first five years, and in 2006, MEXT decided in 2006 to extend the support for another five years.[41]

It is difficult to measure the effect of KSRP on the local economy. However, there is a concern that research done at universities and research institutes does not match well with the existing local technological capabilities. Within the science park, more than 20 professors are working on LSI designs, but few local design firms can use the cutting-edge research done at the universities and institutes. In many cases, the collaborators are located either in Tokyo or on the West Coast of the United States. Given the technological capabilities of existing local firms, it might have been better to attract researchers in the area of material sciences and devices who could interact with local firms. The number of individuals conducting research in material sciences is slowly increasing. The manufacturing strength of Kitakyushu is in material sciences (nurtured through mining and steel) and in processing technologies. Kitakyushu should have accounted for those factors in its incentive packages for universities and research institutes when it was selecting potential entrants to the science park. However, it is not too late to redirect the effort to attract material scientists and process engineers to the park so as to stimulate the links with local firms.

---

39 The facility is currently hosting 10 firms. In addition to incubators, KSRP also offers 130 research labs, of which 45 labs are occupied.

40 MEXT promoted the Fukuoka System LSI Design and Development Cluster and the Kitakyushu Human Techno Cluster. See http://www.mext.go.jp/a_menu/kagaku/chiiki/cluster/ for the list of cluster initiatives supported by MEXT.

41 The park is managed by Kitakyushu Foundation for the Advancement of Industry, Science, and Technology, which has an endowment of ¥800 million. In addition to the endowment, the foundation brings in research projects funded by METI, MEXT, and the New Energy and Industrial Technology Development Organization. In 2005, the amount allocated from such external funding was ¥1.7 billion for 323 projects.

It is difficult to discern which local industries are the most promising or to foresee the direction of their development. However, one can safely say that basic research capabilities that can expand and extend the existing knowledge base are required for local industries to move into nanotechnology, information and communication technology, and robotics, where the future growth prospects are ripe. How university-industry links should evolve in Kitakyushu needs to be evaluated, keeping in mind the likely evolutionary path of local industries. Given the current capabilities in material sciences and advanced processing technologies, collaborations in these areas can lead to the emergence of new industry and business models.

Potential for the Development of Knowledge Clusters in Kitakyushu

Additional effort to transform Kitakyushu's economy into a more knowledge-intensive production system will need to come from the private sector, especially the large firms that have the financial, human, and managerial resources to set the strategic goals. The strength of Kitakyushu lies in the presence of large local firms such as Nippon Steel, TOTO, and Yaskawa Electric, while other cities in Kyushu rely mainly on branches and subsidiaries of major firms. These large firms act as the lead firms for a large number of other firms supporting their operations and can engage in R&D activities. Kyushu also has a large number of subsidiaries and branches of major firms, such as Sony Semiconductor Kyushu, NTT DoCoMo Kyushu, and Toyota Kyushu. Although some of them have managerial autonomy and have begun to engage in R&D, many of them act purely as production platforms.[42] Even though a number of local firms, such as TOTO, Yaskawa Electric, and Mitsui High-tec, can boast of having the largest market share in their specific industries in Japan, their size is still small compared with the largest firms in Japan. For instance, the market capitalization of TOTO, the largest manufacturing firm in Kyushu, is ¥427 billion. This amount is relatively small compared with the market capitalization of Toyota, which is ¥22 trillion (Kyushu Economic Research Center 2007). This difference in size may limit the scope of R&D operations that these firms can undertake and the number of areas into which they can diversify.

---

42 Other cities in Japan face a similar situation. For the case of Sendai in Tohoku area, see Jiang, Harayama, and Abe (2006).

Nonetheless, the role played by these large firms will be critical to the development of new clusters in Kitakyushu, especially through their local R&D efforts. One concern is that some of these firms are not conducting any critical R&D in Kitakyushu. For instance, TOTO has R&D facilities in the Kanto area (in Kanagawa and Chiba prefectures), and about half of the personnel are located there.[43] The R&D conducted in the Kitakyushu area is concentrated on product development and process technologies. In the case of Nippon Steel, the main R&D facility is located in Chiba and no facilities are in Kitakyushu. Yaskawa Electric's main R&D activity is still in Kitakyushu area, with two-thirds of activities located in Kitakyushu city and the remaining one-third in Tsukuba. Nippon Steel Chemical conducts basic R&D in Kitakyushu and Chiba, with about an equal split between the two in terms of personnel. Although other firms are engaging in R&D activities, details of their operations are unknown. The arrival of automobile assemblers and associated parts manufacturers gave much stimulus to the local economy, but in reality, the parts procurement rate is only 50 percent in Kyushu, as noted earlier. Even though the procurement rate is slowly increasing, many of the most complex and advanced parts are still imported from the Chubu and Kanto areas. Any components that are crucial to the performance of the automobile are developed at the early stage of design with the lead firms. Hence, research activities also tend to cluster around the headquarters of major automobile manufacturers. Unless firms in Kitakyushu can capture the production of some of the critical components in automobiles, the likelihood of an increase in R&D activities by these firms is low.[44]

To sustain its economic dynamic, Kitakyushu must rely more on the emergence of local firms that can lead the way, instead of relying on subsidiaries and branches of larger firms with headquarters elsewhere. This shift will require a better support system for start-ups and spinoffs. The current support system is government led, including venture capital.

---

43 The main line of business for TOTO is the production of sanitary wares and household ceramic products such as tiles. TOTO has been able to add value to its products by developing photocatalytic tiles that eliminate odors from organic matters and by incorporating electronics (and, in the future, information and communication technology) into its sanitary wares. Although TOTO invested heavily in its own R&D efforts, collaboration with the University of Tokyo was also instrumental (Kodama and Suzuki 2007).

44 The Hydrogen Technology Research Center at Kyushu University is conducting cutting-edge research in fuel cells (DBJ 2005).

In contrast, in Silicon Valley, the support system is led mainly by the private sector (see chapter 2 by Kenney), although government did play a significant role in providing the conducive environment. The current structure of business organization in Japan tends to be vertically oriented along the traditional industrial sectors. In the future, this structure must change to one that is more horizontal, especially across the traditional industrial sectors. The growth potential is mainly in the multidisciplinary areas such as nanotechnology, biotechnology, and information and communication technology interacting with traditional industries. According to Nishimura and Minetaki (2004), the effect of information technology (IT) investment on productivity in Japan is still quite low. The only industry benefiting from the wider use of IT is the IT-producing industry. This experience is in stark contrast to that in the United States (Gordon 2004a,b). In the United States, IT-using sectors also benefited enormously from investment in IT, which means that there is still large scope for productivity increases from IT investments in Japan if organizational changes and alternative business practices are adopted. This potential provides a possible window for firms in Kitakyushu to capture some of the growing market in providing IT services to businesses such as system integration and customization.

In addition, Japan is a leading producer of chemical products. Similar to emerging technologies such as nanotechnology and biotechnology, innovation in the chemical industry will have a large effect on a wide range of industries, including those engaged in green technology. Kitakyushu has been one of the centers of the chemical industry in Japan. Marrying the current capabilities in this area with other growth areas may be a fruitful direction to consider.[45]

These efforts need to be complemented by policies aimed at making Kyushu a more attractive location for corporate headquarters. Currently, the majority of headquarters are located in Tokyo, Osaka, and Nagoya. Even some of the local firms have moved their headquarters from Kyushu to the Tokyo and Osaka areas.[46] Unless Kyushu becomes an attractive place for local firms and skilled workers, it will face an uncertain future.

---

45 Although similar to other industries, the chemical industry has many establishments in Kyushu that lack the functions offered by headquarters (Kyushu Economic Research Center 2007).

46 Such relocations are not a new phenomenon. For instance, Bridgestone was started in Kyushu, but it moved its headquarters to Tokyo in 1937. In recent years, Tama Home moved its headquarter to Tokyo in 2005, and Royal Holdings (a restaurant chain) moved there in 2004 (Kyushu Economic Research Center 2007).

References

Akita, Takahiro, and Mitsuhiko Kataoka. 2002. "Interregional Interdependence and Regional Economic Growth: An Interregional Input-Output Analysis of the Kyushu Region." *Review of Urban and Regional Development Studies* 14 (1): 18–40.

Calzonetti, Frank J. 2007. "The Role of an Antecedent Cluster, Academic R&D, and Entrepreneurship in the Development of Toledo's Solar Energy Cluster." University of Toledo, Toledo, OH.

DBJ (Development Bank of Japan). 2005. "Towards the Fusion of Clusters: Automotive and Semiconductor Clusters in Kyushu." (Kurasuta yugou no jidai he: kyushu chiiki ni okeru jidoushasangyou to handoutai kurasuta) DBJ, Fukuoka.

———. 2007. "Emergence of New Industrial Cluster: Rapid Investment in Photovoltaic Module Production in Kyushu." (Arata na sangyoushuseki no hauga: kyushu de aitsugu taiyoudenchi kanren toushi) DBJ, Fukuoka.

Glavic, Peter, and Rebeka Lukman. 2007. "Review of Sustainability Terms and Their Definitions." *Journal of Cleaner Production* 15 (18): 1875–85.

Gordon, Robert. 2004a. "Five Puzzles in the Behavior of Productivity, Investment, and Innovation." NBER Working Paper 10660, National Bureau of Economic Research, Cambridge, MA.

———. 2004b. "Why Was Europe Left at the Station When America's Productivity Locomotive Departed?" NBER Working Paper 10661, National Bureau of Economic Research, Cambridge, MA.

Grether, Jean-Marie, and Nicole A. Mathys. 2006. "Is the World's Economic Center of Gravity Already in Asia?" University of NeuchÂtel, NeuchÂtel, Switzerland.

Invest Fukuoka. 2007. "Automobile." http://www.investfk.jp/industry_03.html.

IST and DBJ (Fukuoka Industry, Science, and Technology Foundation and Development Bank of Japan). 2003. "Networks in Hakata and the Feasibility of Development of Semiconductor Cluster." (Hakata youshiki nettowāku to handoutai kurasutā no hatten kanousei) IST and DBJ, Fukuoka, Japan.

Jiang, Juan, Yuko Harayama, and Shiro Abe. 2006. "University-Local Industry Linkages: The Case of Tohoku University in the Sendai Area of Japan." Policy Research Working Paper 3991, World Bank, Washington, DC.

KIAC (Kyushu Industrial Advancement Center). 2006. *Automobile Industry and Organization of Parts Procurement in Kyushu.* (Kyushu no jidhousha sangyou no genjou to buhinchoutatsukouzou) Fukuoka, Japan: KIAC.

Kodama, Fumio, and Jun Suzuki. 2007. "How Japanese Companies Have Used Scientific Advances to Restructure Their Business: The Receiver-Active National System of Innovation." *World Development* 35 (6): 976–90.

Kyushu Economic Research Center. 2007. *Industries in Kyushu (Kyushu Sangyou Tokuhon).* Fukuoka, Japan: Nishinippon Shimbun.

Makower, Joel, Ron Pernick, and Clint Wilder. 2007. "Clean Energy Trends 2007." Clean Edge, San Francisco, CA. http://www.cleanedge.com/reports/ Trends2007.pdf.

Manley, Julie B., Paul T. Anastas, and Berkeley W. Cur Jr. Forthcoming. "Frontiers in Green Chemistry: Meeting the Grand Challenges for Sustainability in R&D and Manufacturing." *Journal of Cleaner Production*.

Maruyama, Yasushi, Makoto Nishikido, and Tetsunari Iida. 2007. "The Rise of Community Wind Power in Japan: Enhanced Acceptance through Social Innovation." *Energy Policy* 35 (5): 2761–69.

Nagamatsu, Akira, Chihiro Watanabe, and Kwok L. Shum. 2006. "Diffusion of Trajectory of Self-Propagation Innovations Interacting with Institutions: Incorporation of Multi-Factors Learning Function to Model PV Diffusion in Japan." *Energy Policy* 34 (4): 411–21.

Nameroff, T. J., R. J. Garant, and M. B. Albert. 2004. "Adoption of Green Chemistry: an Analysis Based on U.S. Patents." *Research Policy* 33 (6–7): 959–74.

Nikkei Weekly. 2007. "Millions of Car Owners vs. the Poor." 2007. June 11.

Nishimura, Kiyohiko, and Kazunori Minetaki. 2004. *Advancement of Information and Communication Technology and Its Impacts on the Japanese Economy*. Tokyo: Yuhikaku.

Nishinihon Shimbun. 2007. "Toyota Kyushu Increases Annual Production Capacity to 500,000." (Toyota kyushu nensan 50 mandai taiou he.) In Japanese. June 5.

Sargent, John. 1987. "Industrial Location in Japan with Special Reference to the Semiconductor Industry." *Geographic Journal* 153 (1): 72–85.

Shin, Sangbum. 2007. "East Asian Environmental Co-operation: Central Pessimism, Local Optimism." *Pacific Affairs* 80 (1): 9–26.

Sony Corporation. 2007. "Toshiba, Sony and SCEI Sign a Memorandum of Understanding Establishing a Joint Venture to Strengthen Manufacturing Capabilities for High-Performance Semiconductors." Press Release. Oct. 18, 2007. http://www.sony.net/SonyInfo/News/Press/200710/07-1018BE/ index.html.

Tomokage, Hajime. 2005. "Semiconductor Business Network in Kyushu and Asia through MAP&RTS Program." Paper presented at the International Conference on ICT Industrial Clusters in East Asia, Kitakyushu, Japan, December 2.

Welch, Eric W., and Akira Hibiki. 2003. "An Institutional Framework for Analysis of Voluntary Policy: The Case of Voluntary Environmental Agreements in Kita Kyushu, Japan." *Journal of Environmental Planning and Management* 46 (4): 523–43.

Yunogami, Takashi. 2004. "Competitiveness of Japanese Semiconductor Industry in Technology Level." ITEC Research Paper 04-07. Kyoto: Doshisha University.

Index

Boxes, figures, notes, and tables are indicated by b, f, n, and t, respectively.